CHARLIE CHASERS
HISTORY OF USAF AC-119 "SHADOW" GUNSHIPS
IN THE VIETNAM WAR

LARRY ELTON FLETCHER

HELLGATE PRESS   ASHLAND, OREGON

CHARLIE CHASERS
©2013 LARRY ELTON FLETCHER

Published by Hellgate Press

(An imprint of L&R Publishing, LLC)

Hellgate Press

PO Box 3531

Ashland, OR 97520

email: info@hellgatepress.com

Editor: Harley B. Patrick

Cover Design: L. Redding

Cover Illustrations: (Front) "Guns Hot," an AC-119 Shadow Gunship attacking enemy targets. Original painting by U.S. Air Force Reservist and aviation artist Darby Perrin. (Back) "Rains of Death," a 2.5 minute time-lapsed photograph taken by 17th SOS Shadow Gunner SSgt Michael Drzyzga, Jr.; Shadow Emblem designed by 71st SOS Illuminator Operator SSgt Philip Bender.

Library of Congress Cataloging-in-Publication Data

Fletcher, Larry Elton, 1943-

Charlie chasers : history of USAF AC-119 "Shadow" gunships in the Vietnam War / Larry Elton Fletcher. -- First edition.

pages cm

Includes bibliographical references.

ISBN 978-1-55571-731-5

1. Vietnam War, 1961-1975--Aerial operations, American. 2. AC-119 (Gunship) 3. United States. Air Force--History--Vietnam War, 1961-1975. I. Title.

DS558.8.F58 2013

959.704'348--dc23

2013021740

Printed and bound in the United States of America

First edition 10 9 8 7 6 5 4 3 2 1

War is an ugly thing, but not the ugliest of things;
The decayed and degraded state of moral and patriotic feeling
Which thinks that nothing is worth war is much worse.
A man who has nothing for which he is willing to fight,
Nothing that he cares about more than his personal safety is a
Miserable creature who has no choice of being free, unless made and
Kept so by better men than himself.

—John Stuart Mill

Contents

CHARLIE CHASERS

Acknowledgments

I was inspired to write this book after reading the memoirs of 17th SOS Fighting C Flight Commander Colonel Tom A. Teal, USAF Retired and the unpublished work *Shadows in Southeast Asia*, written by Colonel Earl J. Farney, USAF Retired. I sincerely thank both men for granting me permission to use any or all of their materials in this book.

In addition to these two officers and gentlemen, other 17th SOS Shadows who deserve special recognition for their contributions to this book include: Lieutenant Colonel Donald "Tiger" Fraker, USAF Retired; Major Henry "Hank" D. Kailianu Alau, USAF Retired; Major William "Bill" Hamilton (Deceased), USAF Retired; Major John Windsor, USAF Retired; Major John "Jack" Nicol, USAF Retired; Major Donald Craig, USAF Retired; Chief Master Sergeant Norman J. Evans, USAF Retired; Captain Ralph Lefarth, Captain Robert Safreno, Captain Bert Blanton, Captain Donald Carlson, Captain Marty Noonan, Captain Gene Van Over, and Captain Robert Mundle. Another gunship fly boy who deserves recognition for helping is AC-47 "Spooky" pilot, Lieutenant Colonel Lyle A. Sproul, USAF Retired.

My heart-felt thanks go to Jenny and Mike Bowman for sharing news clippings and photographs compiled by Jenny's father, Lieutenant Colonel James W. "Bill" James, Fighting C Flight Commander from April thru September 1971.

My admiration and appreciation goes to the men of the 71st Special Operations Squadron who share the Squadron's Shadow story on their website at *www.71stsos.com*, specifically Webmaster James Alvis. With permission to use any or all information on the website, I incorporated a wealth of information about the unit's history in this work. The 71st SOS was the only USAF Reserve Unit activated for combat action during the Vietnam War. Like pioneers exploring and creating a foothold in the American Wild West, the 71st blazed the trail to war and established a firm foundation in Vietnam for the success of AC-119 Shadow gunships. A special thanks to Shadows Herman "Al" Heuss, Tom Newbold, and Dale Burgan for procurement of photographs.

The official website for AC-119 gunships of the 17th SOS Shadows, the 18th SOS Stingers, and the AC-119 Gunship Association is *www.ac-119gunships.com*. The website is the heartbeat of past and current events pertaining to Shadow and Stinger life. My sincere gratitude goes to Webmaster Chief Master Sergeant William "Bill" O. Petrie, USAF Retired for his dedication and professionalism in creating and maintaining this precious source of AC-119 gunship history.

The unclassified *History of 14th Special Operations Wing*, which embodies the history of the 17th SOS, was extensively used in writing this book. Materials were obtained from the U.S. Air Force Library and Historical Research Agency at Maxwell Air Force Base, Alabama. I was unable to obtain a complete roster of all those who served in the 17th SOS during the Vietnam War because the rosters are still classified due to personnel service numbers being the individual's Social Security number. Thus, I could not include all the names of the unsung heroes of the 17th SOS Shadow Squadron in this work. Therefore, I did not list rosters of the 71st SOS. Joe Caver, Archivist Kevin Burge, and the staff at the USAF Library and Historical Research Center were extremely helpful during my research and I thank them for their interest and assistance in this project.

Because the majority of Contemporary Historical Evaluations of Combat Operations (CHECO) reports about USAF aerial operations in Cambodia are still classified after forty years, I was unable to access important CHECO reports involving the 17th SOS for this work. The two CHECO reports that I reference in this work were accessible online through The Vietnam Center at Texas Tech University in Lubbock. The Vietnam Center website is *www.vietnam.center@ttu.edu*. The AC-119 Gunship Association designated The Vietnam Center as its official repository. AC-119 Gunship information can be found at *www.vietnamarchive@ttu.edu*.

Acknowledgments

Much research for this book was simplified by the "Fixed-Wing Gunship Bible," *Development and Employment of Fixed-Wing GUNSHIPS*, superbly written and documented by USAF historian Lieutenant Colonel, Dr. Jack S. Ballard. I respectfully honor and admire him and the Air Force History Program.

The excellent book *Call Sign Rustic*, authored by Colonel Richard Wood, USAF Retired, was a godsend for me in figuring out some of the major campaigns and battles in Cambodia. Shadows and Rustics worked closely together in helping our Cambodian friends and allies. I highly recommend Colonel Wood's book.

Another excellent book, *The Rustics,* published by the Rustic Forward Air Controller Association, also helped in figuring out the U.S. air campaign in Cambodia. Rustics Claude G. Newland and Douglas (Doug) B. Aitken were very cooperative and accommodating while supporting my requests. Thanks to Claude Newland for putting me in touch with Cambodia General Chak Bory, I was able to obtain valuable information for this work.

I am sincerely grateful to aviation artist Darby Perrin for allowing me to use his oil painting "Guns Hot" for the book cover. In the painting, Perrin's extremely accurate depiction of the AC-119G Shadow truly captures the gunship in attack-strike mode during daylight combat action. Perrin's excellent artwork commemorating military aviation can be found on his website: *www.planeart.com.*

Manuscript proofreaders Tom Teal, Earl Farney, and William Culver were vital to the correctness of this work. I am very grateful for their time, effort, and expertise.

It was my pleasure working with Hellgate Press editor Harley Patrick on the publication of this book. I sincerely thank him for his guidance, patience, positive attitude, and commitment during the editing process.

Last but not least, I thank my wife, Sue, for her steadfast encouragement during the years of this project. And a big thank you to graphic artist daughter Tracy Lynn Upschulte and her Design Café for making the excellent maps depicted in this work.

Foreword

I graduated from the United States Naval Academy and was commissioned in the U.S. Air Force at Annapolis in 1958. During my studies at the Academy, I first learned about U.S. involvement in French Indochina, established by President Harry Truman in 1950. That year, the Military Assistance Advisory Group (MAAG) was created in Saigon to work with French forces to regain dominance of their Indochina colony that was lost to the Japanese during World War II. On 3 August 1950, a thirty-five-man MAAG team was the first U.S. military advisors to arrive in Vietnam. In 1958, I had no idea that twelve years later, I would be a combatant in the Vietnam War.

Our nation shared in the Republic of Vietnam's (RVN) struggle against communist armed forces (aka Viet Cong and North Vietnam). As a consequence of Truman's action, the military footprint of U.S. military forces in South Vietnam gradually increased through the years of U.S. presidents Eisenhower, Kennedy, and Johnson. After President Richard M. Nixon was elected, a concerted effort to end the war and bring home American troops evolved. From TET 1968 to the Cambodian Incursion in 1970, every effort was made to gain a peace agreement with North Vietnam. In 1969, the Nixon administration announced the war in Vietnam would no longer be fought by American troops; that the South Vietnamese would take over the war effort.

"Vietnamization" of the War was declared. Drawdown of U.S. ground troops stationed in Vietnam irreversibly started thereafter to bring "Peace with Honor." On 1 May 1970, American and South Vietnamese armed forces invaded Cambodia to destroy North Vietnam Army (NVA) sanctuaries along the border of South Vietnam to help protect U.S. troops stationed in RVN during the withdrawal of American ground forces.

In January 1970, I received assignment orders to the 17th Special Operations Squadron (SOS) in Vietnam. My tour of duty commenced in June 1970, before the withdrawal of American ground forces from Cambodia, and terminated twelve months later in 1971 when American air power continued on without interruption to support and defend the Republic of Cambodia against armed forces of Viet Cong, North Vietnam, and Khmer Rouge.

I was assigned to 17th Special Operations Squadron (SOS) C Flight at Tan Son Nhut Air Base, Saigon, subsequently flying 100 combat missions as a navigator on AC-119 "Shadow" gunships while performing additional duties of Aircraft Maintenance Officer and Executive Officer to the Commander. I was also quasi-historian for C Flight, consequently collecting many documents, news articles, tape recordings of combat missions, and flight events plus photographs. All Shadow combat missions were recorded on Sony cassette tape recorders by the gunship navigator from engine start-up to engine shut-down.

Due to the secrecy of air operations in Cambodia and Laos following the 1970 invasion of Cambodia, little has been published about AC-119 Gunships of the 17th and 18th Special Operations Squadrons. Consequently, the squadrons, the aircraft, and their missions during the Vietnam War are by and large unknown. Historians for the most part have disregarded the uniqueness of AC-119 "Shadow" and "Stinger" gunship missions while paying tribute to the more popular AC-47 "Puff the Magic Dragon," aka "Spooky" and AC-130 "Spectre" gunships. Within this work, the AC-119 Shadow gunships of the 71st SOS and the 17th SOS are forefront in telling the tale of the black twin-tailed attack fixed-wing gunships.

I have and always will remember my tour of duty with C Flight at Tan Son Nhut Air Base, Saigon. Flying combat missions round-the-clock over Cambodia during 1970-71 forged a Brotherhood of Shadow Warriors within C Flight, consequently nicknamed Fighting C Flight. It was an honor to serve with the dedicated men of hard working ground crews and the courageous air crews; all of which were volunteers for special operations. The uncertainties of prolonged low level flight in a slow mover like the AC-119 gunship over hostile enemy territory was the pinnacle of combat for me at the time; but two years later, I would experience the same uncertainties while conducting high altitude bombing raids over Hanoi and Haiphong in a B-52.

I treasured my experiences with Fighting C Flight, enough so that I was inspired to write a document titled "Shadows in Southeast Asia" at the Air War College, Maxwell AFB, Alabama in 1976. I have given permission for author Doctor Larry Elton Fletcher to use any materials from my unpublished document and any other materials that I hold to pursue publication of this long-overdue book.

As a navigator with the rank of major, I flew several missions in Cambodia with Shadow 27 gunship aircraft commander, First Lieutenant Larry Fletcher. Rank held no privileges on Shadow combat crews; only crew positions held rank. There were four officers and four enlisted/non-commissioned officers on each Shadow gunship crew. Teamwork was critical to mission accomplishment. Shadow flyers knew and often reiterated the Mission of the United States Air Force: TO FLY AND FIGHT!

Earl J. Farney
Colonel, USAF Retired

CHARLIE CHASERS

Dedication

This book is dedicated to the following 17th Special Operations Squadron, C Flight Shadow gunship crewmembers who were killed in AC-119 gunship crashes at Tan Son Nhut Air Base, Saigon, Republic of Vietnam.

SHADOW 76 – 11 October 1969

Major Bernard Knapic – Aircraft Commander
Captain John H. Hathaway – Co-Pilot
Major Moses "Mo" Alves – Navigator
Major Jerome J. Rice – Navigator/NOS
Staff Sergeant Abraham L. Moore – Flight Engineer

SHADOW 78 – 28 April 1970

First Lieutenant Thomas L. Lubbers - Aircraft Commander
First Lieutenant Charles M. Knowles – Co-Pilot
Major Meredith "Andy" Anderson – Navigator
Master Sergeant Joseph C. Jeszeck – Flight Engineer
Staff Sergeant Robert F. Fage Jr. – Gunner
Sergeant Michael J. Vangelisti - Gunner

Seven days passed after the crash of Shadow 78 when Staff Sergeant John A. Murdock III was moved to write about his fallen brothers. John was a 17th SOS aerial gunner assigned to C Flight at Tan Son Nhut. His poem was enlarged, printed, framed, and hung on the wall behind the Fighting C Flight Commander's office desk.

THE SHADOW MEN

The SHADOW men fly by night
In the land of Vietnam
They have many tales to tell
Of battles they have won
They fly on night patrols
To help the friendlies out,
To give them some security
With the VC all about.
These crews of courageous men
Fight the battles long
But not always do these crews come home.
Some have made the sacrifice
For a reason they believed.
The rest of us fight the war
So they died not in vain.
Where do they go from here?
To heaven I believe.
They went there to be with God,
To wait for you and me.
Walk proud my friends who fly the SHADOW,
For a crew went down today.
Let us not let them down,
For the sacrifice that they made.
We'll take them with us in memories
For great guys were they all!
Now let us go out and fight the battles,
And bring an end to wars.

— John A. Murdock III
SSgt, USAF
28 May 70

Tastes of Combat

A C-119 Shadow gunship mission is scheduled to launch at 1930 hours military time. Crewmembers are briefed on weather, intelligence, and mission profile prior to aircraft preflight. With the plane already loaded to the hilt with 7.62mm ammunition and flares, each crewmember completes his pre-flight before the black flying machine is deemed CR (Combat Ready). Crewmembers saddle-up with parachutes and survival equipment before boarding the gunship for engine start-up. The twin engines cough at first, belch black smoke, and then purr like cats. Lined-up on runway centerline, engines at full power, brakes released, we roll faster and faster to become airborne; half man, half machine, ready for action. We've got U.S. TIC (Troops-in-Contact) with the enemy, just west of Pleiku.

Radio call sign for the U.S. ground troops is "Corpsman." Corpsman provides enemy locations on the radio to the Shadow gunship. He's taking heavy mortar and rocket fire from NVA and Viet Cong (aka North Vietnam Army, Victor Charlie, VC, or Charlie). Charlie is fixing to kill them all. The Shadow aircraft commander (A/C) pilot eases the gunship into a firing orbit and orders, "Four guns, rapid fire!" The head-gunner acknowledges over intercom and flips all four gun switches online at the high rate of fire, 6,000 rounds-per-minute per minigun. With gunsight pipper on target, the pilot presses the firing button on his yoke and the guns spew out a solid curtain of red tracers in the night sky.

Charlie ducks and quickly retreats as Shadow tracers chase the attackers away. Charlie will wait for another night to attack when the unseen flying dragon is not lurking in the darkness. Word spreads fast on the guerrilla grapevine, "Don't mess with dragon gunships or B-52s." All have but one life, it's precious, no matter your country or nationality.

All is quiet now with enemy mortars and rockets silenced. Corpsman digs deeper for possible counter-attack. He has four wounded. U.S. Army Medevac choppers are on their way. The war is shorter by one more sleepless, fear-filled Vietnam night.

Then come major battles; not every day, but once is enough. Following is a nameless Vietnam War combat veteran's recollection of such a battle as recorded on tape. He knew what hell was like.

It was like just one great nightmare, but then again its reality. Men weren't just hit once, they were hit multiple times. Both arms, both legs, head, chest. I've seen men with three or four holes in 'em say, "Doc, I'm all right, just gimme my rifle. I'll be okay; can't win 'em all. Doc, I don't want to die just laying here, give me my rifle dammit! I'm going to die fightin'."

Bullets were coming in so close you could hear them whistle past your ears. I looked up and saw one come through the trees about three inches from my head. I then looked off to my side and saw one hit the dirt next to my ass. A grenade went off in front of me. I looked at it go off. Just for a second, I thought I couldn't see; thought I was blind. Then I looked up and was okay. But the tracers looked like the 4th of July. Green tracers, yellow, red, and white. None of us thought we'd get out of there alive, believe me, none of us, not one. Rifle fire, machine gun fire, grenades, moans, groans, gooks all over the place. At first I was scared. Then all I wanted to do was kill. I can't explain it in words. Your blood gets hot and you want to shoot 'em. But you can't shoot enough of 'em. Definitely I was scared. Anyone that goes out there and isn't is crazy. You concentrate so hard you don't think about death.

Then came the sky jocks; crazy, sweet fools, napalm was slammin' so close. If I'd had a couple of eggs, I could have fried 'em. They were great. One dropped his bombs so close it nearly ripped my helmet off. They're beautiful, ask any foot soldier.

And the gunships; they'll bring the fire right down on your bunkers if you're really hurtin'. The damn fools don't know when to quit...and they have no place to hide...a circlin' up there.

Prologue

American involvement in Southeast Asia began during World War II when Japanese troops occupied the French Colony of Indochina. Six secret agents, code name "Deer Team," from the Office of Strategic Services (OSS) parachuted from a C-47 near Ho Chi Minh's base camp on 16 July 1945. The Deer Team mission was to train Ho's guerilla force in basic weapons and combat skills to harass and help fight the Japanese while gathering intelligence on Japanese troop movements. In exchange for Ho's cooperation, the U.S. agreed to assist Ho in establishing his "nationalist force" in Vietnam.

Vo Nguyen Giap (to become General Giap) met the Deer Team upon landing and led the six OSS agents to the village of Tan Trao where they were greeted with a banner "Welcome to our American Friends." The banner had been created by two Americans already stationed in Tan Trao. One of the Americans was Lieutenant Dan Phelan who manned the Air Ground Aid Station that assisted in the rescue of downed U.S. aircrew members and the other was Frankie Tan who was part of an espionage network working for Texaco since 1944.

Deer Team members trained Ho's band of Viet Minh guerillas during the weeks leading up to the surrender of Japan on 15 August 1945 which ended World War II. On the second day of September in Hanoi, Ho declared that Vietnam was now independent; no longer under any foreign rule including the Japanese and the Vichy French colonial officials. The Deer Team departed Vietnam from Hanoi seven days later.

France thought different about Ho Chi Minh's proclamation of Vietnam Independence. France demanded reinstatement of colonial control over Indochina which included Vietnam, Cambodia, and Laos. In the aftermath of WWII, France eventually resumed custody of its Indochina Colony when French forces returned in 1946 to assume control of Vietnam. Negotiations between France and Ho Chi Minh's "nationalist" of Vietnam followed but failed, resulting in war between French forces and communist Viet Minh forces.

The Viet Minh led by communist Ho Chi Minh fought for Vietnam Independence from the colonial yoke of France from 1947 through 1954. The Viet Minh under Giap employed unconventional-style warfare, guerilla tactics of ambushes and surprise attacks, followed by quick retreats to vanish into the hills and jungles. In contrast, the French conducted conventional-style WWII warfare used in the European Theater (e.g., establishment of fixed fortifications [forts] and airfields while relying on roads and bridges for movement of troops, supplies, and mechanized support).

Though basically anti-colonialism, the U.S. was drawn into supporting the weak but legitimized French colonial forces fighting the Viet Minh. Regardless of considerable American financial support and war machines/materials provided for French forces, the picture of control soon became clear. The French controlled major cities and towns but the Viet Minh controlled the countryside, especially at nighttime. This picture of control in Vietnam would repeat itself years later in South Vietnam and neighboring countries Cambodia and Laos.

As the situation deteriorated for the French, the U.S. under the Eisenhower administration sent forty B-26 bombers for the French Air Force and two hundred American technicians to maintain the aircraft in an effort to help turn the tide of war. This one act alone was not nearly sufficient to stop highly successful Viet Minh attacks on French Union Forces (units comprised of Frenchmen, Foreign Legionnaires, Vietnamese, Cambodians, Laotians, Moroccans, Algerians, and Senegalese) and French fortifications scattered throughout Vietnam.

The U.S. support of France's Indochina War steadily increased thereafter. Surplus U.S. military equipment and supplies left over from the war against Japan was readily available. Tanks, artillery, armored vehicles, troop transports, supply trucks, jeeps, and planes were given to the

French Union Forces. One U.S. aircraft carrier with a full contingency of fighter/bomber aircraft was turned over to the French navy.

Growing frustrated and tired of chasing the elusive Viet Minh, the French carried-out numerous operations to entrap large concentrations of enemy forces where there was no escaping. Entrapment operations were somewhat successful in some cases but not to any great degree. A plan was needed to entice the Viet Minh generals to assemble a massive force to confront and do battle with French troops where the full strength of French artillery and airpower could be totally employed.

French General Henri Navarre formulated a major strategic plan to concentrate French troops at Dien Bien Phu to repel the Viet Minh offensive in Laos, blockade the communist army from the Red River Delta, and to draw Viet Minh forces out from valley and hillside jungles for a major confrontation of armed forces.[1]

The Viet Minh attack that began the siege of Dien Bien Phu was launched on 13 March 1954. French outer defenses quickly crumbled under the fire of enemy 105mm guns and other artillery pieces surrounding the fortress located in northern Vietnam near the border with Laos. The French struck back at the Viet Minh with artillery and air strikes.

In continued efforts to help save the besieged French garrison at Dien Bien Phu, the French air force bombed and strafed enemy locations with B-26 and newly acquired American A-1E aircraft. C-47 Dakotas were used extensively for delivering supplies and reinforcements. Already in action to airdrop paratroops and supplies into Dien Bien Phu were thirty (30) U.S. C-119 "Flying Boxcars." The C-119 troop/cargo carrier was also used as a bomber to drop napalm on Viet Minh artillery sites. Most of the aircrews flying C-119s were American employees of Civil Air Transport (CAT), the contract airline founded in 1946 by Major General Claire Lee Chennault in China, the head of the World War II "Flying Tigers." Some aircrew members included U.S. pilots from the Military Assistance Advisory Group established by the Truman Administration in 1950. Years later, CAT evolved into the CIA-operated Air America.

The first C-119 napalm strike was conducted against Viet Minh revetted artillery emplacements approximately one-half mile outside Dien

Bien Phu on 24 March. The first and following napalm strikes proved somewhat effective. The Viet Minh commander General Tran Do stated, "Under the enemy napalm bombs, even stone and earth took fire, but our artillery fire continued."[2]

On 6 May 1954, CAT C-119 pilots James B. "Earthquake McGoon" McGovern and Wallace A. Buford were flying in clear skies over Dien Bien Phu on another supply airdrop mission when Viet Minh anti-aircraft gunners found their target and the disabled C-119 crashed behind enemy lines. McGovern and Buford became the first Americans known to have been killed in combat in Vietnam. In spite of valiant efforts by the ground troops defending Dien Bien Phu and the U.S. and French airmen flying support missions, French Union Forces surrendered to the Viet Minh on 7 May 1954.

On 3 June, France granted independence to the State of Vietnam under leadership of Bao Dai. One month later, Bao Dai appointed Ngo Dinh Diem as Premier. On 21 July, France and the Viet Minh signed a cease-fire "Final Declaration" at Geneva, Switzerland, resulting in the Geneva Accords in which the former French Colony, now named the State of Vietnam, was divided at the 17th Parallel into communist North and French South Vietnam to allow both treaty signers time to regroup until a general election scheduled for 1956 could be held to determine the future of the State. The Accords specifically stated that the 17th Parallel was not to be used as a political boundary. Thus as a technicality, neither the State of Vietnam nor the United States were a party to the agreement.

The end of French colonial rule in Indochina marked the beginning of American efforts to promote and support resistance to communist expansion in the world; namely Vietnam. In February 1955, the U.S. Military Assistance Advisory Group (MAAG) Vietnam was established under the Eisenhower Administration in which military advisors were sent to help train armed forces of South Vietnam. In April, troops loyal to President Diem defeated the Binh Xuyen outlaw army near Saigon. Following a lopsided referendum victory in October 1955, President Diem proclaimed South Vietnam as the Republic of Vietnam.

The 1956 general election never happened; thanks in part to U.S. clandestine efforts in creating the new Republic of Vietnam in 1955 and the decision by Diem to not hold general elections as called for in the Geneva Accords of 1954. As a result, to unite South with North into one nation, the North Vietnam Viet Minh communist party under Chairman Ho Chi Minh waged relentless, unconventional guerilla-type warfare against the new republic and its western allies that included the United States.

At first, the Viet Cong (South Vietnamese communists), supported and supplied by North Vietnam, conducted subversive operations to undermine the government of South Vietnam. Terror attacks, assassinations, and kidnapping of government officials were launched by Viet Cong and ever increasing numbers of North Vietnam cadre members from 1956 through 1959. The first American casualties occurred on 8 July 1959 when military advisors Major Dale Buis and Master Sergeant Chester Ovnard were killed in action (KIA) by Viet Cong at Bien Hoa. Years later, Richard B. Fitzgibbon was identified as the first American casualty of the Vietnam War, having been killed on 8 June 1956.

In January 1961, Radio Hanoi announced the formation of the National Liberation Front (NLF) in South Vietnam. In March, a cease-fire in Laos was agreed to and a Geneva Conference of fourteen nations met to make Laos a neutral country. In May, U.S. Vice President Lyndon B. Johnson visiting President Diem in Saigon announced expansion of U.S. defense and economic aid to South Vietnam.

Under the Kennedy Administration, the line in the jungle sand had been drawn to halt any communist aggression in Southeast Asia. The expansion of communism had to be stopped and Vietnam was the place to make a stand. After WWII, the Russians had established communist satellite nations in Eastern Europe, creating an "Iron Curtain" against the West; China had been lost to the communist and the Korean War had proven that communist would again wage war to spread party doctrine.

On 11 May 1961, President Kennedy approved the deployment of 400 Green Beret Special Forces to South Vietnam as special advisors to train

South Vietnamese troops in counter-insurgency methods to fight the Viet Cong. The first USAF tactical unit was deployed to Vietnam at Bien Hoa Air Base on 15 November 1961. A detachment of 155 airmen of the 4400th Combat Crew Training Squadron (CCTS) under Code name Farm Gate, aka "Jungle Jim" was assigned the overt task of training South Vietnam airmen. Under covert conditions, Jungle Jim airmen flew C-47, TF-28, and B-26 aircraft in combat while conducting counter-insurgency operations. In November, use of defoliant chemicals (Operation Ranch Hand) were authorized by the governments of U.S.A. and RVN to clear major transportation routes of foliage in South Vietnam to deny cover for the VC. On 11 December, two U.S. Army CH-21 helicopter companies (8th & 57th Transportation) consisting of 380 men were the first helicopter units to arrive in South Vietnam to assist the Army of the Republic of Vietnam (ARVN) operations, consequently raising U.S. forces in Vietnam to 3,000 personnel.

On 7 January 1962, four USAF C-123s equipped for chemical-spraying arrived at Tan Son Nhut AB to commence Operation Ranch Hand. MAAG personnel were officially authorized to accompany and advise the ARVN during combat on 20 January and officially authorized to return enemy fire on 14 February. On 2 February, the first U.S. aircraft, a C-123 of the 309th Tactical Carrier Squadron, 464th Tactical Carrier Wing was shot down by enemy gunfire during a defoliant training mission between Bien Hoa and Vung Tao, RVN. On 8 February 1962, U.S. Military Assistance Command, Vietnam (MAC-V) was established with General Paul Harkins as Commander. On 11 February, six airmen of Detachment 2A, 4400th CCTS and two MAAG GIs were KIA when their "Farm Gate" SC-47 was shot down near Bao Loc during a leaflet-drop mission.

On 15 March, the U.S. Army/Navy Advisory Campaign in Vietnam officially began as more military advisors and assets arrived in Vietnam. During the month, South Vietnam initiated the Strategic Hamlet program that forced peasants to relocate into defended compounds.

In May, President Kennedy deployed U.S. Marines and jet fighters to Thailand in response to communist activities in Laos. On 23 July 1962, the neutrality of Laos was recognized by the Geneva Accords. In September, the U.S. Special Forces (Green Berets) in Vietnam were formed in Saigon. The 1st Special Forces Group located on Okinawa had been sending Green Berets to Vietnam, starting with a sixteen member detachment in June 1957. In October, the 2nd Air Division was created to coordinate U.S. Air Force activities in Vietnam.

By the end of 1962, U.S. forces employed in Vietnam reached 11,326. Army and Marine aviation units flew approximately 25,000 combat sorties during the year. Thirty-one American GIs were killed in action (KIA) and seventy-eight wounded in action (WIA). Seven fixed-wing aircraft and four helicopters were lost during combat during the year. The Kennedy administration had demonstrated its determination and commitment in opposing communist expansion in Southeast Asia.

During January 1963, Viet Cong forces continued offensive actions throughout South Vietnam. The VC destroyed five U.S. helicopters, damaged nine others, and inflicted heavy casualties on ARVN units at AP BAC. The Chieu Hoi program was started in April to grant clemency to Viet Cong who surrendered to RVN forces. On 11 June, the Buddhist monk Thich Quang Duc drenched himself with gasoline and set himself afire on a Saigon street in protest of Catholic President Diem's policies against Buddhists. Riots consequently broke out in Saigon during the summer, causing the country to be placed under martial law in August.

On 8 July, the USAF 4400th CCTS stationed at Bien Hoa was reorganized and designated the 1st Air Commando Squadron (ACS). Three airmen of the 1st ACS were KIA when their B-26 was shot down during an escort mission over Kontum province on 2 September.

On 1 November, a new provincial government for the RVN was established under Major General Duong Van Minh after a military coup deposed President Diem. The next day Diem and his brother Ngo Dinh Nhu were assassinated in Saigon's Cholon district. On the twenty-second day of November, President John Kennedy was assassinated in Dallas, Texas. Two days later, President Lyndon B. Johnson proclaimed his determination to support the Republic of (South) Vietnam.

On 6 December, the 1st ACS lost four commandos when their RB-26 was shot down near Binh Dai at the mouth of the Mekong River during a Farm Gate photo reconnaissance mission. During the year, a total of fourteen fixed-wing aircraft and nine helicopters were lost to enemy ground fire. Seventy-eight American GIs were KIA and 411 were WIA during the year. By the last day of 1963, U.S. military personnel in Vietnam reached 16,263.

The beginning of 1964 saw the war escalate with initiatives on both sides. MAC-V created its Studies & Observation Group (SOG) to conduct highly classified clandestine operations throughout Southeast Asia. North Vietnam infiltrated more cadres and supplies for support of the Viet Cong operating in South Vietnam. The U.S. ordered American dependents out of Vietnam in February. American concern over the strength and effectiveness of RVN forces grew with each action. Viet Cong activity in and around the capital city of Saigon and in the Mekong River Delta steadily increased with time. Compounding this problem was the political turmoil created in Saigon with the Diem government eliminated. After all, Diem had governed since 1954.

On 20 May, the first U.S. Marine ground combat unit arrived in RVN. Marine Advisory Team One was based at Da Nang to provide security on Tiger Tooth Mountain. Team One consisted of thirty communication personnel and seventy-six infantry riflemen from G Company, 2nd Battalion, 3rd Marines.

The Republic of Vietnam, now under provisional governance of General Van Minh, was highly vulnerable to another military coup and to political attacks instigated by North Vietnam to be carried out by Viet Cong in the south. On the first day of June, General William Westmoreland took command of MAC-V. One month later, the Army of the Republic of Vietnam suffered a major defeat at the hands of the VC in the Delta region.

Three Special Forces Green Berets and forty-seven ARVN were KIA in Tay Ninh province in a human wave attack by a full VC battalion on 19 July. Two of the three Americans were captured and executed by the VC. The ARVN's ability to repel VC and NVA attacks quickly deteriorated with low troop morale, losses of weapons, and high desertions. Recruiting problems were severe. The enemy was bold, professional, and hungry for battle. "Incidents" surged to 1,800 per month. Two hundred of 2,500 villages were controlled by the enemy.

On 2 August 1964, North Vietnam PT boats attacked the U.S. Navy destroyer *Maddox* in the Gulf of Tonkin. F-8s from VF-51 on the *Ticonderoga* responded and sank one of the PT boats. Two days later, enemy PT boats attacked the *Maddox* again.

Consequently, five days later the U.S. Congress passed the Gulf of Tonkin Resolution that authorized President Johnson the use of armed force to defend and aid any nation of the Southeast Asia Collective Defense Treaty, which included South Vietnam. As a result of the resolution, President Johnson initiated Operation Pierce Arrow. Sixty-four airstrikes launched from Navy aircraft carriers USS *Ticonderoga* and USS *Constellation* were conducted against North Vietnam targets on 5 August. Two aircraft were lost to enemy anti-aircraft fire. Navy Lieutenant Everett Alvarez became the first U.S. prisoner of war (POW) imprisoned in North Vietnam.

On 24 October, six airmen of the 309th Troop Carrier Squadron (TCS) and two soldiers from the 5th Special Forces Group were KIA when their C-123B was shot down by Cambodian anti-aircraft artillery (AAA) near Phum Dak Dam inside Cambodia during an ammo drop to Bu Prang. On 19 November, two T-28 aircraft of Detachment 6, 1st ACW were shot down in South Vietnam en route to Thailand. Four crewmen were KIA.

In November, the Viet Cong again attacked Bien Hoa Air Base, destroying five aircraft and heavily damaging numerous other U.S. and South Vietnamese Air Force (VNAF) warplanes while inflicting twenty-three American casualties. The continuing success of VC attacks cast severe doubts on the ARVN security of airbases and other United States installations in RVN. The infiltration of a North Vietnam Army regiment into Kontum Province in December marked the beginning of continued escalation in the war. Within the month, three more NVA regiments quietly penetrated into South Vietnam and bordering territories.

On 28 December, the Viet Cong 9th Division attacked ARVN troops stationed at Binh Gia located approximately thirty-five miles east of Saigon. ARVN troops took heavy casualties as the Cong overran Binh Gia.

By 31 December 1964, U. S. troop strength in Vietnam had reached 23,310 which included 1,300 Green Berets. One hundred forty-seven Americans were KIA and 1,039 had been WIA. Thirty-eight fixed-wing aircraft and twenty-two helicopters were lost in combat. The number of Viet Cong troops was estimated at 51,300 that included main forces and local forces for sixty-nine battalions, including 17,000 NVA infiltrators. U.S. troops were outnumbered but there were greater numbers in ARVN uniforms.

During 1964, the role of the U.S. drastically changed from advisors/trainers for South Vietnamese armed forces to outright combatants to help fight Viet Cong attacks. The stage was set for major intervention of the latest American airpower to retaliate against Vietnamese communists, plus the commitment of U.S. combat ground forces to defend U.S. airfields/installations and to fight in the defense of South Vietnam in 1965.

The Johnson Administration lost no time in responding to North Vietnam for action in South Vietnam. In retaliation for an attack on U.S. forces stationed at Pleiku, U.S. jet warplanes attacked targets in North Vietnam in Operation "Flaming Dart" on 8 February 1965. Three days later, "Flaming Dart II" was conducted against North Vietnam in retaliation for a Viet Cong attack at Qui Nhon that killed twenty-three U.S. personnel. Tit for tat!

On 2 March 1965, Operation "Rolling Thunder" began sustained air attacks on North Vietnam targets. Six days later in a show of Johnson's resolve to counteract communist Vietnamese attacks, the first "official" U.S. combat troops, the 9th Marine Expeditionary Brigade (two Marine battalions), either flew into Da Nang Air Base aboard USAF C-130s from Kadena Air Base, Okinawa, or made USN amphibious landings north of Da Nang to wade ashore on Red Beach One and assume positions to defend the airfield. The show of force was telecasted worldwide where television was available.

The Vietnam War, though not officially declared by the U.S. Congress, had begun in earnest by the Johnson Administration. The Gulf of Tonkin Resolution approved by Congress in August 1964 had given the President the power to wage war against North Vietnam in Southeast Asia.

Author's map of Southeast Asia.

ONE

Emergence of USAF Fixed–Wing Gunships

B y 1964, events strongly indicated the need for more U.S. military support if South Vietnam was to be saved from communist aggression and possible takeover. Increased airpower would be a critical part of the equation. But, what kind of airpower was most useful in guerrilla-style warfare? The French Air Force had effectively used F-8 and B-26 fighter/bombers against the Viet Minh, strafing and dropping bombs and napalm on enemy troops during VFR (visual flight rules) daylight conditions.

Nevertheless, during the hours of darkness when most Viet Minh attacks occurred, there was very little if any aerial support for French ground forces. Therefore, the question for the U.S. military remained: What kind of aircraft could really provide prolonged protection of airbases, firebases, cities, towns, hamlets, forts, outposts, and road and riverine convoys while providing direct fire support for friendly troops in combat with the enemy, particularly during the hours of darkness, and even during inclement weather conditions?

The Farm Gate detachment at Bien Hoa established in 1961, flying prop-driven FT-28, B-26, and C-47 aircraft, had already proven to be successful in counterinsurgency operations, but their capabilities were limited. Consequently, the U.S. Air Force was seeking new methods of aerial weapons systems to combat the Viet Cong guerilla-style warfare tactics of ambushes and "attack and withdraw" to the jungle forests. The need for an aircraft with night capabilities; a night fighter with a large load capacity and long flight endurance that could loiter over targets for extended time periods with substantial firepower became clear to Air Force personnel like Captain Ronald W. Terry.

The aerial weapon system needed in Vietnam did not spring out of the Research and Development "think tanks"; it did not move from the drawing boards to the wind tunnels, or undergo exacting scientific engineering and analysis. Instead, the weapon system evolved from the minds of regular Air Force personnel improvising with aircraft and equipment already in the inventory, parts from various systems matched with new operational concepts to create a new weapons system; the fixed-wing gunship or gunplane, so as to not to be confused with a helicopter gunship. The fixed-wing gunship concept took initiative and a lot of tinkering; it was a story about good old "Yankee Ingenuity."

At Wright-Patterson AFB, Dayton, Ohio, Captain Terry rejuvenated an old theory of delivering ordinance on ground targets. While Terry was on a tour of duty in South America, he witnessed mail and supplies lowered to remote villages from the air in a unique operation. As a slow flying plane circled in a steep pylon turn, a bucket was suspended on a rope from the cargo door of the aircraft. The bucket tended to orbit in one spot over the ground and the villagers easily gathered their mail and supplies from the bucket. Terry could visualize the substitution of the suspended rope with the ballistic path of bullets from an aircraft with side-firing guns. A pilot should be able to fly an aircraft with a fixed side-firing gun in a continuous circle above a stationary ground target, aim through a fixed side-window gunsight, and fire a steady stream of bullets to hit the target. It was something to prove and Terry would prove it.

In 1963, Captain Terry was working as a member of the U.S. Air Force Systems Command team, investigating new ideas for counterinsurgency warfare. Captain Terry pushed the fixed-wing gunship theory and took his argument to anyone who would listen. After highly successfully tests of lateral-firing Gatling guns (aka miniguns mounted in

C-131 aircraft) at Eglin AFB, Florida firing ranges, requests were made to mount miniguns in the C-47 "Gooney Bird" of World War II fame. Test firings and the stability of the flying gun platform proved just as successful.

The fixed-wing gunship concept was a simple one; to fly slow and low above the target in a firing orbit of 360 degrees around the target, all the while keeping the target in sight and then saturating the target with devastating minigun and/or cannon firepower even during the hours of darkness and inclement weather conditions. It was an unlikely conversion of relatively slow propeller-driven transport aircraft with abundant cargo space large enough to house guns, ammo, and flares into heavily armed gun platforms. An aerial offensive weapon system like fixed-wing gunships was desperately needed and requested to fill a void in the USAF arsenal of preferred jet fighter/bombers.

The fixed-wing weapon system was ideal for night and counterinsurgency operations and its excellent slant range capability enabled it to strike targets on steep slopes that had long been considered inaccessible to jet fighter/bombers. Unlike the "fast-movers" of jet aircraft (in and out of target areas with very little loiter time while requiring forward air controllers), fixed-wing gunships (aka "slow-movers") could loiter for hours waiting for targets, change attack plans and firing patterns quickly, correct malfunctions inflight, provide illumination at night with flares, and then saturate targets with accurate and devastating firepower from miniguns and cannons during the hours of darkness, in difficult terrain, and under varying weather conditions. The Viet Cong and NVA had learned very quickly that daylight operations were vulnerable to air strikes. Hence, communist forces had traditionally used darkness as their ally. They moved supplies at night; they trained at night, and they attacked at night.

Captain Terry's briefings on side-firing gunplanes moved steadily up the chain of command. On 2 November 1964, Terry and Lieutenant Sasaki gave their presentation to General Curtis B. LeMay, Chief of Staff, USAF. General LeMay reacted favorably and sent a Systems Command team to Vietnam to modify and test the C-47 in combat.

Three conversion kits were shipped to Bien Hoa Air Base, South Vietnam. Two C-47s were reconfigured for Project Gunship I combat tests. Thus, the venerable U.S. Army Air Corps/U.S. Air Force C-47 (aka DC-3) became the first fixed-wing gunship employed in Vietnam.

One sortie of the combat test typified the instant popularity of the "Flying Fire Dragon." On 23 December 1964, the aircraft was on airborne alert out of Bien Hoa Air Base. The moon was high; there was a layer of light scud on the horizon. At 2237 hours, the crew was directed to Thanh Yend, west of Can Tho in the Mekong River Delta area. A little outpost was under heavy attack by the Viet Cong.

The FC-47 went in blacked-out (lights out), and turned into a firing orbit, and quickly brought fire on enemy positions. Apparently this Viet Cong unit had not seen the "fire breathing dragon-ship" before; therefore, when the gunship attacked, the VC immediately broke off the assault.

A second aircraft was diverted just after midnight on the same night to Trung Hung, an outpost twenty miles west of Thanh Yend. A South Vietnam Air Force (VNAF) C-47 was there dropping flares, but the Viet Cong continued to attack. The FC-47 arrived at 0040 hours and pumped a stream of 7.62mm rounds into the surprised Viet Cong. Trung Hung defenders were awed at the fire from the sky; the VC attack stopped their attack with the first burst of fire. At night, the Gatling guns of the flying dragon ship, with its steady stream of red tracers, was a fearsome sight for enemy troops, resulting in quite a psychological impact. Consequently, requests for the fire-spitting dragon ship were in high demand because of its accuracy and firepower. The need for fixed-wing gunships was everywhere but there were only a few of the gunships available.

The success of the gunship in night defense was easy to understand. The entire South Vietnamese hamlet pacification program was at stake. Under the cover of darkness, the Viet Cong assaulted and sometimes overran forts and strategic hamlets in government designated "safe areas." The VC showed that the South Vietnamese Army could not protect the villages and outposts, thus frustrating the South Vietnam government and ARVN attempts to reestablish control over vast rural areas of the country.

The C-47 gunship was first designated FC-47. Because of objections from jet fighter/bomber commanders and pilots to a cargo plane being designated a fighter aircraft, the "F" that designated the C-47 gunship as a "Fighter" aircraft was eventually changed to an "A", which designated "Attack" aircraft, thus the FC-47 became the AC-47. Fixed-wing gunships were thereafter designated Attack Cargo (AC) (i.e., AC-47, AC-130, and AC-119). At first, the FC-47 carried the popular names and radio call signs of "Puff the Magic Dragon" and simply "Puff" followed by a number, but ultimately became "Spooky" for the signature prefix to its radio call sign.

With all the successes of the FC-47 gunship during combat tests in Vietnam, justification was now warranted for the formation of a full squadron of C-47 gunships. Subsequently, training for the 4th Air Commando Squadron started on 29 August 1965 at Forbes AFB, Kansas. Two and one-half months later on November 14, twenty AC-47 aircraft of the new 4th ACSq arrived at Tan Son Nhut Air Base, Saigon, RVN. Four of the twenty aircraft were designated for command support and attrition. When the 4th Air Commando Squadron arrived in-country, the 1st ACS FC-47 crews were transferred from Bien Hoa to Tan Son Nhut and incorporated into the 4th ACS. FC-47 operations had been conducted as part of the 1st Air Commando Squadron which included O-1 Bird Dogs FACs, A-1s, and cargo/psyops C-47s aircraft stationed at Bien Hoa Air Base.

The squadron was assigned to the 2nd Air Division. A forward operating location (FOL) was immediately established at Da Nang and four of the gunships were sent from Tan Son Nhut to Udorn Royal Thai Air Force Base (RTAFB) to support the secret war in "neutral" Laos. Flying day armed recon missions in the "Steel Tiger" region of southern Laos proved that the gunship was extremely vulnerable to heavy anti-aircraft fire. It wasn't long before one AC-47 was lost over Laos. Another gunship was lost to enemy ground fire while flying from Tan Son Nhut to Phan Rang Air Base, RVN.

Regardless of AC-47 successful interdiction efforts on the Ho Chi Minh Trail in the Steel Tiger region and the defense of small towns,

hamlets, and outposts in southern Laos, the primary mission of the 4th
ACSq was still protecting hamlets, forts, outposts, and military installations in all four corps of South Vietnam.

Seventh Air Force Operations Order 411-65, November 1965 stated
the mission of the 4th Air Commando Squadron of AC-47s was to support hamlets under night attack with firepower and flares, to supplement
strike aircraft in defense of friendly forces, and to provide long endurance escort for convoys.[1]

With the fixed-wing gunship concept proven to be highly successful
and firmly established by the AC-47 "Spooky" in 1966, gunship operations expanded with increased fighting in South Vietnam during the new
year of 1967. With the 4th SOS operating out of DaNang (A Flight),
Pleiku (B Flight), Nha Trang (C Flight), Bien Hoa (D Flight), and Bien
Thuy (E Flight); the basic operations plan for all flights was to have two
aircraft orbit on airborne alert to cover assigned areas while one backup
aircraft stood ground alert for reinforcement in needed areas. Only E
Flight at Bien Thuy had two aircraft on standby ground alert. AC-47 operations continued strong aerial support for ground troops in contact
with enemy forces while defending hamlets, outposts, forts, USA Special Forces camps, and air bases.[2]

Spooky's six-man combat aircrew consisted of pilot, co-pilot, navigator, flight mechanic, loadmaster, and one gunner. On target, the pilot
and copilot worked together in flying the AC-47 in the firing orbit to
maintain a stable firing platform. The pilot had complete control of the
gunship and crew, but the copilot would nudge his control column forward or backward to keep a consistent firing altitude which was usually
around 3,000 above ground level (AGL). Many AC-47 pilots flew
lower, depending on targets, weather, and enemy anti-aircraft fire.

In the left-turn firing orbit, the copilot watched for signs that the pilot
might experience vertigo while concentrating on the target, especially
during nighttime. Target affixation was real. The copilot controlled the
Master Firing switch located on the copilot's overhead control panel,
but was under commands of the pilot to switch between guns hot and
guns safe position. The navigator worked closely with the pilot to verify

the correct location of the aircraft in the target area and to confirm targets before firing. The flight mechanic (aka flight engineer) monitored all gauges in the cockpit for potential problems with the aircraft from engine performance to fuel consumption.

The loadmaster was responsible for the flares carried onboard (thirty-six flares as late as early 1968; then twenty-four flares later to reduce aircraft weight due to the mandated flare box). He set the flares and dropped them at the directions of the pilot. On February 1969, Spooky 71 of the 3rd SOS sustained a mortar round explosion in its right wing causing the aircraft to bounce uncontrolled into a steep right turn. Amidst the catastrophe, loadmaster Airman First Class (A1C) John L. Levitow saved a fellow-crewman from falling out of an aircraft opening and then recovered an activated flare rolling around on the floor to push-out the deadly flare before it exploded once clear of the aircraft. Levitow was awarded the Medal of Honor for his heroic actions.

The gunners (aka weapons mechanics) loaded and cleared malfunctions while keeping the three 7.62mm miniguns ready for firing. At the direction of the pilot, the gunner would select the number of guns the pilot wanted to fire at any one time and the rate of fire that the pilot wanted (i.e., low rate = 3,000 rounds-per-minute; high rate = 6,000). The gunner would select which single gun to fire as he was the only one who knew which gun was ready to fire. Once the pilot ordered the copilot to switch the Master Firing control to guns hot, the pilot could fire the guns by pressing the firing button on his control yoke.

It was normal to carry 21,000 rounds of 7.62mm ammunition on a typical Spooky mission. The three guns were initially loaded with 2,000 rounds each. Ten ammunition cans containing 1,500 rounds each were stored onboard. As each gun was fired out (i.e., emptied of ammo), the gun was reloaded by the gunner with 1,500 rounds. Occasionally, two gunners were assigned an aircraft, but because of never-ending shortages of gunners, one gunner assigned to a mission was the standard. The addition of another crewman to watch out for anti-aircraft fire was always welcomed. Throughout combat operations, all available eyes onboard Spooky scanned for enemy anti-aircraft fire.

During 1967, AC-47 operations experienced major increases with an additional squadron of AC-47s (The 14th ACS became operational in January 1968 and was redesignated the 3rd ACS on 1 May 1968) and additional aircraft for the 4th ACS authorized to expand operations and to replace lost gunships. The 4th ACS lost a total of five aircraft; three of which were confirmed losses to enemy ground fire during the year. The need for the aerial weapon system had become absolutely essential to directly support ground troops in contact with enemy forces and to defend air bases, artillery fire bases, towns, hamlets, forts, and outposts. The standard had been set high by the AC-47 Squadron during 1967; not one friendly outpost had been overrun when there was a Spooky gunship overhead.

To insure even greater success of fixed-wing gunships by adding advanced technology on the warbirds, the Air Force started investigating possible aircraft to replace the aged fleet of AC-47 gunships. The Air Force looked for bigger and better airframes to carry more and/or bigger guns into prolonged battle. Despite its combat successes and reliability, the old C-47 lacked adequate cargo space thus payload capacity, and its low wing prevented the pilot full view of the target and the placement of minigun fire. The "Gooney Bird" had proved to be extremely efficient and effective as the first USAF fixed-wing gunship, but a larger aircraft that could provide more firepower, greater loiter time on target, and accommodate advanced warfare technology equipment was essential.

The C-130 "Hercules" airframe was determined ideal for the next fixed-wing gunship; a four engine turboprop aircraft with more than sufficient engine power, payload, and fuel capacity to correct these deficiencies. In 1967, a modified C-130A prototype Gunship II arrived at Nha Trang AB on September 21 to undergo combat evaluation. The gunship carried four 20mm Vulcan cannons, four 7.62mm miniguns, and a variety of sophisticated sensors, illumination devices, and navigational aids. Seventh Air Force had recommended the C-130 aircraft to replace the highly effective but aging AC-47.[3]

A major problem surfaced with AC-130 gunships replacing the AC-47s right away. There was a shortage of C-130 airframes available for conversion to gunships and the fact that C-130s were in critical demand worldwide as cargo and troop carriers, especially in Southeast Asia. Nonetheless, the demand in Vietnam for more fixed-wing gunships was deemed paramount for saving Vietnam. Therefore, the Air Force reconciled that the C-119G "Flying Boxcar"—with its high wing configuration affording a clear line of sight along the length of the fuselage for both firing and sensor operation, greater cockpit/cargo space for advanced equipment, flight crews operating computer firing control and sensor systems, larger payload, longer loiter time, and better survivability—was the best and most aircraft available for Project Gunship III. The aircraft was the quickest solution to filling the void of AC-47 gunships until more AC-130 gunships became obtainable. A sufficient supply of C-119Gs was readily available with U.S. Air Force Reserve units.

As follow-on to the C-82 Packet, the C-119 "Flying Boxcar" was developed shortly after World War II and was the largest U.S. cargo/troop/paratroop carrier transport aircraft at the time. The newly formed U.S. Air Force in 1947 fully utilized C-119s in support of American and allied activities worldwide, including the Korean War and first Indochina War in Vietnam and Laos.

On 8 June 1967, Secretary of the Air Force Dr. Harold Brown approved the selection of C-119G aircraft as the immediate successor to the AC-47. Modifications to transform 52 C-119G aircraft into AC-119 gunships were planned in two phases. In phase one, twenty-six C-119G aircraft were modified to carry four 7.62mm miniguns, advanced firing control system, infrared and white light detection equipment, jettisonable flare launcher equipment, and ceramic armor to protect crewmembers and essential aircraft components. These aircraft became the AC-119G "Shadow" gunships. In the second phase, twenty-six C-119G aircraft would be further modified with the addition of two J-85 engines to carry two .20mm cannons and four 7.62mm miniguns plus an advanced fire control system, even more sophisticated sensors such as infrared and Doppler radars, and an advanced illumination system. These became the AC-119K "Stinger" gunships.

TWO

Gunship III

The first phase of Project Gunship III was committed to developing improved replacement gunships for the aging fleet of AC-47 gunship missions currently employed in Vietnam. The AC-119G model was the most expedient remedy to the need for more fixed-wing gunships in the war zones. Thus, the G model of the AC-119 gunship took priority over its more sophisticated brother, the K model AC-119 gunship.

Fairchild-Hiller, manufacturer of the C-119, was the most logical aircraft company to convert the cargo plane into a gunship. Warner Robins Air Materiel Area (WRAMA) awarded the modification contract to Fairchild-Hiller on 17 February 1968. Upon activation of the USAF Reserves 930th Tactical Airlift Group, C-119G aircraft were sent to Fairchild-Hiller's Aircraft Service Division plant at St. Augustine, Florida for modification to AC-119 gunships. The Air Staff designated the AC-119G/K Gunship III project "Combat Hornet" on 21 February 1968. Problems soon arose which caused delays in converting the troop/cargo transports into gunships and the eventual deployment of the 71st SOS to Southeast Asia. The first AC-119Gs were scheduled to arrive in Vietnam by July.

Among the problems were procurement of electronic components and miniguns for the gunships not on schedule, the procurement of aircraft

Conversion of C-119G Transport/Troop Carrier "Flying Boxcars" into Attack
AC-119G "Shadow" Gunships at Fairchild-Hiller Aircraft Plant in St. Augustine,
Florida, 1968.

support equipment, and defining supply procedures. A smoke removal
evacuation system became a must modification to clear smoke from the
aircraft within ten seconds in case a magnesium flare ignited in the
cargo (gun) deck. The survival of the gunship and crew was at stake because a flare fire would fill the aircraft with blinding and toxic smoke,
impairing the vision and reaction capabilities of aircrew members.

A serious problem evolved with the AC-119G's gross weight. The first
AC-119G was delivered to TAC (Tactical Air Command) to begin limited
flight testing on 9 June 68. Test personnel immediately identified the
combat configuration of the AC-119G would be over the take-off maximum gross weight limit of 62,000 pounds, thus forcing lighter fuel loads
and in turn loiter time over targets. Consequently, the gunship failed to
meet Air Force profile standards of sustaining a 200 feet-per-minute rate

of climb with one engine feathered during hot day conditions at a gross weight of 62,000 pounds. The final test report recommended a weight reduction in the gross weight of the aircraft in order to fulfill desired SEA combat capability.

Representatives from Headquarters USAF, PACAF (Pacific Air Forces), TAC, AFLC (Air Force Logistics Command), Seventh Air Force, and Fairchild-Hiller conferenced at WRAMA on 26-27 July 68 to determine alternatives for improving the aircraft performance to meet combat mission requirements. Conference attendees identified thirty items that could be removed to reduce aircraft weight by 3,277 pounds. The conferees had already been briefed that the AC-119G weighed 66,282 pounds when ready for take-off with a full load of fuel, ammunition, and flares. Removal of the thirty items would reduce the weight of the gunship to 63,005 pounds. The conferees believed that PACAF and Seventh Air Force needed to adopt the weight reduction plan and at the same time relax the single engine climb rate standard from 200 feet to 100 feet-per-minute.

Air Force Headquarters encouraged PACAF to accept the recommendations of weight reduction and lowering single engine rate of climb standard to 100 feet-per-minute and by doing so, the SEA mission profile for the AC-119G could be met while stressing the lower standard of performance afforded "adequate operational safety" with the pilot operated jettisonable flare launcher. Jettisoning the flare launcher in an emergency would boost the single engine rate-of-climb to around 150 feet-per-minute. On 15 August 1968, PACAF agreed to lower the rate-of-climb criterion to 100 feet-per-minute. Consequently, the aircraft were recycled through the St. Augustine plant for weight reduction modifications and on 11 October 68, the Air Force officially accepted the modified AC-119Gs.[1]

Twenty-six C-119Gs were converted to AC-119G gunships. Serial Numbers of those aircraft were: 52-5898, 52-5905, 52-5907, 52-5925, 52-5927, 52-5938, 52-5942, 53-3136, 53-3138, 53-3145, 53-3170, 53-3178, 53-3189, 53-3192, 53-3205, 53-7833, 53-7848, 53-7851, 53-7852, 53-8069, 53-8089, 53-8114, 53-8115, 53-8123, 53-8131, 53-8155.

The Fairchild AC-119G gunship was a fixed high-wing, twin boom, land monoplane of all metal construction. Modifications to the C-119G cargo/troop carrier aircraft to provide a side-firing aerial weapons system for day and night combat operations during all-weather conditions included the following:

1. Four SUU-11 Pod or four MXU-470/A Module 7.62 millimeter mini-guns (Gatling-type guns with revolving barrels). Eventually all Shadow gunships were fitted with G.E. MXU-470 mini-gun modules with flash suppressers, specifically designed for gunship use. Any number of guns could be fired at one time. At high rate of fire, each gun fired 6,000 rounds-per-minute. At low rate of fire, each gun fired 3,000 rounds-per-minute. When all four miniguns were on-line at high rate, a five second burst of fire sent 2,000 bullets at the target. The barrage of bullets was called "Rain of Death".

2. A Computerized Gunsight Fire Control System was installed for pinpoint placement of bullets. The system operated in fully automatic, semi-auto, manual, and offset firing modes with Lead Computing Optical Gun Sight and Fire Control Display.

3. A LAU-74A Flare Launcher, housing twenty-four Mark 24 flares, was installed in the starboard paratroop doorway (the door was removed) at the rear of the cargo deck. The launcher could be jettisoned in case of a "hung" flare fire or for use of the doorway for crew bailout. A small doorway was cut out just forward of starboard paratroop door for crew entrance/exit on the ground.

4. AVZ-8 Illuminator, a 20-kilowatt, 1.5 million candlelight Xenon "white spot light" with a variable beam that could light up a football stadium during the darkest of nights. It was aimed out the port paratroop doorway (the door was removed) at the rear of the cargo deck. When used, the light literally turned night into day on the ground.

5. Night Observation Scope (NOS) that magnified starlight and moonlight several thousand times to provide the NOS operator with a clean, though green, picture of the terrain below. The NOS, which

utilized moonlight, starlight, and infra-red light, enabled the gunship to see in the dark of night. The framework for the NOS was installed in the port forward doorway (the door was removed).

6. Auxiliary Power Unit (APU) 60 KVA.

7. Ceramic armor plating for cockpit crew protection against enemy ground fire.

8. Twenty-two self-sealing fuel tank bladders in the wings. Bladders were filled with reticulated polyurethane foam to suppress explosions.

9. Updated flight, navigation, and standard radio equipment for
Southeast Asia Operations.

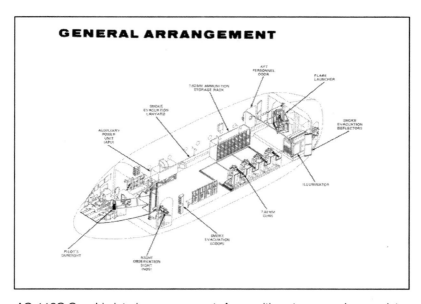

AC-119G Gunship interior arrangement. Ammunition storage racks were later
removed to reduce aircraft weight. Cans of ammunition were thereafter
strapped-down to the floor.

With dimensions of 109 feet, 3 ¼ inches (wing span), 86 feet, 5 ¾ inches (length), and 26 feet, 7 ¾ inches (height), the gross weight of the aircraft was 64,000 pounds while powered by two Wright R-3350 radial piston-driven engines at 3,500 horse-power per engine. The aircraft's cruising speed was 180 knots, while speed during combat was reduced to 140 knots. Attack altitudes above ground level (AGL) were: A (Alpha)—1500 feet; B (Bravo)—2500 feet; C (Charlie)—3500 feet; and D (Delta)—4500 feet. Most combat missions for the AC-119G gunship were flown at or below Charlie altitude because the 7.62mm miniguns maximum effective range of fire was 3500 feet. Existing weather conditions and enemy anti-aircraft fire also dictated the firing altitude. Maximum sortie (aka mission duration) was six hours with thirty minutes reserve fuel. Usually, combat sorties ranged from four to five hours in duration.

Mission priorities of the AC-119G squadrons were to provide: 1) Close-fire support of U.S. and friendly troops in contact with enemy forces; 2) Close-fire support of U.S. and friendly military installations including artillery fire bases, forts, outposts, strategic hamlets, villages, and district towns; 3) Pre-planned armed reconnaissance and interdiction of hostile areas and infiltration routes; 4) Search and Rescue support; 5) Night and day armed escort for road, river, and close off-shore convoys; 6) Illumination for night fighter strikes; and 7) Harassment and Interdiction of enemy.

The AC-119K Gunship

In the second phase of Gunship III development and modification at Fairchild-Hiller Aircraft Service Division plant located at St. Augustine, Florida, twenty-six more C-119Gs were converted into AC-119K gunships. The K model C-119 gunship was actually preferred by the Air Force over the G model gunship but the urgent need of gunship replacements for the AC-47 in Vietnam justifiably pushed the production of AC-119G gunships ahead of the K model.

In addition to all the modifications made to transform the C-119G into the AC-119G gunship, two J-85 jet engines were added for greater take-off performance to accommodate heavier payloads that included two 20mm Vulcan cannons and ammunition, beacon tracking radar, for-

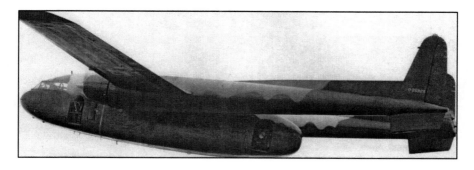

AC-119G Gunship's "Business" port side with pilot gunsight, night observation scope, four miniguns, and white spotlight.

ward looking infrared radar (FLIR), and associated fire control system computers on K models. Polyurethane foam bladders were installed in both the G and the K models for explosion protection against hits sustained from enemy anti-aircraft weapons.

The AC-119Ks were assigned to the 18th Special Operations Squadron, activated under the 1st Special Operations Wing for training at Lockbourne AFB, Ohio on 25 January 1969. The squadron would eventually be assigned to the 14th Special Operations Wing at Phan Rang, RVN. The first AC-119K gunship arrived at Phan Rang on 3 November 1969 and flew its first combat mission ten days later. In keeping consistent with fixed-wing gunship call signs starting with the letter "S", (i.e., Spooky, Spectre, and Shadow), Seventh Air Force officially approved the radio call sign of "Stinger" for the AC-119K gunships on 1 December 69. Stinger airmen soon created their squadron patch with the motto of "Vengeance By Night." The primary mission for Stingers was interdiction of enemy supply routes on the Ho Chi Minh Trails, Steel Tiger, and Barrel Roll in Laos while also flying direct fire support missions for allied ground forces in combat with enemy forces and defending friendly air bases.

THREE

Call to War

On Thursday morning 11 April 1968, news flashes from public radio stations in the state of Indiana announced the activation of the U.S. Air Force Reserve Unit, the 930th Tactical Airlift Group, stationed at Bakalar AFB in Columbus, Indiana. The recall alert came four days after many C-119 reserve units were involved in transporting troops to trouble-spots following the Martin Luther King assassination.

That day in April 1968 became monumental in the lives for many reservist of the 930th who would eventually become the members of the 71st Special Operations Squadron. At the time, they had no clue that they would be flying, maintaining, and supporting AC-119G gunship combat operations in Vietnam.

Reserve officer and pilot, thirty-three-year-old Captain Marvin Evens had taken off a few days from preparations for his final examinations in medical school. He was senior at Indiana University and was looking forward to an internship. Captain Evens and crew flew a C-119G "Flying Boxcar" from Bakalar AFB, Indiana to MacDill AFB, Florida during Operation Garden Plot to transport troops to various locations in the United States. On the 11th, Evens' flight engineer, Master Sergeant Owen Stickles, shocked the captain by announcing the news of being called to active duty.

Technical Sergeant Harold Morgan, age thirty-seven, served in the life support section of the 930th. His full-time civilian job was at Trane Company in Lexington, Kentucky, where air handling units were built. Like most men of the 930th, Sergeant Morgan assumed the call to active duty would only involve moving cargo from base to base in the States; i.e., the 930th would be full-time "Trash Haulers."

On 13 May 1968, the following C-119 units of the 930th Tactical Airlift Group (TAG) of the U.S. Air Force Reserves were officially called to active duty and assigned to the 838th Air Division (TAC), Forbes AFB, Kansas, with duty at Bakalar AFB, Indiana: 930th Group Headquarters, 930th Consol. Aircraft Maintenance Squadron, 930th Aerial Port Squadron, and the 71st Tactical Airlift Squadron. The 930th Group was mobilized with strength of eighty-three officers and 254 airmen.

On 14 May 68, TAC Movement Order 11 directed the 930th to move from Bakalar to Lockbourne AFB, Ohio. Upon receipt of 930th TAG Operations Order 1-68 on 1 June 68, the activated units started their permanent-change-in-station (PCS) move to Lockbourne. On 17 June 68, the 930th TAG was reorganized into the 71st Air Commando Squadron with Lt. Col. James E. Pyle as Squadron Commander. Squadron personnel were in place and functioning at Lockbourne by 21 June.

On 3 July 68, the first training class in the AC-119G gunship destined for duty in Southeast Asia was accepted by the 4413th Combat Crew Training Squadron (CCTS) at Lockbourne. The vast majority of personnel in the 71st were qualified and experienced C-119G aircraft veterans. Training stressed crew coordination, operational equipment, and procedures peculiar to the fixed-wing gunship. Live fire training flights were conducted at firing ranges on Lake Erie and Camp Atterbury, Indiana.

On 8 July 1968, the Air Commando Command of the United States Air Force was redesignated Special Operations Command. Thus, on 8 July 68, the 71st Air Commando Squadron was designated the 71st Special Operations Squadron (SOS) of the Parent Unit, the 1st Special Operations Wing, England AFB, Louisiana. The 14th Air Commando Wing with headquarters located at Nha Trang Air Base, Republic of Vietnam (RVN) aka South Vietnam was consequently redesignated the

14th Special Operations Wing (SOW) on 1 August 1968. The 71st SOS would be assigned to the 14th SOW under Seventh Air Force; PACAF upon arrival in Vietnam.

Major Bill Hamilton wrote about his experience becoming a gunship navigator:

> My assignment to the AC-119 came in the disguise of orders to the C-119G, as an advisor to the Vietnamese Air Force. Although I had been volunteering for Vietnam for two years straight in any of the following aircraft, A-26, AC-47 and F-4; I was always turned down as a critical resource. I was a B-52 Radar Navigator and SAC said no! Additionally, I had no experience in airlift or cargo aircraft, nor had I been an instructor navigator, so I was floored. I was to report to Clinton County Air Reserve Base, Ohio for checkout. The 302nd TAC Airlift Wing was responsible for my checkout and it was to last fifteen days. I expected to arrive alone but was surprised to find six other Nav's in my class. We were all flabbergasted to be there, especially the other Nav's as they were not volunteers. We received orders to report to the 4413 CCTS at Lockbourne AFB and with the next issue of Aviation Week we knew we were going to the new gunship. We reported to AC-119G training on August 2, 1968 and were to graduate on August 22, 1968.[1]

Deployment to Vietnam

By the end of November 1968, 71st SOS flight crews had successfully completed training with the 4413th CCTS program at Lockbourne and were designated combat ready. On 27 November 1968, deployment orders to Vietnam were received by the 71st SOS as approved by the Deputy Secretary of Defense Paul H. Nitze. Eighteen AC-119G gunships had undergone or were undergoing modifications at the Fairchild-Hiller Facility at St. Augustine in preparation for the ferry missions from the Florida facility to South Vietnam. The most significant modification was the removal of the four minigun pods and mounts and the installation of a 500 gallon rubberized auxiliary fuel tank for greater fuel capacity. The miniguns and mounts were shipped to Nha Trang.

The eighteen gunships were ferried by eighteen different crews consisting of a pilot (P), copilot (CP), navigator (N), flight engineer (FE), and crew chief (CC) to Nha Trang Air Base, Republic of Vietnam. The approximately 9,800 nautical mile ferry route to Vietnam from Florida via England AFB, Alexandria, Louisiana; March AFB, Riverside, California; McClellan AFB, Sacramento, California; McChord AFB, Tacoma, Washington; Elmendorf AFB, Anchorage, Alaska; Adak Island NAS, Midway Island; Anderson AFB, Guam; and Clark AB, Manila, Philippine Islands required about seventy-two flight hours.

On 4 December 1968, Crew #8 departed Florida in aircraft #53-7852 for Vietnam. The pilot was activated reservist Major Roxy R. Rupe. His CP was Captain Richard E. Rudkin. Other crewmembers were: Major Franz Schmucker (N), SSgt Earl McDaniel (FE), and Sgt Ronald Cross (CC). After numerous aircraft system failures along the route, Rupe's gunship arrived at Nha Trang on 26 Jan 1969.

Crew #15, Lt. Col. John W. Lewis (P) and crew members Major Edmon G. Tucker (CP), Major Kyle Jones (N), SSgt Bernie Westendorf (FE), and Sgt David A. Antle (CC) departed St. Augustine on 5 December in aircraft #53-3192, arriving in Vietnam on 25 Jan 1969 after repeated aircraft problems.

Also on 5 December, Crew # 18 with Major Clyde Sherrill as pilot and crewmembers Capt Howard Mangin (CP) , Major Byron D. Feather, (N), SSgt Herb Loveless(FE), and Sgt Warren Hinton (CC) launched from Florida for destination Vietnam in aircraft #53-3189. The crew arrived at Nha Trang on 27 Dec 1968; one of the first two AC-119G gunships to arrive in the Republic of Vietnam on that date.

Also arriving at Nha Trang on 27 December was AC-119G aircraft #53-8069 piloted by Major Herbert Zumhingst and copiloted by Major Gene R. Tippy. Major Joseph Derscavage (N), SSgt Ronald D. Penrose (FE), and Sgt David Farmer (CC) completed ferry mission crew #20. The crew departed the Fairchild Aircraft Plant in St. Augustine on 6 December.

Left to right: Lt. Col. Mel Gebhart from 14th SOW and Maj. Bill Brown greet 71st SOS Commander Lt. Col. James E. Pyle at Nha Trang. (Courtesy of Al Heuss)

The "New Kid on the Block." Just arrived AC-119G Shadow Gunship at Nha Trang Air Base, Republic of Vietnam, to start replacing AC-47 Spooky Gunships (*seen in the background*). (Courtesy of Al Heuss)

With two gunships in-country on the 27th, Crew # 9 and Crew #23 arrived on 30 December to add to the force of AC-119s at Nha Trang.

Crew #9 had departed for Vietnam on 6 December but ran into problems along the route with aircraft #53-3178. Crewmembers were Major Ben R. McPherson (P), Capt Marvin A. Evens (CP), Capt Michael R. Kiely, (N), SSgt Ron N. Eddington (FE), and SSgt John M. Burkes (CC).

Crew #23 departed St. Augustine in aircraft #53-5905 on 10 December. Crewmembers were: Lt. Col. Burl G. Campbell (P), Lt. Col. William L. Horrell (CP), Major Harold R. Crawford (N), MSgt Ronald E. Wheeler (FE), and Sgt Roy L. Lawson (CC).

All other 71st SOS personnel (258) and unit equipment were airlifted to Vietnam from Lockbourne by three C-141s. The first C-141 flight departed Lockbourne on 10 December with the squadron advance party (ADVON) headed by Lt. Col. Donald L. Beyl and unit equipment onboard. The ADVON arrived at Nha Trang on 12 December and began preparations for the arrival of the main force of squadron personnel and the gunships. The second C-141 flight departed Lockbourne on 22 December and arrived at Nha Trang 24 December with mostly personnel. The third and last C-141 arrived as scheduled at Nha Trang in mid-January 1969 with the remainder of squadron personnel and equipment.

Thirty officers and sixty enlisted personnel of the original three hundred thirty-seven personnel recalled for active duty did not deploy to South Vietnam with the 71st SOS for various reasons including overage of personnel, medical, hardship, humanitarian, and lack of retainability.

The last two AC-119G aircraft departed St. Augustine on 29 January 1969. By the second day of March, all eighteen AC-119G gunships of the 71st SOS had arrived at Nha Trang and the combat theater of South Vietnam.

As gunships arrived at Nha Trang, maintenance crews removed the temporary ferry fuel tanks from the cargo decks and reinstalled the gun mounts and miniguns while fixing any aircraft write-ups to make the aircraft operational ready for combat duty. Aircrew members were scheduled for and attended training at the PACAF Jungle Survival School at Clark Air Base, Philippines.

The first radio call sign authorized by higher command for the 71st SOS gunships was "CREEP." Who in the world thinks up such names? The squadron and air crew members protested and were allowed to request

71st SOS Pilot Lt. Col. Don Beyl and Navigator Capt. Bill Joyce ready at sunset for another night mission in South Vietnam. (Courtesy of Al Heuss)

their own call sign. They requested "SHADOW." The request was approved to become effective 1 December 1968. The call sign fit the black and camouflaged color of the war machine that only flew combat missions during the hours of darkness. Shadow also reflected the moral fiber of its mission to deny the enemy sanctuary from aerial attack from dusk to dawn.

Introduction to Combat

The first AC-119G Shadow combat mission was flown on 5 January 1969, call sign Shadow 41. Aircraft Commander Lt. Col. Donald Beyl took off from Nha Trang at 2226 hours in aircraft number 905. Shadow 41 fired only 1,300 rounds that night, but friendly folks on the ground were grateful for the help.

Combat evaluation of the Shadow gunship continued until 8 March 1969 by a team from the Tactical Air Command under Major Darrell E.

Wood. The team analyzed Shadow's performance in interdiction, base/hamlet defense, armed reconnaissance, close-air support, and forward air controlling. During the combat evaluation period, a mission statement for the Shadow emerged:

> To search out enemy infiltration routes, installations, and destroy his means to wage war. Respond with firepower and illumination in close support of strategic hamlets under night hostile attacks. Supplement strike aircraft in defense of friendly forces and provide harassing interdiction fire support. Insure escort for convoys and respond as directed in support of defense of friendly forces.

The evaluation report confirmed combat effectiveness of the gunship with the exception of forward air controlling. The gunship was judged not suitable for forward air control work. Size and speed of the AC-119 made it impossible to maintain visual contact with the fighters that was necessary to safely direct a fighter strike and adjust ordnance delivery. The aircraft proved to be slow and hard to maneuver while vulnerable to enemy fire, which was not conducive to the role as a Forward Air Controller (FAC). The 71st SOS achieved combat-ready status (C-1) on 11 March 1969.

The Shadow had limitations. Regardless of powerful twin 3350 radial engines, the gunship was still underpowered at take-off for safe single engine climb performance at gross weight. The aircraft was not equipped for all-weather capability which hampered operation in adverse weather conditions and mountainous terrain. The gunship was slow at 140 knots firing circle speed, making it highly vulnerable to enemy ground fire below altitudes of 3,500 feet; therefore, it couldn't logically be used in a high-threat triple-A environment, specifically the Ho Chi Minh Trail in Laos.

Armed reconnaissance missions were designed to interdict enemy supply lines and harass enemy units. The AC-119s were assigned an area to patrol. The area was bounded by precise coordinates, usually using TACAN (Tactical Air Navigation) radial and distance. Soon, aircrews called them "Shadow Boxes." The first boxes were located west of the cities of Kontum and Pleiku. Cambodia, Laos, and South Vietnam converged there in the so-called "Tri-Border" area, one of the Ho Chi Minh Trail terminus areas. The gunship crews quickly showed their aggressiveness in searching for targets. Some of the more aggressive crews would "take 'er right down on the deck" to get at the target. They frequently pressed in at 500 feet using the white spot light illuminator and flares to find Viet Cong and North Vietnamese forces. There was one report on hitting sampans at 300 feet in the night. Shadow put the white spotlight on the sampan and the VC immediately jumped into the water before the sampans were destroyed.

When Shadow received firing clearance, land targets were marked with an MK-6 flare (marker log) and then the Shadow would climb to firing altitude. This was usually 2,500 or 3,500 AGL because the guns were bore-sighted for these altitudes and they couldn't fire as accurately below 1,500 feet AGL. The threat of anti-aircraft guns and/or inclement weather conditions sometimes limited target acquisition and/or attacks.

To enter a "Firing Circle" to attack a target, the pilot (aircraft commander) banked the gunship left into a 30 degree turn to orbit the target in a 360 degree, approximately circular path around the target. Once the target was identified and firing clearance obtained, the pilot focused on the target through a side-looking, side-mounted optical gun sight located at his command station gunsight to his left while maneuvering the gunship with ailerons and rudder. As he maneuvered the aircraft, the pilot held the target in his gun sight reticle (crosshair).

Upon entering the firing circle, the pilot had directed his copilot to "hold the pitch" (i.e., to maintain the designated firing altitude). In addition to maintaining altitude with his flight control column, the copilot monitored radios, engine and flight instruments (especially the airspeed indicator), calling-out banks over thirty degrees, and watching for anti-aircraft fire. It was the responsibility of the copilot to take control of the aircraft if the pilot exceeded forty-five degrees bank in the firing circle. Pilot vertigo was always possible especially during night missions. It was critical that the aircraft maintain a constant speed in the firing circle; approximately 140 knots indicated. The FE sat on an empty ammo can placed behind the pilot's console located between the pilot and copilot. The FE also monitored engine instruments, especially fuel gauges. It was his duty to inform the pilot when fuel tanks needed switching. Two fuel tanks were located in the each wing. Figuring "bingo fuel" was also a critical duty of the FE.

If all parameters were met, the guns pointed broadside to the target would fire when the pilot pressed the trigger button on his yoke to expend a continuous barrage of projectiles down on the enemy. If the pylon turn was perfectly coordinated, the target theoretically was hit repeatedly until the pilot stopped firing.

This brought nearly continuous, accurate delivery of ordnance from a firing point at any bearing angle from the target. The attack permitted little recovery time for the enemy. He was constantly being flanked or attacked from the rear unless he had 360 degree shielding.

One Shadow was directed to an outpost under attack near Dak To. Victor Charlie (VC) was lobbing mortars on the outpost's perimeter. The ground unit requested flares. Flares were launched and eventually the 20KW white light activated. The gunship fired all four guns at high rate, creating a blanket of red tracers on the enemy locations. The Viet Cong made a hasty retreat, thus showing a high respect for the flying fire dragon. Nighttime close-air support and hamlet defense by the AC-119G Shadow proved to be very effective.

Aircraft and crews continued to arrive at Nha Trang. By the conclusion of the combat evaluation period, all eighteen aircraft assigned were on station. The 71st Special Operations Squadron was fully deployed under the command of Lt. Col. James E. Pyle. The old "Flying Boxcar" had truly been transformed from a cargo/troop transport to an aerial attack weapon system that had proven itself worthy of combat action.

***

The 71st SOS was assigned to the 14th Special Operations Wing headquartered at Nha Trang Air Base. Nha Trang also served as 71st SOS headquarters and the main support base for the AC-119G gunships. As air

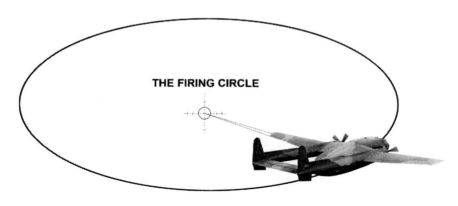

The firing circle.

crews were checked-out as combat ready (CR), FOLs were established and activated. FOL Flight C at Tan Son Nhut Airport first activated in January 69 with five gunships and then Flight B at Phan Rang Air Base with six gunships became operational by 15 February. Flight A was assigned to Nha Trang with five gunships combat ready and two spare gunships. Spares were flown from Nha Trang to forward locations and exchanged for aircraft due for periodic Inspection, Repair As Needed (IRAN). All three FOL flights flew three fragged (fragmentary order) missions each night with first mission take-offs at 1830 hours. Second and third mission take-offs followed at two to three hour intervals.

The 71st SOS and A Flight Commander at Nha Trang was Lt. Col. James E. Pyle and the operations officer was Lt. Col. Warren L. Johnson. B Flight commander at Phan Rang was Lt. Col. William E. Long and operations officer was Lt. Col. Earl W. Scott. Lt. Col. Donald F. Beyl was C Flight commander at Tan Son Nhut with Lt. Col. Robert S. Mulgrew as flight operations officer.

Shadow navigator Major Bill Hamilton was a member of the Nha Trang Shadow crew that flew the first Shadow gunship combat sortie in Vietnam on 5 January 1969. After several more checkout missions at Nha Trang, his crew was moved to Tan Son Nhut AB, Saigon to establish C Flight, FOL Det. 1, on 17 January 1969. Hamilton wrote about his initial impressions of Tan Son Nhut, "We were a tenant unit on the base and were not very welcome. We had to beg, borrow and steal most all of the equipment we needed to operate. We were given the oldest trucks, jeeps, etc. We were just not wanted!"[2]

Before any missions were flown in III Corps by C Flight at Tan Son Nhut, crews were recalled to Nha Trang. Major Hamilton explained why:

> Upon arrival (at Nha Trang), several of our officer crewmembers, to include myself, were sent to Nakhon Phanom AB, Thailand. While there we flew sorties with the C-123 Candlesticks over the Ho Chi Minh Trail. This was to prepare us to fly Armed Recon and FAC missions with our AC-119G's. After our arrival back at Nha Trang, our crew flew the only out of country missions flown by the AC-119G/Shadow. We flew with a F-100 fast FAC on board and it was our and all of the Shadow crews good luck, that the powers to be, after we told them about the narrow misses you have in a plane that flies a 360 circle around its target and that 7.62 mini guns were not the thing to do combat with on the trail, cancelled all further missions on the trail. [The AC-119K Stinger with its 20mm cannons did a great job on the trail later on.] That one mission with the Candlestick crew and the five (Shadow) missions on the trail were the six worst missions I flew in South East Asia. Although I only saw it six times, I will never forget what that big AAA looks like coming up at you. Especially in a slow mover! My crew and I were the first members of the Field Goal Club! That is where you have 57mm rounds go between the twin booms that extend from the engines to the vertical stabilizer. No points for the bad guys, thank goodness![3]

Upon returning to Tan Son Nhut from missions conducted out of Nha Trang, the 71st SOS FOL Det 1 "C" Flight eventually earned overdue respect from the host air base located on the outskirts of Saigon. Major Hamilton wrote: "The local Security Police were our best friends at first because we could get the gun barrels they needed for their APCs. We were also the only offense, firepower carrying (aerial) unit on the base. After we were able to stop some of the base attacks and provide some defense to the base we were more than welcome at last. We flew the first mission in III Corp on Jan 28, 1969, with the first mission in IV Corps on February 1, 1969. Our main mission at first was armed recon along the Cambodian/Vietnam border. We operated in the areas of the Parrot's Beak, Angel Wing, Dog's Head, and areas due west of Tay Ninh. We later expanded that area to include War Zone C as well. With our night scope and infrared light we were able to pick up movers, camp fires under the jungle canopy, sampans, etc. on moonless nights, which had previously been Charlie's safe time. The fact that we could fire without dropping flares caught the enemy unprepared. This proved to be an additional harassment, as they now had to respect all aircraft noise as a potential threat, not just when the flares came out.

Our first major troops-in-contact (TIC) came on February 15, 1969. The next one occurred the night and morning of February 22 and 23, 1969 and was in support of Fire Support Base (FSB) Thunder II on Highway 13 running north out of Saigon. We flew two sorties totaling 9.8 hours and fired 150,000 rounds of 7.62 Ammo. It was during these two missions that the ground forces found that with our equipment, we could fire right up to the perimeter wire without exposing their positions. We stopped the base from being overrun that night and for our efforts were awarded the Distinguished Flying Cross. But more importantly to us, we were made honorary members of the Big Red One and become the most requested air asset in-country at night. Our success in this mission was underlined by the GI who on a later encounter with the VC and was about to be overrun said, "Screw the F-4s—get me a SHADOW!" Or the famous good night message we often received, "Good night, thank you, and God bless you Shadow!'"[4]

When the 71st Tactical Airlift Squadron was called to active duty, the C-119G aircraft crew consisted of two pilots, one navigator, one flight engineer, and one loadmaster. The AC-119G gunship crew required two pilots, two navigators, one flight engineer, two gunners, and one illuminator operator. Loadmasters cross-trained as illuminator operators (IOs) and volunteers from other Reserve Units were accepted to fill other vacancies in addition to the Air Staff ordering men from various Air Force sources to fully man the 71st SOS.

The AC-119 Shadow gunship combat aircrew was comprised of four commissioned officers and four enlisted/noncommissioned officers (NCOs). Aircraft Commander (AC) pilot and the copilot (CP) were both officers as were the two rated navigators. One navigator was stationed at the chart table directly behind the copilot's seat on the flight deck. He was called the "NAV" or the "Table Navigator;" whereas, the other navigator was called the "NOS" because he operated the infrared/starlight Night Observation Scope (NOS) located in the cargo deck of the aircraft.

The NOS stood in the open doorway (the door had been removed) where the scope was installed to find, identify, and track targets in the dead of night for the pilot to shoot. If the pilot could not actually see the target or if the pilot wanted to pinpoint bullet impact, he would take guidance from the NOS through the onboard fire control computer into his gunsight. Navigators were qualified to perform either one of the navigator positions on the gunship and commonly alternated positions between missions.

Four enlisted crewmembers, many of which had attained the ranks of noncommissioned officers, were the flight engineer (FE), the illuminator operator (IO), and two airborne weapons mechanics aka aerial gunners (AG).

The FE was a highly knowledgeable and experienced aircraft mechanic/maintenance man on flight status who helped pilots operate, monitor, and troubleshoot performance of engines and aircraft systems. He was one of the AC pilot's right hand men when it came to flying in a firing circle, leaning fuel/air mixtures for maximum fuel performance and the least amount of exhaust stack emissions so enemy gunners couldn't spot the gunship at night, conducting burnouts so sparkplugs didn't foul, and adjusting throttles in order to maintain a constant indicated airspeed of between 138 and 140 knots in the firing circle. The FE closely monitored fuel gauges and was responsible for advising the pilot when fuel tanks (four fuel tanks on the gunship) needed to be switched before a tank ran dry. The FE was also responsible for fuel consumption calculations and figuring "BINGO" fuel, i.e., when the gunship had enough fuel left onboard to return to home base to make at least one go-around before making a full stop landing or possibly running out of avgas before safely landing.

The IO/Spotter operated the flare launcher that contained twenty-four flares and the big white spot light that turned night into day on the ground. He was also the gunship's eyes to the rear of the aircraft. He scanned for and spotted AAA and called for break-outs from the firing circle when enemy fire was about to hit the gunship. The IO was the gunship's designated "jump-master," in case the crew had to bailout. He was responsible for ejecting the flare launcher (at the AC's command) to make an exit from the aircraft and insuring that crewmen had parachute chest and leg straps secured before jumping.

Two aerial gunners, one of which was designated senior or lead gunner and the other his assistant, maintained, loaded, cleared jams, and safe guarded the four 7.62mm miniguns onboard Shadow gunships. For the pilot to have one, two, three, or four guns in firing mode (online), he ordered the gunners over the aircraft intercom to activate the gun(s), (e.g., "Give me two guns online, low rate"). At low and high firing rates of 3,000 rounds-per-minute and 6,000 rounds-per-minute respectively, the pilot would call for a gun or guns at low or high rates of fire which the gunner would set. The gunner would then and only then switch a gun(s) from "safe" mode to "firing" mode on his control panel located in the cargo deck. Then the pilot could press the gun trigger on his yoke and the gun(s) would fire. Once the number of guns to be brought online and the rate of fire was ordered by the pilot and activated by the gunners, the guns were HOT!

Changing firing altitudes because of enemy AAA fire or inclement weather caused Shadow gunners heartburn. Adjusting minigun azimuth to another flight level created mayhem on the gun deck. Gunners sometimes moaned and groaned but always got the job done.

Shadow gunners proved to be a special breed of aerial warriors; red, white, and blue thru and thru. They may have been the heart and soul of Shadow spirit. Seldom if ever did a Shadow pilot not have guns ready to fire upon his orders. The guns were always loaded and operational for combat action, thanks to the dedicated aerial weapons mechanics called gunners who flew on the Shadow.

The business card of the 71st and the 17th Special Operations Squadrons, with its motto "Deny Him The Dark," read:

> When Uninvited Guests Drop In…Call for "The Shadow."
> We Provide: Lighting for All Occasions, Beaucoup 7.62
> Mortar Suppression. We Defend: Special Forces Camps, Air
> Bases, Outposts, Troops in Contact. Who Knows What Evil
> Lurks Below the Jungle Canopy? THE SHADOW KNOWS.

The Shadow business card was instigated and designed by 71st SOS aerial gunner SSgt Alvin Reynolds at Nha Trang Air Base in early 1969 as the follow-on to the business card of AC-47 Spooky gunships.

(*From top, clockwise*): 71st SOS patch, 17th SOS patch, Shadow calling card.

FOUR

71st SOS Combat Operations

After nearly four years of war, starting in November 1965, 1969 would mark the final year of AC-47 Spooky gunship operations as the 3rd and 4th Special Operations Squadrons were inactivated and their aircraft were turned over to the VNAF and to the RLAF.

The arrival of AC-119 gunships in Vietnam signaled the start of planned one-for-one tradeoff of AC-47 gunships to allied forces. In August, the 3rd SOS flew its last mission before inactivation on 1 September 69. On 1 December 69, the last mission of the 4th SOS was flown and the squadron was inactivated on 16 December 69. The legacy of USAF AC-47 gunships would live on thereafter.

Initially, upon the arrival of the 71st SOS, Shadows joined AC-47 Spooky gunships to protect hamlets, outposts, Special Forces camps, district towns, and other fixed military positions. The "Spooky" Air Patrol became the "Spooky/Shadow" Air Patrol. Ground commanders and air controllers even interchanged the call signs, but nobody cared except for Shadow navigator Major Frank J. Emma. On his second solo combat mission, Emma was flying the desk position for navigators on the AC-119 flight deck while continuously monitoring the UHF, HF, VHF, and FM radios onboard the Shadow. As he monitored the radios, a U.S. Army ground unit in danger of being overrun requested the Direct Air

Support Center (DASC) for immediate air support from a Spooky gunship. Emma contacted the DASC and informed them that Shadow was a
gunship only five minutes from the Army unit and could provide fire
support. DASC replied that our Shadow could not respond because the
ground contact had specifically requested a Spooky, not a Shadow gunship. Consequently, DASC scrambled an AC-47 Spooky gunship and
the Army ground unit waited for nearly thirty minutes for air support.

On the next day, Emma met with the Ground Liaison Officer (GLO),
an Army captain named Doug, and reported the incident. Doug confirmed that ground soldiers only knew of the Spooky and were unaware
of the new Shadow gunship. With the approval of Emma's aircraft commander, Lt. Col. Knie, Emma and copilot Tommy Peterson set out to
educate U.S. ground troops as to the capabilities and utilization of the
Shadow gunship. They were first flown to Landing Zone Bayonet and
thereafter to other U.S. units to get the word out for ground units "to
simply request the most available gunship!"[1]

With its night observation scope, automatic flare launcher containing
twenty-four flares, and its searchlight of a million candlepower, the AC-
119 Shadow gunship backed-up its motto "Deny Him The Dark." No
longer could the nighttime attacks by Viet Cong and NVA units strike
without detection from the Shadow in the sky. The steady red stream of
7.62mm tracers spoke a common language among enemy and friendly
forces. Die from the sky if attacker; survive if friendly defender. The
71st SOS AC-119s defended 1,296 positions during the first three
months of 1969. Not one friendly position was overrun when there was
a Shadow flying overhead. That combat performance record helped
Shadow aircrews build great morale and confidence in their mission

A typical night combat mission began in the intelligence briefing
room where targets were assigned by direct air support control agencies.
Enemy actions were briefed and in case of bail-out, escape and evasion
plans, safe ground havens and rescue procedures were covered. Navigators planned routes to targets while obtaining information on friendly artillery activity and heavy bombing strikes. Later, Aircraft Commander
Pilots briefed their crews on the mission profile before crewmembers

donned approximately seventy pounds of flying and survival gear in preparation for boarding the gunship for the mission.

Checklists were completed from engine start-up to engine run-up checks before taking the active runway for takeoff. The copilot communicated with ground control for taxi instructions and later with the control tower for take-off clearance. The NAV conducted air-ground radio communications, many times over three separate radios to obtain flight clearance through U.S. Army artillery sections prior to take-off and en route to target areas. Flying slow and low during artillery firings could result in disaster.

The table navigator (aka NAV) utilized ground control radar vectors, TACAN stations, and his charts to direct the aircraft commander to the target area. Approaching the target area, the NAV and the NOS worked together to accurately acquire and identify the target. All the while, the pilots, gunners, and illuminator operator were accomplishing checklists in preparation for striking the target. After the target was positively identified, the NAV requested clearance to fire on the target, usually from province chief control, to avoid firing on friendly troops or civilians.

If firing clearance was obtained, the NOS and the NAV worked closely with the aircraft commander as he maneuvered the aircraft to enter a firing circle and to affix his gunsight crosshairs with the crosshairs superimposed on his gunsight from the NOS. With the copilot maintaining the designated firing altitude, the pilot pressed the firing button on his control yoke to fire on the target.

Along with the pilot, the NAV and the NOS made assessments of target damage from the firings, especially through communications with the ground contact's confirmation of hitting enemy troop positions and subsequent cessation of enemy action. When not in radio contact with ground controllers, any secondary explosions or indications of a kill were reported by the NOS to the gunship aircraft commander pilot and navigator to report upon mission completion.

***

In early 1969, a village compound near Tay Ninh was under Viet Cong attack and electrical power to the compound was lost as a local doctor bent over a wounded Vietnamese soldier, prostrate on a stretcher. The night was muggy, too muggy for a delicate surgical operation, especially without substantial lighting. A call for help was answered by a Shadow, piloted by Lt. Col. Burl G. Campbell, who was supporting the Vietnamese forces in efforts to clear the enemy out of the besieged village. The DASC at Bien Hoa directed Shadow to fly up the river to Go Dau Ha, then direct to Tay Ninh. Campbell pushed up the throttles a bit more, the auxiliary power unit (APU) was brought on-line, and the illuminator "white spotlight" was activated and ready to go.

Campbell rolled the bird into its 30 degree left pylon turn with the white light focused on the target, the doctor, and patient. A disciplined orbit was held for more than thirty minutes despite enemy fire as minutes dragged on until the surgery was completed. The Vietnamese soldier did survive to fight another day.

***

During his 210 missions in Southeast Asia, AC/IP Major Robert J. Allen logged 678 hours combat flying time in the AC-119G Shadow gunship. Flying out of Nha Trang, Phan Rang, and Tuy Hoa, RVN included missions in South Vietnam and Laos and if his Shadow navigator got mixed-up reading his map, inadvertent intrusions into North Vietnam and Cambodia. Nonetheless, corrections in flight paths were implemented.

One mission that Major Allen flew early in his tour of duty was patrolling the Ho Chi Minh Trail in Laos. His four miniguns were strictly loaded with ball ammunition without red tracers. Locating several trucks moving down the trail, he rolled in to hit the lead and the last truck to stop the enemy convoy. With the lead vehicle targeted by the NOS and clearance to fire, he pressed the firing button and was amazed when a steady stream of red tracers left the aircraft and headed for the target. Almost immediately, several enemy anti-aircraft weapons of varying sizes began returning fire, which drove away his Shadow gunship before getting shot down.

On another mission near Dak To, ground troops reported taking fire from a hillside, but as soon as Allen's Shadow flew into the area, everything got quiet. After flying around for a while, Shadow left the area and flew approximately twenty miles south, turned out all navigation and anti-collision lights, and then returned to the target area blacked-out. The enemy had resumed their attack and support weapons were firing, which the NOS could pinpoint on his scope. Allen immediately fired on the enemy weapons, subsequently witnessing several large secondary explosions. The attack was stifled.

***

The reputation of Shadow grew with time and successful missions. Some thought the Shadow could see anything in the dark. The Shadow was even directed to checkout the unidentified flying objects (UFOs) under Operation "Whiskey Box" in the Duc Co area of western II Corps. That's right, UFOs! Tactical radars were picking up low flying objects. The matter had aroused operational interest. The enemy might be transporting men and equipment by helicopter. The logistics line of enemy covert operations ran from Cambodia to strategic locations in South Vietnam. The AC-119s were sent to investigate. They worked with U.S. Army Hawk radar elements and Army helicopter gunships. Shadow made several runs into the area. The crew saw UFOs of helicopter speed and altitude, but couldn't identify or intercept them. When the unidentified flights stopped, the matter was left unresolved.

***

Major Bill Hamilton wrote about expanded capabilities of the Shadow. "In March we began a new phase of our operations. We began to assist the Forward Air Controllers (FACs) in putting in airstrikes. We would drop flares, mark ground positions with log flares, and also use our white light to change night into day. We also gave the FAC a ready ground fire suppression capability...."[2]

***

Most gunship crews assumed alert status at some time during their tour at FOL Shadow Operations, waiting for a call for immediate air support to fight off an enemy attack somewhere in their area of operations (AO). Such was the case at Tan Son Nhut for the crew of Shadow 77 of C Flight in response to an air support request in Tay Ninh Province.

Sergeant Louis Gabor, a twenty-four-year-old draftee from Pomona, California, assigned to Company D, 2/5, 1st Calvary Division in Vietnam as an RTO for the company commander, wrote about Shadow 77 arriving overhead during an encounter with NVA troops in early March 1969:

> As part of a battalion-sized operation to interdict enemy units crossing into Vietnam on 07 March 1969, we were on patrol in III Corps, SSE of Nui Ba Den (Black Virgin Mountain) and WNW of Trang Bang, between the Vam Co Dong River and the Cambodian border. In the late afternoon we established our FOB [forward operating base] in a rectangular lot with trees and other vegetation planted around the perimeter. Nearby were dwellings, apparently abandoned and dry rice patties. We established fighting positions (foxholes) all around the FOB perimeter and set out claymore mines and trip flares. The 1st and 2nd platoons left our location after dark to set up ambush sites. The 1st platoon's ambush site was located approximately 500 meters south of our FOB and the 2nd platoon took up an ambush position approximately 500 meters to the west of the FOB. The sky was clear with some moonlight, so we could see shapes and shadows on the ground as we scanned the surrounding terrain for enemy movement. Our primary focus was to the west, toward the Cambodian border.
>
> Around midnight, we were alerted by the sound of small arms fire and explosions coming from the west. The 2nd platoon had gotten hit hard by NVA troops, but was able to disengage from the enemy and return to our FOB location with one KIA and eleven WIA. We called in Medevac choppers to carry out the casualties. We had just gotten the Medevac's out when we heard the sound of mortars being fired coming from the west of the 1st platoon's position. They fired so

many, and so fast, that from our location, the mortars sounded somewhat like popcorn popping and I thought that either the 1st platoon's position, or ours, was going to be hit. Mortars are fired at a high angle, so a few tense moments passed before we started hearing the explosions coming from the 1st platoon's location. It sounded like they were going to get hammered but, probably alerted by the 2nd platoon's fire-fight, they had managed to leave their ambush position just before it was hit.

It wasn't long after the mortars had stopped that I heard our people talking to Shadow 77 on the radio. Our radio contact and fire controllers on the ground were artillery forward observers with the call sign "Birth Control 29." Our company call sign was "Ready Navajo." In a few minutes, Shadow 77 was over the 1st platoon's location.

Shadow 77 came over blacked-out and I couldn't see the gunship even after he kicked out three flares to light up the ground. If twelve o'clock is west, the Shadow launched the flares from about one to ten o'clock (counter-clockwise orbit for the gunship) and immediately started taking machine gun fire from the NVA. Between eight and four o'clock in its orbit, it looked like Shadow fired three miniguns at enemy positions. Red tracers streamed from the sky. I could hear the prolonged growl "Grrrrrrrrrrrr" of Shadow's guns but could not see the aircraft. After Shadow 77 finished its firing run, things got real quiet. The 1st platoon came back to our position a short time later with no casualties.

Considering that the NVA weren't stopped by the 2nd Platoon's ambush, that they continued on to hit the 1st Platoon's position with a mortar barrage, and that they knew our location because the Medevac choppers had landed in our FOB, I think the situation could have gotten really serious if Shadow 77 hadn't helped us out. "Thank you, Shadow 77."[3]

While unable to identify the Shadow 77 crew members that supported Sgt Gabor's company, Captain Gene Schaltenbrand, a pilot assigned at the time to 17th SOS C Flight based at Tan Son Nhut AB, wrote in response to author's inquiry via e-mail: "Shadow Aircraft Commanders were not assigned individual call sign numbers. We flew four frags every night with radio call signs of Shadow 74, 75, 76, and 77 (the latter being the alert aircraft). As I recall, Shadow 74 patrolled IV Corps, Shadows 75 & 76 covered III Corps, and Shadow 77 would go where needed."

***

Upon returning to base (RTB) from a mission, the Shadow navigator obtained friendly artillery clearances for the route home while the pilot, copilot, and flight engineer recomputed fuel reserves and fuel consumption while making power adjustments, running post-mission checklists, and assessing any battle damage or performance write-ups. The aircraft was evaluated by crewmembers for a possible "turn-around" mission in case there was a need for additional air support in which the aircraft would be immediately refueled and rearmed with ammunition and flares at the base.

Gunners reported the number of rounds expended, reported and repaired malfunctioning miniguns if possible, reloaded functional guns if sufficient ammunition remained onboard, and policed spent casings on the gun deck floor on the way home just in case the gunship would be "turned around" for another combat mission upon landing at homebase. The IO reported the number of flares launched during the mission and any discrepancies with the flare launcher or the white light.

If there was no need for a turn-around mission, the gunship landed and crews attended debriefings where crewmembers provided information to intelligence personnel for mission reports.

Many combat missions flown by the 71st SOS were simply routine fire support missions while others were far more intense with actual duels with enemy .51 caliber machinegun sites. Such was the case for a Phan Rang B Flight Shadow commanded by Lt. Col. William E. Long who explained the mission:

We were working in an area of heavy enemy movement (target #1) when a friendly unit called for assistance against a small arms and mortar attack (target #2). Firing on enemy locations, the attack was broken off. Later on we were again called to help another unit under intense automatic weapons fire. We turned on our (white) spotlight to draw enemy fire so he would reveal his position. It worked, and Charlie opened up on us with .50 caliber machineguns.[4]

Long shot back destroying three of the six positions while causing four secondary explosions. Colonel Long stated, "That was the heaviest automatic weapons fire we have encountered in several weeks. We sometimes found ourselves in crossfire from several (enemy gun) positions, but our guns caused all the damage—to them."[5]

Most missions were scheduled for five hours. Many times, crews returned to homebase and refueled, rearmed, and relaunched for another five hours of combat. Targets ranged from interdiction of infiltration routes and troops-in-contact to defending villages under attack. A frantic radio call to divert to another target up to 100 miles away required full power to race across the night sky in order to arrive in time to provide aerial support for American or South Vietnamese troops under attack.

Another crew saved many lives of friendly troops by calling off a B-52 bombing strike in the friendly location. "Thank you very much. You made my DEROS possible" and many other expressions of appreciation from U.S. ground troops were radioed to the Shadow gunships for support during combat operations in Vietnam.

***

The organizational structure of HQ 71st SOS in the spring of 1969 showed Lt. Col. James E. Pyle, squadron commander; Lt. Col. Richard E. Knie, deputy commander, Lt. Col. Warren L. Johnson, operations officer; Lt. Col. William L. Horrell, executive officer; Major Duane C. Oberg, administrative officer; MSgt Harold W. Peach Sr., first sergeant; Major Kenneth B. Richardson and Captain Edwin C. Humphrey, aircraft

maintenance officers; Major Clyde Sherrill, flying safety officer; and
Major Herman A. Heuss, stand/eval officer.

Nine crews and seven gunships were assigned to A Flight at Nha
Trang. Lt. Col. Russel A. O'Connell was A Flight commander and Lt.
Col. John W. Lewis was assistant operations officer. The 71st SOS operations officer, Lt. Col. Warren L. Johnson, also served as the ops officer for A Flight.

Nine crews and six gunships were assigned to B Flight at Phan Rang.
Lt. Col. William E. Long was B Flight commander. Lt. Col. Earl W.
Scott was operations officer.

Seven crews and five gunships were assigned to C Flight at Tan Son
Nhut. Lt. Col. Donald E. Beyl was C Flight commander. Lt. Col. Robert
S. Mulgrew was ops officer.

The 71st SOS Flight Crew Roster on 15 March 1969 shows twenty-
five complete combat crews of eight men per crew and twenty-two
unassigned aircrew members for a total of 222 combat aircrew men in
the squadron. Of the 222 air crewmen, 81 were activated reservist and
141 were assigned to the 71st from other active duty assignments. All
fifty-six aerial gunners came from active duty status.

***

One day in May, 71st SOS B Flight based at Phan Rang proved that
Shadow was not just a "fly by night" combat aircraft. Aircraft commander Lt. Col. F.J. Rostkowski and his Shadow crew had completed
their night mission and were relieved for crew rest. At 1150 hours, B
Flight received a request to provide aerial support for troops in contact
eleven miles east of Phan Rang. Roused from their beds, Rostkowski's
crew rushed to the flight line and their assigned gunship.

Airborne by 1212 hours, they were over the target area within five
minutes to support South Vietnam (RVN) Marine forces attempting to
make a beach landing to recover dead and wounded ARVN soldiers.
Phan Rang-based F-100 Supersabres arrived to bomb and strafe enemy
locations under directions from the on-site FAC before Rostkowski's
Shadow expended 18,000 rounds in six minutes out of a total of 21,000

rounds into enemy positions. Shadow gunner Sgt Wade Dunn was credited with keeping the miniguns online during the fierce hail of fire. Even so, Shadowmen still regarded the primary mission of the Shadow gunship as a night stalker/attacker to "Deny Him The Dark," i.e., deny enemy forces the protection of darkness to attack.[6]

During May 1969, replacements for activated reserve troops of the 71st SOS began to arrive in Vietnam. In-country training for incoming regular AF troops was accomplished thru on-the-job training. Squadron transition from the 71st SOS activated reserves to the 17th SOS regular forces would prove to be flawless.

The accomplishments of the 71st SOS during the period from 1 January 1969 through 31 May 1969 were most impressive. The Squadron operated from three locations in Vietnam: Flight A based at Nha Trang flew 2,697 hours on 764 combat missions; Flight B based at Phan Rang flew 1,985 hours on 372 combat missions; and Flight C based at Tan Son Nhut flew 1,568 hours on 350 combat missions.

During its six-month tour of duty in Vietnam during 1969, the 71st SOS flew a total of 1,209 fragged sorties (1,516 combat missions), 6,251 combat hours, fired 14,555,150 rounds of 7.62mm ammunition and dropped 10,281 flares. Seventh Air Force credited the 71st with 682 confirmed enemy killed by air with an estimated total of 1,104 enemy killed by Shadows. The Squadron was also credited with forty-three enemy vehicles destroyed.

The 71st Shadows were involved in a number of U.S. Army and Marine Corps ground operations. Shadow gunships supported Operations "Purple Mountain" and "Dewey Canyon" in I Corps, "Green Basket" and "Putnam Panther" against the VC in II Corps, Operation "Toan Thang" in III Corps, and "Speedy Express" in IV Corps. Air support provided by the 71st SOS proved essential in destroying enemy troop movements throughout assigned areas during these land operations. Additional Air Force operations supported by the 71st while in the combat zone included a UFO hunt, Operation "Whiskey Box," the chock-point interdiction operation, and support of Ben Het area operations.[7]

On 1 June 1969, the 17th Special Operations Squadron was activated at Nha Trang under the command of Lt. Col. Richard E. Knie to replace the 71st SOS. The final 71st SOS action in Vietnam was turning over unit command of the eighteen (18) AC-119G Shadow gunships to the 17th SOS.

Activated reservists of the 71st SOS departed Nha Trang Air Base, RVN (South Vietnam) aboard three Military Airlift Command (MAC) C-141 Starlifters on 5 June 1969. Five reservists of the 71st extended their tour of duty in Vietnam: MSgt Dale Stickles, MSgt Herb Weaver, SSgt George Dragoo, SSgt Len Swallom, and SSgt Hector Trevinal.

The 71st was deactivated on 18 June 1969 at Bakalar AFB, Indiana. As of 19 June 1969, the 71st SOS reverted to USAF Reserve Status and continued training at Bakalar through December 1969 when the squadron was reassigned to Grissom AFB, Indiana.

The 71st SOS had successfully completed its mission of establishing AC-119G Shadow gunship operations in Vietnam. From active duty call-up on 13 May 1968 to deactivation on 18 June 1969, the squadron blazed the trail from combat training and deployment to combat operations in Vietnam. The Squadron was most deservingly honored with the Air Force Outstanding Unit Award for exceptionally meritorious achievement in support of operations during the period from 19 December 1968 to 30 April 1969, the Presidential Unit Citation Award for the period from 19 December 1968 to 30 June 1969, and The Republic of Vietnam Gallantry Cross with Palm for combat duty from 14 February to 4 June 1969.

Members of the 71st SOS were also submitted for 751 Air Medals, 143 Distinguished Flying Crosses, 18 Bronze Stars, and 47 Air Force Commendation Medals. Purple Hearts were awarded to two men who sustained injuries on combat missions.

Campaign Streamers for the Shadows of the 71st Special Operations Squadron included: Vietnam Air Offensive, Phase IV and TET 69/Counteroffensive.

FIVE

17th SOS Activation and Take-Over

The 17th SOS Shadows immediately picked-up where the 71st SOS left-off while absorbing approximately 65% of 71st SOS personnel. The 17th SOS Shadow replacement personnel pipeline to Vietnam was well underway, having begun months before. A steady stream of regular USAF personnel arrived just prior to and following the departure of the activated 71st SOS reservists. Pilots, navigators, and flight engineers were trained in C-119Gs at Clinton County Air Force Base, Wilmington, Ohio before reporting to the 4413th CCTS at Lockbourne AFB, Columbus, Ohio for AC-119 gunship training that included full crews of pilots, navigators, gunners, and illuminator operators in training.

By 30 June 1969, Headquarters for the 17th SOS had been moved from Nha Trang to Phan Rang Air Base. A Flight at Nha Trang was moved with four gunships to Tuy Hoa Air Base. B Flight was based at Phan Rang with seven gunships. C Flight stationed at Tan Son Nhut Air Base had five gunships. Two more squadron gunships were undergoing phase maintenance at Phan Rang.

Sorties flown in I Corps by 17th SOS A Flight based at Tuy Hoa Air Base were Frags 45 and 47 (tactical air missions assigned by TACC) and were under the control of Horn DASC (Big Control). In II Corps, Frag 48 was under the control of DASC Alpha (Ragged Scooper). B

Sgt. LeRoy Frahm, avionics specialist in the 71st and 17th SOSs, created the "Charlie Chasers" emblem after many Shadow aircrews returned to base reporting that they were "chasing Charlie" everywhere. Frahm was then summarily commissioned to paint the emblem on all 17th SOS "B" Flight gunships at Phan Rang.

Flight at Phan Rang AB Frag 61 was also tasked to II Corps. In III Corps, B Flight Frags 62 and 64 were assigned to III DASC (Pawnee Target) and were used by Pawnee in accordance with priorities. Tan Son Nhut C Flight III Corps Frags were 76 and 78 under the control of III DASC. The Shadow 76 sortie was usually fragged as an armed recce mission with specific boxes, but was on-call to respond to a TIC or TOC

(Tactical Operations Center) at any time. Shadow 78 was the III Corps alert frag at Tan Son Nhut and was usually launched only for TICs. IV Corps could also scramble Shadow 78 through TACC in cooperation with Corps DASC.

Sorties flown by the 17th SOS in IV Corps were Frags 77 and 79 and under control of IV DASC (Brute Alpha), usually contacted through the IV Corps GCI site, call sign "Paddy." Both Shadow 77 and Shadow 79 missions were fragged as armed recce missions within specific "Shadow" boxes, but could be called to respond to a TIC or TOC at any time.

Shadow radio call signs were identified by the Frag number, e.g., Shadow 61 or Shadow 77, etc. Shadow aircraft commanders were not assigned an individual radio call sign number until the beginning of 1971. Thereafter, aircraft commanders flew missions under the same Shadow number.

Typical Shadow sorties included: Combat Air Patrol (CAP) in which a specific base or area was in need of aerial defense; Armed Reconnaissance (Recce); A & I Boxes of special interest, i.e., known enemy troop concentrations or special strike zones; and TIC or TOCs where specific targets were identified by radio communication with ground controllers.

Major Bill Hamilton, Shadow navigator assigned to C Flight at Tan Son Nhut during the transition from the 71st to the 17th SOS, wrote in his memoir:

> Our Mission as the 17th SOS remained the same except in August we began to work with the Australians in Vung Tau province. We also increased our operations with the Navy SEALS and riverine forces in the Rung Sat Special Zone as well as IV Corps. We now took on the task of interdiction along the waterways of IV Corps and moved into the U Minh Forest. In November we saw an increase in our usage in the Search and Rescue (SAR) mission, but only at night. In an effort to recover two downed Army Pilots shot down near Binh Thuy, our white light and infrared light coupled with our Night Sight (night observation scope) helped slow down their (en-

emy) movement toward the U Minh Forest, enabling them (Army pilots) to be rescued by Special Forces troops and to use their words "saved our asses from a long time in captivity.[1]

Communication and cooperation between Shadow gunship aircrews and U.S. Army units had greatly improved since the arrival of the 71st SOS, thanks to the concerted efforts of people like navigator Major Frank Emma. Air controlling agencies like the crucial Direct Air Support Centers (DASCs) and allied ground troops in distress soon recognized the Shadow call sign and its capability as a gunship.

Sergeant Bobby Jones, HHB 2/20th Arty, Republic of Vietnam, wrote the following poem on 7 June 1969 about U.S. Army Fire Support Base entitled "CROOK":

As the night moves in on a fire base
And the rain starts to fall,
Here stand many sentries, these men
Are the bravest of all.
First they pick up movement, then
The bullets start to crack.
Now the soldier is ready for
The main attack.
Although the enemy are all around
These fighting men hold their ground.
Gunships are called up to their aid.
The enemy know the mistake they've made.
The battle is over, they're on the run.
For these brave men, a job well done.
But they all know they'll be back again
And these brave men will fight to win.

Fire Base "CROOK" was nestled near an enemy infiltration route in Tay Ninh Province. Army Captain Larry B. Thomas of the 22nd Infantry, Bravo Company was the Commander of CROOK. The night was corrosive, hot and sticky, too heavy for mosquitoes.

Suddenly, Charlie was on the perimeter. III Corps DASC echoed the distress call. A Shadow gunship raced to the fire support base and powered into a good pylon orbit. Clearance to fire was granted. The pilot opened with rapid fire, rocked the wings just a bit and worked the rudders to cover the enemy location. The VC faced solid red sheets of lead from the gunship but held ranks and charged time after time. Eventually, they fell back, badly bloodied bad 323 killed; no one knowing how many wounded. VC prisoners were awestruck by the aerial firepower.

Captain Thomas wrote to the Shadow outfit, expressing gratitude from Bravo Company that made Shadow men feel ten feet tall. When fellow GIs were in trouble, flight crews pulled out all the stops to help them.

> COMPANY B
> 3D BATTALION 22ND INFANTRY
> APO SAN FRANCISCO 96385
> 17 June 1969
>
> SHADOW,
>
> We in the Infantry usually complain about the support we receive; however, we know this criticism isn't necessarily justified. The perfect example of this is the tremendous support we received in the "Battle of Crook," the sixth and seventh of June 1969.
>
> Due to your outstanding performance, extremely accurate firepower, and professionalism, a determined enemy force was turned back time after time. The staggering losses suffered by the enemy and minimal amount of injury upon our own men was due to the direct result of your efficiency and effectiveness.
>
> We of Bravo Company wish to thank you for your support. If there are any questions concerning awards on your personnel who participated, contact me at Tay Ninh.
>
> Larry B. Thomas, Captain
> Infantry Commanding

***

The role of the AC-119 gunship in close-air support for the U.S. Army was of great concern. To enhance this capability, the Air Force added a variety of special sensors. Included was UHF homing and ranging device on the Shadow gunship and an X-band transponder tracking radar on the AC-119Ks.

Visits were arranged between gunship crewmembers and U.S. Army unit commanders. These informal sessions sought to strengthen perspectives and pinpoint requirements for effective operations. Crewmembers of the 17th Special Operations Squadron at Tan Son Nhut AB visited the Americal Division in the last quarter of 1969. A written guide for aiding Army commanders on gunship employment techniques grew out of these exchange visits.

Regardless of the many successful combat missions being flown during the hours of darkness, nagging problems ensued for the 17th SOS. Personnel redeployment, reorganization, and ceaseless retraining of replacement aircrew and support personnel arriving in-country from CONUS was endless. Aircraft maintenance became a significant factor in the effectiveness of the squadron. Shadow gunship maintenance was usually behind the power curve because of equipment failures, a lack of spare parts supply or disruptions in delivery of spare parts in-country, and faulty replacement engines shipped from CONUS. Some called the camouflaged boxcar a "maintenance nightmare."

Of the eighteen Shadow gunships in-country, two or three aircraft were not operational ready for combat on a regular basis due to mandatory periodic maintenance inspection and repair as necessary (IRAN) conducted at Phan Rang Air Base and corrosion control (C&C) performed at Kadena Air Base, Okinawa.

At the beginning of August, four gunships had been grounded for battle repairs. On 6 August, one more gunship took .51 caliber hits in the fuselage and one engine. The engine caught fire and extensive damage resulted. Consequently, the 17th SOS requested temporary relief from one mission (scheduled sortie) per night during this time of operations. Nevertheless, Shadows continued night support of ground troops in trouble.

***

It was 19 August 1969 and 17th SOS C Flight Shadow 77 was on alert status at Tan Son Nhut Air Base. At 0315 hours, Shadow 77 was scrambled; mission number 4038. Engines coughed to life and the mags (magnetos) checked good. The black bird lifted into the night and headed toward the target. Everything in the machine vibrated, worse than a corn blower in August. The navigator wondered at the decibel level of noise. It was tough on the ears and made the mission duration deceptively long. But what the hell, in this business, if engine noise wasn't the problem, something else was. And the aircraft radios and their nonstop diatribe put any auctioneer to shame.

Assistance was urgently needed. Five U.S. advisors were on station. Two were killed by direct hits on their building. Dust and debris was everywhere. The weather was sticky and muggy. A GI feverishly worked the radio. He was wounded with blood caked on his left arm. Red and yellow, it resembled the South Vietnam flag.

The radio crackled. Shadow 77 arrived on station within minutes with clearance to fire. Six enemy gun positions opened fire with their automatic weapons trained on the sluggish Shadow gunship. Two of the six positions were fortified. At 0334 hours, Shadow 77 took her first hit. The enemy had lost interest in their attack on "Skilled Trench Bravo." The nasty night bird had to be killed. Tracers passed abeam off Shadow's right wing, but the gunship continued to circle above its target, firing on every pass. The cockpit was hectic. It was dark as hell. The pilot maneuvered the gunship to evade ground fire. Staff Sergeant Benzi, the IO, took a deep cut in the index finger of his left hand from the sharp edge of a flare. "Death to the Communists!" someone shouted. The gunship crew was frenzied. One of the gunners pulled out his personal .38 caliber revolver and fired a few shots through a gun port. Insanity!? The enemy guns at WS 982963 and WS 975962 were silenced.

Shadow 77 called in the remaining active gun positions to IV Corps DASC for fighter strikes. 77 remained on station for Medevac choppers and flare illumination. Spat 04 and a VNAF flare ship arrived in the area to aid in air strikes. Enemy ground fire erupted again. This time it was from WS 981973. Shadow 77 poured in a few bursts of fire on high rate of 6,000 rounds-per-minute. Enemy guns were silenced at 0530 hours.

At 0550 hours, the dead and wounded were evacuated from "Skilled Trench Bravo." Army reinforcements arrived via helicopter. Shadow 77 returned to base (RTB). Sergeant Benzi required six stitches in his finger. The crew of 77 hit their party hootch for beer until noon. The mission was re-flown and critiqued ten times over.[2]

***

On the night of 3 September 1969, another Tan Son Nhut C Flight Shadow, Shadow 76 commanded by pilot Major Boschian, headed for action. The "Quarterhorse" unit of the U.S. Army was in trouble. First Squadron of the 4th Calvary could vouch for that. Headquarters and Bravo Troops were garrisoned at Thunder I near Nha Trang.

Lights appeared near the perimeter fence. The sensors began to indicate heavy movement on three sides. Friendly snipers located and killed one Viet Cong in the wood line to the south. Thunder I was under attack. Powder smoke was everywhere. Not a breath of fresh air existed because of a persistent low bank of fog.

U.S. Army Lt. Col. John T. Murchinson, Jr. was calm. He liked the Army, armor, and Vietnam. This was his kind of war. Those that didn't believe in it could get the hell out. But even Murchison needed help on the 3rd. But, why did they call in that sorry flying boxcar? It wasn't much faster than a tank, and had a lot less punch.

Shadow 76 rolled into a firing circle over Murchinson's Marauders. It was time to get the respect of these "grunts." But conditions favored Victor Charlie because Shadow 76 had big problems seeing the targets due to ground fog and smoke.

Then came a break in the layer of fog and smoke and the NOS sensor operator got a fix on the perimeter. The gunship's miniguns whined at high rate. Ground spotters adjusted the gunship fire for deadly accuracy right on the fence. Siege, smoke, fog, and spirits all lifted around midnight. And the war was shorter by one more goddam day.

Colonel Murchinson wrote: "There is no doubt in my mind that

SHADOW 76's magnificent crew was instrumental in stopping enemy action against Thunder I on 3 September 1969. The men of the 1st Squadron, 4th Calvary, commend the men of 'SHADOW 76' and look forward to operating with them in the future."[3]

***

Army field units showed their appreciation for Shadow support in many ways. Regardless of method, they all had a profound meaning to the Shadow men of C Flight. One of the more common gifts of gratitude was captured enemy weapons. Three of the best weapons were mounted and displayed in the Shadow Operations building: a Soviet 7.62mm light machinegun, RPD; a Soviet 7.62mm assault rifle, AK-47; and a Soviet antitank grenade launcher, RPG2, VC B-40.

One problem; the captured weapons were unauthorized. The solution was mounting the weapons on plaques with quick disconnects. This allowed for rapid removal and storage of the weapons in the minigun shop if the 7th Air Force Inspector General arrived.

The funny thing about the minigun shop at Tan Son Nhut was that it also was unauthorized. This fact was discovered when a telephone was requested for the shop but was disapproved. Someone had constructed the shop for only the good Lord knows what and without the approval of civil engineers. The shop appeared nowhere on their official engineering drawings. Yet, in the building, miniguns were repaired for as many as fifteen gunships. But back to the phone; due to the nonexistence of the minigun shop, another phone was ordered for the Shadow Operations building with a mighty long extension cord that reached the shop. GI ingenuity is tough to beat.

***

"Psyops" refers to psychological operations. It consisted of means short of combat designed to convince the enemy to desert and join the friendly side. It's rather unusual how the AC-119 gunships got into the psyops business. It wasn't planned that way. Certain weapons or strikes were tremendously feared by Charlie. A good one for instance was the B-52 Arc Light strikes. They were awesome. They turned many enemy underground tunnels into shambles. Craters pockmarked the landscape where enemy hid. Charlie was never sure just where the massive iron bombs would impact.

Similarly, the AC-119 gunships gave the enemy fits. The Shadow could put four guns on high rate of fire (24,000 rounds-per-minute) and "rock the wings." The barrage of firepower would cover every square inch of a football field in six seconds; enough coverage to deny easy camouflage or unlimited movement. Charlie couldn't expose his backside or fight in the open for danger of getting mowed-down by 7.62mm bullets. From the ground, the tracers (every fifth bullet fired) looked like a solid sheet of red steel coming down. And an accomplished pilot could accurately fire to within twenty-five to fifty meters of friendly forces.

Against the night sky, the gunship was tough to see, let alone hit. Charlie anti-aircraft gunners repeatedly miscalculated the lead angle to hit the unseen source of red fire. He had a tendency to lead the aircraft too much or not enough, and usually to the outside of the gunship's firing orbit. But he'd see that curtain of red tracers spewing earthward at him. His respect grew and so did the story. He called the gunships "Dragonships."

Since the enemy had such a healthy fear of the flying machine guns, it was only natural for gunships to leave a calling card for psychological purposes. One bird was assigned duty to distribute leaflets to enemy troops. The propaganda leaflets were dropped from the flare launcher doorway after a successful attack. Hopefully, the leaflets encouraged enemy survivors to convert to the friendly side.

Printed in Vietnamese, the front side of the propaganda leaflet designed for the AC-119K Stinger gunship was titled "RAIN OF DEATH" with a photo of the gunship and the caption "Here is the AC-119 gunship that just attacked you." The English translation of the backside of the leaflet read:

> Men in the Communist ranks, you were just attacked by the AC-119 gunship. This gunship is equipped with two 20mm cannons and four 7.62mm miniguns. Each has a rate of 6,000 rounds-per-minute, meaning that it can fire six

rounds into each square meter in your area in a few seconds. The aircraft can carry great quantities of ammunition, enough to saturate its target. Moreover, the AC-119 is equipped with modern electronic devices to determine your positions, your hideouts even at night. We will continue to attack you. Next time, will you escape death? We hope you will make the clear-sighted decision to rally to the National Just Cause to bring peace soon to the nation and allow you to escape a dreadful death.

Whether or not this psychological ploy had any effect was a mystery. The dead weren't talking and prisoners gave no feedback.

Not to be outdone by psyops, crewmembers of the 17th SOS now had their own calling card that was a modified calling card from the 71st SOS. The card again briefly summarized the 17th SOS operations of the AC-119 Shadow. Great pride was taken when leaving the card as a mark of excellence. Shadow men never passed up a chance to give them away to any American. Calling cards cropped up at every Shadow FOL and so did stencil-painted decals of the Shadow emblem on Shadow barracks and vehicles. The masked man from radio fame was proudly displayed on squadron patches. Only The Shadow knew what evil lurked in the minds of enemy and also what lurked in the night jungles below. Morale was kite-high. The 17th SOS had proven its effectiveness on the battlefield while growing into a seasoned combat unit.

***

In the midst of tremendous self-confidence based on so many combat missions and accomplishments achieved since the introduction of the AC-119G Shadow gunship into the Vietnam War, tragedy would strike at the least expected time. The 17th Special Operations Squadron experienced its first aircraft (tail number 538069) fatality on the night of 11 October 1969. C Flight Shadow 76 crashed shortly after takeoff from Tan Son Nhut Air Base.

The aircraft commander pilot, Major Bernard "Bernie" Knapic, had just returned to Tan Son Nhut from seeing his spouse on R & R. Copilot Captain John Hathaway was scheduled to depart Tan Son Nhut for his R & R upon completion of the Shadow 76 mission. His spouse was already in en route to Hawaii to meet him there.

Other members of the veteran crew were navigators Major Jerome Rice and Major Moses "MO" Alves; SSgt Abraham Moore (FE); gunners SSgt Bill Slater and Sgt John Lelle; and SSgt Gale "Pat" Jones (IO).

Also aboard the ill-fated flight was USAF SSgt Ellsworth Smith Bradford from the 600th Photo Squadron and Vietnamese officer/interpreter Lieutenant Biu Kien.

With all preflight inspections and mission briefings completed, scheduled takeoff time was met. Upon becoming airborne, engine #1 erupted into a blazing fire. Emergency procedures for engine fire were followed to shutdown the engine but in the process, power for flight was lost, resulting in the crash landing off the end of the runway.

Three U.S. Army soldiers were the first to arrive at the crash site. They helped rescue survivors before the aircraft became too dangerous to enter. The aircraft burst into an inferno upon fuel ignition and explosions resulted from live ammo and flares. Sergeant Lelle pulled IO Jones from the burning wreckage. Survivors were immediately flown by a rescue helicopter to 3rd Field Hospital in Saigon. Lelle, Jones, and Slater were the only crewmembers to survive the crash. USAF photographer Bradford died in the crash. Lt. Biu Kien survived the crash only to die weeks later of sustained injuries. A Vietnamese civilian was also killed when the aircraft crashed into his house located a short distance from the end of the runway.

In all, a total of eight men died from the crash of Shadow 76; five 17th SOS C Flight members, one USAF photographer, one Vietnamese officer, and one Vietnamese civilian. It was the first heart-breaking tragedy of the war for the 17th SOS but unfortunately it would not be the last.

On 10 November, another Shadow gunship sustained severe damage when its right landing gear collapsed on landing at Chu Lai Air Base, RVN. Fortunately, no crewmembers were lost or injured in the accident.

The old flying machine had certainly gotten the attention of Shadow flyers, young and old.

Major Bill Hamilton stated, "Our final operating area was with the Special Forces. We were used as diversions for insertions, extractions, and were called upon when they had contacts that could not be broken. I have flown several sorties during which we whispered to each other over the radio while we covered their movements or positions till daylight. The enemy was that close!"[4] Major Hamilton flew his last combat mission on 7 December 1969 and shortly thereafter returned to the Real World.

***

As the year was coming to an end, the weather worsened, enemy activity declined, and there was a drop in the squadron sortie rate. Less time was spent looking for Charlie. Missions became "combat air patrol" operations for protection of U.S. and friendly forces and installations. By mid-December, most of the squadron's problems resulting from the loss of men and airplanes were addressed and adjustments made to strengthen squadron posture as the 17th SOS prepared for the New Year while bidding good riddance to 1969.

Nonetheless, the 17th SOS had set a blazing pace of night missions, exceeding 2,000 sorties and 8,000 combat hours from the first day of June through December 1969. Shadows fired twenty million rounds of ammunition, expended 12,000 flares, killed 800 enemy troops and destroyed 150 sampans. The 14th Special Operations Wing laid claim to a hard fact: No allied outpost had been overrun while the gunships were on station.

SIX

Good Morning Vietnam, 1970

T he year 1970 ushered in the second year of Shadow operations in Southeast Asia. Shadow gunships had proven themselves as deadly defenders of artillery fire support bases, air bases, Special Forces camps, villages, hamlets, and outposts in South Vietnam. Aerial support of American and allied ground troops in contact with enemy forces and flying "Shadow Boxes" on armed reconnaissance missions proved productive during the past year of operations.

Command positions at squadron level occurred during the start of the New Year with completion of tours of duty and rotation back to the states. Lt. Col. Don O. Clark replaced Lt. Col. Richard E. Knie as 17th SOS Commander. Lt. Col. James M. Roach replaced Lt. Col. Matthew A. Boonstra as squadron operations officer and Major Robert G. Mems replaced Major William R. Scott as squadron executive officer.

Key personnel assigned to A Flight were Flight Commander Lt. Col. William E. Reeter, Operations Officer Lt. Col. Charles "Chuck" M. James, Administrative Officer Major Francis A. Nealon, Maintenance Officer First Lieutenant Joseph R. Maly, Jr. (replacing Major Otis W. Jones), First Sergeant MSgt James H. Lewis (replacing MSgt John P. W. Schwartz).

Commander of B Flight at Phan Rang HQ 17th SOS was the Squadron Commander Lt. Col. Don O. Clark. Flight Operations Officer was Lt. Col. James M. Roach, who also served as Squadron Ops Officer. Flight Administrative Officer was Major Charles H Meier, Jr. and Captain Robert H. Thompson was Flight and Squadron Maintenance Officer. Master Sergeant Nelson L. Horner was the Squadron and B Flight First Sergeant. Double duty was normal for many at 17th SOS Headquarters at Phan Rang.

At Tan Son Nhut Air Base, Lt. Col. Harry A. White became C Flight Commander when Lt. Col. Paul J. Buckley departed on 2 January. Flight Ops Officer was Major Remo A. Boschian, Major Richard L. Stoner was Administrative Officer, and MSgt Clarence B. Weber was First Sergeant for the Flight.

With the arrival of an AC-119G gunship from CONUS now in-country to replace the Shadow 76 aircraft lost on the October 11th crash at Tan Son Nhut, the squadron resumed its full force of eighteen gunships. Five gunships were assigned to each FOL located at Tuy Hoa, Phan Rang, and Tan Son Nhut. At Phan Rang, two gunships were undergoing phase inspections and one gunship was being repaired.

Enemy action had slowed in South Vietnam; therefore, several missions were directed to the Cambodia border areas that had lucrative interdiction targets. Specific strike zones called "Shadow Boxes" were designated for armed reconnaissance missions throughout South Vietnam. Seventh AF Intelligence set the priorities and a Shadow "patrol" box would be assigned a line number for the night sortie. En route to the box, the Shadow navigator secured artillery (arty) clearances. These approved routes often dictated a roundabout approach to the target area. To permit Shadow gunships a direct route to troops-in-contact with the enemy, a request for friendly artillery "shutdown" was made and usually granted.

Shadow pilots commonly flew a TACAN radial to a prominent landmark in the box. TACAN provided the pilot and navigator with direction and distance information from the selected station, e.g., TACAN Channel 102 located at Tan Son Nhut. The night sensor operator (NOS) would lock on a prominent landmark in the box for reference, and the crew dropped an MK-6 ground marker for positive positioning. The pilot then eased to firing altitude and took up a search pattern.

Crewmembers, especially the table navigator, put in hours of detailed study on these "Shadow Boxes." Before becoming airborne, pilots and navigators were intimately familiar with all roads, trails, rivers, and canals in the box. Crews were also expected to reconnoiter any new parallel routes. Shadow strikes during the darkest of nights created havoc on VC infiltration routes.

As the year wore on, Charlie became more aggressive. Viet Cong and even NVA troops overtly probed hamlets, Special Forces camps, Army artillery fire support bases, and military installations. Enemy logistic pipelines were a beehive of activity. The AC-119 Shadows were repeatedly called to defend U.S. troops and allies located on enemy supply routes, while working extensively with U.S. Special Forces from DaNang into the Mekong Delta. Requests for gunships soon became prefaced with "Shadow" gunship rather than "Spooky" gunship. Ground troops and DASCs had learned! And it wasn't unusual to have the ground commander demand Shadow's presence in preference to other airpower options. They knew by now that the Shadow could loiter for hours and keep Charlie down or chase him away. The besieged could eat, sleep, and somewhat relax in some degree of safety with a Shadow overhead.

Shadows could place bullets right on the edge of bunkers inside friendly troop perimeters. It was not advisable, but the request was normally granted on more than one bloody skirmish. Troops-in-contact was top priority of Shadows. Time and again, Shadows provided nighttime illumination and/or fire support for U.S. Army Special Forces camps and artillery fire support bases under attack. Any time, any place American troops were in contact with enemy forces, airborne Shadows were diverted or Shadows on alert status were scrambled to provide support. Still, units of VC and/or NVA troops were constantly on the offensive, especially during the hours of darkness.

Shadow navigator Captain Hank Alau wrote about one of his most rewarding missions; the support of Long Khat, a small town just south of the Parrot's Beak during this time:

We were flying a routine mission [out of Tan Son Nhut] when we received a request from Paddy to support troops-in-contact. About a minute later, Paddy advised us that the situation had become a tactical emergency and that artillery could not be shut down because it was supporting the emergency. We decided to fly through the artillery.

I got a sitrep from the ground controller, Bingo Marvel 49, who assured me there were no 50 cals in the area. We flew less than one-half of the first firing circle when the sky lit up with tracer fire and unmistakable popping [sound] of 50 cal. [bullets]. I called back to 49 who then acknowledged there were five guns in the area including one set up in the dispensary. We eventually managed to shutdown three of the gun positions.

Meanwhile, 49 asked us to walk our bullets in towards his camp; we moved in to within fifty meters of his perimeter. We could see it was going to be a long night for 49, so I radioed Paddy to scramble the Shadow alert bird [at Tan Son Nhut]. We pushed our on-station time to the limit. When I finally told 49 we were at bingo fuel, you could hear the panic in his voice. I then got a call from Major Rick Stoner, the navigator on Lt. Col. Mac McCullough's crew. Rick reported they [the alert bird] were only one minute out. You could hear the sigh of relief in 49's voice when I gave him the news.

On our approach to Tan Son Nhut, our fuel gauges read 400 pounds remaining. The number one engine quit [from fuel starvation] as we turned off the active [runway]. A couple of nights later I contacted 49 while flying near his AO. He reported he was doing well and thanked us for making his DEROS good in ten more days."[1]

USAF Staff Sergeant Allen Chandler wrote,

I was going back to Viet Nam to become a crewmember on a combat gunship, but not the type that saved me on my first tour of duty during the TET offensive at Tan Son Nhut in 1968. This was a fixed-wing AC-119G "Shadow" gunship, not a helicopter "Cobra" gunship. I would be flying onboard the gunship as a combat crewmember [Illuminator Operator], helping fight the enemy. I arrived in Viet Nam in February 1970 at Phan Rang Air Base for in-country processing with the 17th Special Operations Squadron (SOS) and Shadow gunship flight duty check-outs. I was assigned to and reported for duty with C Flight of the 17th SOS at Tan Son Nhut Air Base in late February 1970, almost two years to the day from the time I left Tan Son Nhut in 1968. My first combat missions were flown with several different crews as I filled-in where needed. By mid-March, I was permanently assigned to the crew of Aircraft Commander [AC] Pilot First Lieutenant Thomas L. Lubbers. Our work schedule was to fly combat missions five nights in a row [all flights were flown between sunset and sunrise], then pull one night on alert (even though we also flew most of those nights) and then got a night off. One night right after we went Winchester [out of ammo] and were heading home, we spotted a convoy of sampans; so, the pilot flew low and we dumped the empty brass on them. We thought at least we would scare them and it did work. Everybody on those sampans started jumping overboard into the river. However, when we got back to base; we got in trouble for not turning in the empty brass casings."[2]

During the months of March and April 1970, Shadows of C Flight primarily flew in III Corps, the military region surrounding Saigon and areas north of Saigon, and in IV Corps, the military region in the Mekong Delta south of Saigon. The 17th SOS navigator assigned to C Flight at Tan Son Nhut, Major Robert Bokern, stated, "Navigators, who flew in southern Vietnam, knew there was a vast difference for the table navigator flying in III Corps compared to flying in IV Corp. When we flew in III Corps, we worked every second of the flight with all of the FM radio artillery [arty] calls, navigating, clearances, firing clearances, etc. We were really worn out after a mission. On the other hand, flying in IV Corps was a "piece of cake" compared to III Corps. Little or no arty, very few radio calls, and clearances were easier to get. It was almost a "joy ride" compared to flying in III Corps."[3]

In late March, 1970, Fire Support Base (FSB) Illingworth was hastily established directly on top of a heavily trafficked enemy infiltration route from Cambodia. Perimeter defense at Firebase Illingworth for the eight-inch howitzers consisted of only earthen berm and a few culvert bunkers with no timber, not much wire, and not many claymores. Crates of artillery ammunition stacked at ground level (not bunkered) also created a situation for disaster. To stay more than four days in one location was an invitation for enemy attacks on fire support bases. Illingworth was being used as bait.

FSB Illingworth was located next to the invisible Cambodian border in the Dog's Face of War Zone C (north of Tay Ninh). FSB Jay, which had been established weeks earlier, was also located in the Dog's Face, south of Illingworth. The NVA attacked FSB Jay but met with stiff resistance from Jay defenders with artillery support from other artillery bases in the area and with aerial support from gunships, flareships, tactical air, and a Shadow gunplane. Sustaining heavy losses but not overrun by attacking forces, FSB Jay was consequently abandoned and moved to another location and renamed FSB Hannas .

Two nights later after attacking Jay, the NVA made a full frontal assault on FSB Illingworth on 1 April 70. At 0218 hours, mobs of ghostlike figures wearing pith helmets and carrying weapons advanced through the mist toward the base perimeter of Illingworth. American defenders opened fire. Enemy automatic weapons fire and rocket-propelled grenades shot across the fire base. A battalion of the 272nd NVA Regiment was charged with capturing and destroying FBS Illingworth. The FSB was located in a dried-out lake bed surrounded by dense jungle on the border of Cambodia.[4]

Illingworth had been reinforced with additional artillery pieces to supplement their 105mm howitzer units and ammunition in anticipation of enemy attacks. A bloody battle quickly ensued with furious fighting. Defenders of Illingworth, such as Echo Recon, bravely fought off the onslaught of NVA troops. The area around Illingworth was pre-designated killing zones for coordinated U.S. Army artillery and Cobra helicopter gunships attacks plus orbiting Shadow gunplanes with miniguns blazing.

According to Keith Nolan, in *Into Cambodia*, "The Cobra pilots dodged 12.7mm AAA fire while strafing tree lines around Illingworth. The defoliated trees resembled skeletons in the austere light of parachute flares launched by USAF flareships, and the sky rained more fire as two AC-119 Shadow gunplanes orbited in their established aerial tier. Their miniguns shrieked like buzz saws as they flashed down solid streams of red tracers."[5]

Before daylight, the NVA withdrew, leaving behind eighty-eight bodies. Twenty-four Illingworth GIs were killed and fifty-four were wounded during the assault. Surviving defenders of Illingworth were battle fatigued but eventually stood tall after the shock of vicious combat wore down and realizing that they had defeated the NVA.

***

If the 17th SOS Shadows had to isolate one of their proudest moments up to this point in their short history, one of them would be the defense of Dak Pek located sixty-five miles southwest of DaNang and seven miles from the Laotian border. The Civilian Defense Group (CIDG) had a U.S. Special Forces contingent assigned there. Dak Pek overlooked a significant communist supply route. A dozen hills surrounded Dak Pek. One of them was called the U.S. or American Hill. It was hit by Charlie at 0200 on Sunday, 12 April 1970. The following account of events at Dak Pek was compiled and written by Earl J. Farney:

> On the afternoon of 15 April 1970, it was sultry hot in the bunker atop the American Hill. A U.S. Special Forces sergeant dropped an 81mm shell into a mortar and hollered, "Hanging one round!"
>
> The situation was awful. The defenders needed more than mortars to hang in against the enemy. CIDG troops used ma-

chine guns and hand grenades. Shadow gunships poured in curtains of red tracer bullets. Fighter bombers pounded the hills with 750 pound bombs.

Despite bombs, bullets, and mortars, Charlie was relentlessly tough. He fought head-on and didn't flinch using AK-47 assault rifles, recoilless rifles, machineguns, 122mm rockets, and even tear gas against the defenders of Dak Pek. Over 200 assorted rounds pounded the hapless camp daily.

Communist sappers nearly destroyed a highly fortified U.S. Special Forces bunker complex. One hill was taken by the NVA and held for two and a half days; but then was recaptured by the ARVN.

The sappers came up through the wire from the northeast. Before any warning was sounded, they were blowing bunkers with powerful satchel charges. The main U.S. bunker crumbled in a flaming pile of concrete. One U.S. advisor was temporarily trapped inside. A guard, a CIDG soldier, and the soldier's wife were killed. For thirty minutes, U.S. Green Berets held only one circular mortar pit. They escaped through bunker tunnels. The enemy had them and blew their chance. They blew it, partly, within ten minutes after the thirty-odd sappers hit the hill. One of the VC stood and hauled the Viet Cong flag halfway up a pole in a symbolic climax.

Sergeant First Class Thomas Weeks raised his M-16 above the bunker and fired. The VC at the flagpole dropped. Trenches were aflame and there was in-fighting on the hill. Enemy tear gas was heavy. Allied troops wore gas masks. A Viet Cong jumped in the mortar pit and flung a satchel charge at Weeks. The explosion blew Weeks back into the tunnel, but he came out fighting with his comrades following.

CIDG security leader, Dan Van Ban, led his group up the back side of American Hill. Together, the allies held out. Thirty sappers were killed.

Hill 203 did not fare as well. The VC tied up the Vietnamese company commander and cut off his head off before killing his wife and children. The communist attackers had inside help. Lieutenant Nguyen Quy Dinh knew something was wrong. He couldn't raise his commander on the radio.

The enemy struck and burned villages surrounding the camp while the civilians made for a district compound south of the camp. On Sunday morning, air strikes were called in on Hill 202 and on villages that could be cleared by bombing. Fighter/bombers dropped 750 pound bombs carpeting the friendly perimeter.

Sunday afternoon, preparations to take Hill 203 were made. Assaults were made up the steep face of the hill squarely into the face of the enemy. Bloody. Unadulterated trench warfare ensued with five assaults across the saddle and into the fire. What good had those goddam fighter strikes done?

Sunday's assault by CIDG troops, mobile strike force reinforcements, and U.S. and Vietnamese Special Forces were unable to take the hill. CIDG forces were really spooked. They were trained as jungle fighters. Direct assaulting was a new ball game for them. They needed a victory and they needed it now.

On Monday, more bombs and napalm were dropped on Hill 203 which proved worthless. The enemy captured an outpost near the hill. Enough of this horse crap; bring on the gunships. Shadows operating out of Air Bases at Phan Rang and Tuy Hoa, the 17th Special Operations Squadron doubled their sortie rate. They stationed a Shadow gunship continuously over Dak Pek. Consequently, beleaguered friendly forces gained a toehold.

On Tuesday, direct enemy fire was taken from both the hill and the outpost. U.S. and Vietnamese Special Forces, mobile strike forces, and CIDG forces forced their way through two wire gates under the enemy fire in what appeared to be a deadly suicide mission. But then an AC-119 gunship arrived to cover the grunts in their three bloody assault rushes. The hill and outpost were taken. Search and destroy followed from bunker to bunker, lobbing in hand grenades and hitting the deck. Thirty-one enemy soldiers were killed. Eight AK-47s, four B-40 rockets, satchel charges, and Bangalore torpedoes were captured. Hill 203 and outpost camp were in friendly hands.

And the war was over by one more miserable, stinking, lousy hill. And who the hell cares, now that they gained the high ground? The sniping, firefights, and probes continue. There's an estimated two enemy battalions in the ridges and valleys around Dak Pek. To American Special Forces troops, Dak Pek is a "damn difficult camp." War is not nice; it's ugly.

On Wednesday night, defenders at Dak Pek were waiting for Charlie. The flares and moon silhouetted the complex of fortified hills. In the command bunker, there was only a flickering candle. Next to the candle was an ashtray full of cigarette butts. Sergeant Doug Hull, a Green Beret advisor, was hunched over a radio. The only personal belongings Hull had left were his boots, undershorts, and trousers. The rest he burned or buried in the enemy sapper attack on Sunday.

Incoming rounds hit regularly, twenty meters away. It was only last night that a 122mm rocket hit just outside his door. Still, this was what Hull wanted to do. He was tough. Doug wanted to practice his profession with soldiers he respected and civilians he loved.

Sergeant Charles Young, twenty-one, was lying on the concrete floor. He nursed his wounded foot and tried to get some sleep. Three days ago when he was in the main U.S. bunker, he got a rude awakening. A satchel charge blew the bunker in on top of him. He said, "I felt like a rat in a trap."

His buddies dug him out. Four nights later they were still prying open the trap. Green Beret Captain Gordon Strickler sat atop the bunker in the moonlight. The air had cooled. He briefed the battle plan. He could barely see the other hills. In the black silence came the hushed, nervous voice of a GI over the radio. It was from a hill to the west. "It's quiet out here—too quiet."

Yes, too quiet. The breather in war is always an uneasy one. It's borrowed time. Things will be worse. A plane droned toward Hill 203. Streams of red tracers shot earth-ward and then the sounds of guns firing from above. An eerie, brittle screech echoed across the valley. Over the radio, the soldier stammered, "Too close, SHADOW!"

The controller growled, "One hundred meters." The radio man was Lieutenant Don Andrews. He had a bandage on his head which he claimed was the result of sticking his ear in a fan. His map, marked and numbered, was his pants. That af-ternoon, Sgt Tom Weeks had called the numbers out to An-drews who wrote the numbers on the most available place, his pant legs. "My pants are like a damned secret document," Andrews stated. Apparently the document was good. The fire was accurate, "Looking good, looking real good!"

In the Dak Pek camp, a CIDG fighter named A Jong was making the round of his platoon. He had led the successful charge up Hill 203. They called Jong "the camp hero." He was recommended for a U.S. Silver Star.

"Tonight," Jong said, "I want the VC to come, and I wait."

But only the aggressive or the stupid would wish for the VC to return with the smells of his last visit and the stench of rotting bodies still on the ground. When the VC return, peo-ple at Dak Pek die during the hyenas in the night. That is the unforgettable fact of Dak Pek.[6]

Following is an article titled "Shadow Destroys Bunker Complex In Support of Dak Pek," published in the Phu Cat Air Base *Cobra Courier* on May 18, 1970:

An Air Force AC-119 Shadow gunship crew of the 17th Special Operations Squadron at this base [Phu Cat] was recently credited with destroying a large bunker and munitions complex near the Dak Pek Republic of Vietnam Civilian Irregular Defense Group camp, sixty-five miles west of Da Nang. The Shadow was target bound at sunset on a recent evening to support the CIDG camp at Dak Seang when it was diverted to respond to a troops-in-contact call in the Dak Pek area. Crewmen on the flight were Lt.Col. Charles M. James of Rantoul, IL; Lt.Col. Stanley J. Merrick of Atwater, CA; 1st Lt. Michael W. Golden of Golden, CO; TSgt. Robert H. Spencer of East Freetown, MA; SSgt David M. Hammerlund of Puyallup, WA; Sgt John R. Weaver of Manaffey, PA; and A1C Jon D. Jacobson of Moraga, CA.

The camp was taking automatic weapons fire from several positions about 250 meters to the north and west of the camp," stated Colonel James, aircraft commander. "We began pouring our minigun firepower on these positions under the direction of the ground commander, and almost immediately he commented that he had heard a large secondary explosion.

Opposite Page: In the firing circle, the coordination and communication between the aircraft commander/pilot (AC), his copilot (CP) and flight engineer (FE) were crucial, let alone the AC's coordination/communication with the remainder of his flight crew. The AC banked the aircraft in a left turn between 30 to 45 degrees to align his gunsight crosshairs on the target while depending on his CP to maintain an indicated airspeed of 140 knots and to maintain the firing altitude. The AC also relied on the FE to monitor engine performance instruments, leaning fuel mixtures, fuel consumption, switching gas tanks, and propeller adjustments.

(*Left to right*): The Shadow's aircraft commander/pilot (AC), flight engineer (FE), and copilot (CP). The FE's seat was an empty ammo can passed up to the flight deck from the gun deck and placed just behind the pilot's center console. Strict coordination by all three was essential in the firing circle. (Courtesy of Shadow IP Capt. Bert Blanton)

(*Left to right*): Copilot 1/Lt. Don Craig, Flight Engineer TSgt Bill Posey, and Pilot Capt. John Hope. The pilot's gunsight is located just left of Capt. Hope's face. (Courtesy of FE Bill Posey)

The ground controller asked the Shadow crew to hit a location where an enemy 75mm recoilless rifle had been sighted. The rifle was located on the opposite side of the hill from which the camp was taking automatic weapons fire. The AC-119 hit the target and touched off a secondary explosion. The ground contact working with the Shadow relayed his thanks to the crew and said that the explosions resulting from the last hit on the target continued for the next six hours. He credited the crew with destroying a large enemy complex of bunkers and munitions.[7]

With the siege of the Dak Pek and Dak Seang Special Forces camps beginning on 1 April 1970, AC-119 gunships displayed their unique capability of providing continuous air cover during the hours of darkness. This is particularly noteworthy, since the movement of A Flight from Tuy Hoa FOL to Phu Cat FOL was accomplished in the same time frame of April. During this action, Shadow gunships pioneered the tactic of night aerial re-supply by using the gunship's illuminator "white spotlight" to mark the drop zone while providing fire support. Prior to the development of these tactics, three C-7A "Caribou" cargo aircraft had been lost to hostile ground fire while trying to deliver supplies. In the new tactic, the gunship would orbit the outposts and provide fire support until the Caribou reached the initial point for its drop. At that instant, the gunship turned on the illuminator to show the drop point and to draw attention away from the inbound Caribou. Once supplies were dropped and upon a signal from the C-7 Caribou, the Shadow switched off the white light and the Caribou escaped from the drop zone into the darkness of night.

The tactic worked in a total of sixty-eight drops from 6 April to 1 May without a Caribou being hit by enemy fire. The commander of the C-7 Caribou squadron sent a letter of thanks to the gunships for their efforts in protecting his crews and aircraft. During the first ten days of the siege, Shadow gunships compiled seventy-three hours on station at Dak Pek and Dak Seang. In that time, Shadows expended 817,000 rounds of

The White Spot Light (*top*) and the Flare Launcher were operated by the illuminator operator (IO) upon commands from the aircraft commander/pilot. The IO was also the main scanner for enemy anti-aircraft fire, protecting the six o'clock of the gunship. In case of bailout, the IO was designated "jump master" after jettisoning the Flare Launcher at the command of the pilot.

(*Top*): Shadow Gunship 7.62 mm miniguns aimed out the port side. On low rate of fire, each gun fired 3,000 rounds-per-minute; on high rate of fire, 6,000 rounds-per-minute. (*Left*): Shadow Gunship gun deck looking aft. Two aerial gunners loaded/reloaded guns and repaired gun malfunctions in flight to keep guns online for firing on targets by the aircraft commander/pilot. Gunners also helped the IO scan for enemy ground fire and warned the pilot to take evasive action. (*Right*): Phu Cat Shadow gunners Sgt. Tuttle and Sgt. Brown loading miniguns.

ammunition and dropped 440 flares. On many occasions, as the sun rose, the last AC-119 was still on station. The crew was greeted with comments from the ground like, "Beautiful, just beautiful."

Night after night, Shadows continued to orbit the camps until the siege was broken on 22 May 1970. During and after the siege, a high degree of mutual respect and admiration was formed between Shadow crews and the defenders of Dak Pek and Dak Seang. The Shadows certainly respected the likes of Andrews and Weeks.

While action was heavy at Dak Pek and Dak Seang, C Flight AC-119G Shadow gunships at Tan Son Nhut Air Base participated in the Duffel Bag Unit Systems Evaluation of newly developed airborne equipment to monitor signals from ground sensors between 3 April and 31 May 1970. Code Name Duffle Bag sensors were highly classified first-generation acoustic, seismic, and magnetic sensors that originated on the ill-fated "McNamara Line," a wall that U.S. Secretary of Defense Robert S. McNamara was attempting to have built in the demilitarized zone. Duffle Bag sensors were sown along the (Cambodian) border, trails, rivers, canal banks, outposts, and other enemy infiltration routes into South Vietnam by detachments assigned to the Army and Navy. The sensors were connected via line-of-sight radio communications to operators who listened for coded tones. The receivers were called "portatales," about the size of a PRC 77 radio. When the operator picked up a tone code on the portatale, a number would be displayed that indicated which particular sensor had activated. If the sensor was an acoustic or magnetic sensor, the operator could hear in his headphones what was going on in the sensor area.[8]

Shadow gunships carried a portable UHF receiver capable of receiving, decoding, and displaying ground sensor signals and audio transmissions. On 18 April, Shadow 77 detected signals indicating movement in the sensor field and fired approximately 6,000 rounds into the area. The next night, the Shadow again detected more signals of movement from the same area and fired 28,500 rounds into the area. A ground sweep of the area on the following day revealed 150 enemy dead. Seventeen enemy troops were captured during the ground sweep. Because of this action it was recommended that the new sensor monitoring equipment be installed as standard equipment on AC-119s.[9] Nevertheless, this sensor monitoring equipment was not installed as standard equipment.

Someone once joked, "If the monsoons or enemy guns don't kill us, then the aircraft will." Shadow gunships flew under and around thunderstorms with high gusty winds and driving monsoon rains without weather radar onboard to meet scheduled sorties in providing direct aerial fire support for friendly troops in combat with Charlie. Shadow gunships usually operated in reduced or non-threat anti-aircraft artillery (AAA) environments because of their slow speed at low altitudes during combat conditions. Low or non-threat triple-A environments meant there was little chance of one getting knocked out of the sky by enemy fighter planes, surface-to-air missiles, or big AAA in Shadow areas of operation in South Vietnam, Laos, and Cambodia. The biggest danger was the aircraft itself, especially losing an engine on takeoff. The crash of Shadow 76 at Tan Son Nhut in October 1969 had proven that. So there were fundamental feelings of trepidation and mistrust for the aircraft among aircrews and for the combat missions flown. Shadow pilots and crews did not knowingly fly any aircraft suspected of potential malfunctions nor did they intentionally fly into the teeth of enemy anti-aircraft fire.

Shadow flight crews respected their ugly "Lady of the Night" black beast. Flight crews sweated-out low manifold pressure and fluctuating oil pressure on take-off roll, engine failure right at or immediately after lift-off with landing gear in transit, engine fire on take-off, runaway propellers, single engine flight while over-grossed on weight, and climb rates of less than 100 feet per minute. The aircraft could be very unforgiving and fail you in a minute. With virtually no crash landing capability; the airplane would break-up on impact. She was hard to handle in bad weather. But in her better moods, she would forgive all weaknesses of flight with stellar performance becoming a reliable fighting machine, a real "Charlie Chaser" Lady.

The following account of events surrounding the Crash of Shadow 78 was compiled and written by Earl J. Farney:

On 28 April 1970, Shadow 78 waited for takeoff clearance at Tan Son Nhut Air Base. The target was a "Shadow Box" of coordinates in IV Corps. While waiting for tower clearance to take the active runway for takeoff, the flight engineer recommended de-fouling the engines to the pilot and with an okay from the pilot, the FE nursed the throttles to keep the engines clean so sparkplugs didn't foul.

Shadow 78 carried a regular crew of eight consisting of the Aircraft Commander, Lt. Thomas L. Lubbers, Copilot, Lt. Charles M. Knowles, Navigator/NOS, Maj. Meredith "Andy" Anderson, Navigator/NOS, Maj. Robert "Bob" Bokern, Flight Engineer, MSgt Joseph C. Jeszeck, Gunner, SSgt Robert F. Fage Jr., Gunner, Sgt Michael J. Vangelisti, and Illuminator Operator, SSgt Allen Chandler.

The pilot, Lt. Tom Lubbers, ran a good crew. He was young but mature, competent, and dedicated. Always thinking of others, he had a fine sense of humor. They relaxed and bantered remarks over the interphone while waiting for takeoff clearance from Saigon Tower. Just another mission; the tour would be one day shorter. This crew was over the hump; past the half way mark. In fact, the war had reached a routine stalemate. Almost complacent, they felt South Vietnam would stand. Despite the riots, criticism, and the Tet offensive, the combined U.S. / RVN war effort was paying off.

Major Bob Bokern, the sensor operator, secured his flight lunch and stepped up to the Instructor Navigator (IN) fold-down seat on the flight deck. The seat was not recommended for takeoff or landing. But, Bob wanted to watch the takeoff. He sat down and fastened the skimpy nylon belt across his waist. His fireproof Nomex flight suit seemed extra hot.

A Trans International airliner landed and tower cleared Shadow 78 to take the active runway for takeoff. Lined-up on runway centerline, 78 was cleared by Saigon tower to takeoff. Lubbers pushed the throttles forward for takeoff roll

to make their scheduled midnight takeoff time. All engine instruments read within limits as the aircraft accelerated with
full power. Funny how the 119 made more noise on takeoff
than other planes. With the props in sync, the vibration was
felt all the way to the Officer's Club.

At Shadow Operations, native Hawaiian Captain Jose
Cachuela had just assumed the duty as Ops officer. Shadow
Navigator First Lieutenant Rod Sizemore had just left the
Ops building to catch the flight line shuttle bus outside
Shadow ops to the Shadow barracks.

Quiet minutes passed while Jose prepared to make entries
in Shadow ops log book. Seconds earlier, Jose had heard the
loud roar of the twin engines of Shadow 78 revving up to
maximum power for takeoff roll. He had heard the distinctive
sound of the AC-119G gunship roaring down runway 27 Left
just behind Shadow Ops for its scheduled midnight takeoff
time. Then slowly the sound faded after the gunship roared
farther down the runway and into the night. As was their
usual habit, the maintenance crew watched as Shadow 78
lifted off. But this night was different. The gunship rose, fal-
tered and did not gain altitude. Eventually, the maintenance
crew could no longer see the aircraft.

For Jose, silence within operations was broken with a
screech. And it wasn't the UHF radio. Lt Rod Sizemore
screamed through the doorway, "Shadow 78 just crashed on
takeoff just off the end of the west runway!"

Jose's heart sank. My God! His closest friend Bob Bokern
was onboard Shadow 78. Jose quickly found and ignited the
emergency checklist. Call tower. Not a hitch. Damn it, why
was everything so impersonally efficient? Buddies were
probably dying.

The phone on Jose's desk rang. He answered to hear a
distant sounding voice that informed him that an Army helicopter pilot had just notified TSN (Tan Son Nhut Air Base)
Base Ops about an airplane that had just taken off and

crashed, exploding in flames. Stunned by the phone call, Jose immediately initiated emergency procedures.

It was dark outside; pitch black and the air was sticky hot. Low level Army rescue choppers raced toward the flaming wreckage. Get back to the checklist, notify C Flight's commander. Go through GCI radio, called "Paris" to notify Lt. Col. White who was aboard a Shadow, flying in III Corps. Prompt acknowledgment. Notify Headquarters at Phan Rang AB. The DO, Colonel Bruce Brown, issues terse instructions. "Notify the safety officer."

Then the lull, like in most disasters, the adrenalin slows. Jose felt weak, even dizzy. He wanted to wretch. The song, "Cecilia" by Simon and Garfunkel drifted into his brain, pulsing louder and louder like a cicada staccato. Worse than a rain forest, it echoed off the walls and the gun racks. Jose's head throbbed with the melody. It was weird.

Tom Lubbers was the aircraft commander of Shadow 78. He lived in the BOQ next to Jose. Every day, Tom turned his stereo on high volume and played "Cecilia" over and over. Tom was a gentleman bachelor and a hell of a fine officer; one of the best pilots in the C Flight.

Usually, Shadow Ops was filled with people; crewmembers, maintenance personnel, and staff. Even in the night; after all, this was a "fly-by-night" operation. Jose almost swore. No people, no telephone calls, no word on the crash. Deathly silence settled within Shadow Ops, impossible for C Flight at Tan Son Nhut. He glanced at his disaster checklist but it didn't help. It was just him and Cecilia, over and over. He couldn't leave his post as duty officer, chained to a damn desk and telephones. They normally violate all rules of privacy and decency, except now. It could be a morgue.

The armored flying beast fully loaded with fuel, ammunition, and flares rotated and clawed its way into the night air at maximum gross weight. Then it happened; the one disaster that could defeat the feisty Shadow. Engine number 2 failed with the landing gear still down. Level off and feather the prop. The good engine #1 whined in desperation, not enough. Shadow 78 began to mush in. No time for bailout. Tom made a controlled crash with little if any chance of survival. Shadow 76 had proven that in October 1969.

Nothing was said. No panic, just professional airmanship. Hitting and bouncing over a rice field dike, then the grinding touchdown. Bob Bokern lurched forward. The seat belt cut into his stomach. Horrified, he saw a dike fifty yards away. The nose hit it and folded under, instantly killing the pilot and copilot, quickly followed by the flight engineer and navigator sucked under in the debris. Mercifully, the craft ground to a halt in its tangle of death next to another dike. Then the flames and smoke of burning fuel and the explosions of live ammo and flares erupted. Bob saw the overhead sextant mount and scrambled to get out. He wedged himself through the small hole and escaped from the wreckage. IO SSgt Allen Chandler had also survived in the crash with critical burns. Riding in the cargo section of the aircraft, Allen had gotten out of the wreckage by going through a hole on the left side of the fuselage created by the engine that had broken loose. The two survivors met and watched in wonderment and horror at the fiery wreckage that no doubts in their minds had claimed the lives of their fellow-crewmembers

Almost too efficient, U.S. Army choppers descended around the crash site. Bokern and Chandler were loaded on a chopper and flown to the 3rd Army Field Hospital in Saigon.

Captain Jose Cachuela was still at the operations desk when C Flight Commander Lt. Col. White landed. Shadow Ops had started to fill with people, but no one talked. Was it bereavement for the dead or apprehension for the future? You couldn't tell. In either case, it didn't last. Colonel White broke the silence.

"Gentlemen, press on. We got a war to fight!" Under the circumstances, it was a godsend that Colonel White said that.

The phone rang at the duty officer's desk. Captain Cachuela answered. Everyone on board had been killed, Jose was told. Not long after, the phone rang again. Jose delayed to clear the grime from his throat. He again felt the urge to vomit. The muggy heat was stifling. Don't they ever fight where it's cold? Sweaty everything. The place stunk of sweat. Death was a pungent odor. Friends get killed. It's a new ball game.

Jose answered the call, "Shadow Ops, Captain Cachuela."

"Hey, Jose. Bob here!"

Jose just about fainted.

Thank God, Bob was alive and so was Allen Chandler, the IO on Shadow 78. They were the only survivors of the crash.

Bokern and Chandler had been flown to the Army 3rd Field Hospital in Saigon by Army helicopters. Suffering from severe burns and other injuries, Chandler was in surgery within ten minutes after the crash. A corpsman said to Chandler, "We are going to have to cut your boots off to check your feet! Is that OK?" Chandler answered, "Do anything you want to; just keep me alive."[10]

Less than thirty-six hours after the crash, Chandler was stabilized and air evacuated to the burn unit at Camp Zama, Japan. After two weeks there, he was flown back to the States for further treatment and healing.

Major Bokern suffered a compression fracture in his lower back. Upon his release from the hospital and return to C Flight, Bokern was taken off flying duty (DNIF); consequently, becoming a permanent duty officer at Shadow operations. Approximately three months later, Major Bokern resumed Shadow navigator flying duty.

Following are excerpts from personal accounts of the crash by Major Robert Bokern and Staff Sergeant Allen Chandler:

Major Bokern wrote, "The pilot, copilot and engineer were fighting to do everything to keep the airplane flying but being overweight, the AC-119G would just not maintain altitude, much less climb on a single engine. Then we hit, there was a horrible scraping, crunching sound from underneath and other noises I can't describe. I felt myself turned and flung in a somersault head to toe and I thought that this was it. But suddenly everything stopped. I was just there in total silence. All the noise had stopped. Then I was aware that the plane was burning. I could hear the roar of the fire and feel heat, but it was completely dark where I was. I could hear the ammo 'cooking off' in the fire. All I could hear was: POP, POP, POP, POP, POP! My next thought was that I had survived the crash and now I was either going to burn to death or get shot by one of our own bullets flying around."[11]

Allen Chandler wrote, "We had two of the best Shadow pilots in the unit and no one on the crew could have prevented the crash. It was well known that the AC-119s had a lack of horsepower. We tried to cram in all the ammo we could on each flight so we almost always took off at or near maximum weight."[12]

From that April night of horror until the last 17th SOS combat flight prior to deactivation of the squadron, most if not all pilots and crewmen never trusted the Flying Lady Beast again, especially at take-off. Weight of the aircraft was reduced somewhat by eliminating the ammunition rack and tying down ammo cans with cargo straps and reducing the amount of ammunition carried onboard. Every flight safety precaution and every checklist item from preflight to postflight were taken deadly serious. Any indication of a faulty engine resulted in ground aborts or airborne aborted missions.

Just as World War II B-24 Liberator aircrews had nicknamed their bombers, "The Flying Boxcar" and "The Flying Coffin," the C-119 had long been called "The Flying Boxcar." But after the crash of Shadow 78, AC-119 crews started calling the gunship "The Flying Coffin" because there was little chance of surviving a crash on land or ditching at sea. Depending on the severity of airborne catastrophes, bailout from stricken aircraft offered some hope of survival for cargo deck crewmembers, but not much for flight deck crewmembers.

Shadows of 17th SOS C Flight were devastated by the disastrous crash of another AC-119G gunship. Solemnness settled within Shadow Ops and Shadow quarters. Lively chatter of excitement and joking was missing in conversations. Each man had his own private thoughts about the whole ordeal and the devil aircraft that killed her own. C Flight was mourning over the loss of their Shadow brothers.

SEVEN

Prelude to the Cambodia Incursion

Approximately the same size as the State of Missouri in land area, Cambodia was a sleeping, docile nation prior to the overthrow of Prince Sihanouk. Sihanouk had allowed his country to be used for NVA and Viet Cong supply lines and sanctuaries in exchange for peace within his kingdom. Primarily an agricultural society, the basic needs of food, clothing and shelter were being met as the world and time passed by the villages and small towns. Farmers lived peacefully in homes of wood with tiled roofs. Rice paddies and rubber plantations complimented the landscape of beautiful, lush green forests.

With the overthrow of Prince Sihanouk and the Cambodian Incursion, the tranquil country of seven million people, 95% Theravada Buddhist, had become a nation entangled in war. The westward infiltration of NVA and Viet Cong troops from the Vietnam border sanctuaries just before and during the Incursion created disorder and mayhem in the lives of Cambodians. Communist Cambodians (aka Khmer Rouge, literally "Red Khmer") and the North Vietnamese joined efforts in exerting pressure on the Lon Nol government troops.

For years, Prince Norodom Sihanouk and his monarchy form of Cambodian government had maintained a state of neutrality in the Vietnam War, thus avoiding outright confrontations with the warring factions. In doing so, Cambodia allowed herself to be used and abused by Communist and Free World Armed Forces. Communist intrusion of sovereign territory along Cambodia's five-hundred mile border with South Vietnam was begrudgingly tolerated. The NVA and VC used secure sanctuaries located in the eastern provinces of Cambodia to assemble, train, and supply troops to wage war on South Vietnam.

Clandestine missions up to thirty kilometers into Cambodia were being conducted by small bands of local mercenaries led by U. S. Special Forces. The special teams conducted reconnaissance missions, set ambushes, and captured enemy soldiers to gather information about the Communist sanctuaries.

In December 1967, Sihanouk publicly stated that the communist sanctuaries were not officially sanctioned by the Cambodians and that no objections would be raised by his government if American ground troops pursued the communists across the border into Cambodian territory. Consequently, the number of covert military operations across the border steadily increased with time.

Eventually, anti-Vietnamese and anti-communist factions in the Cambodian government demanded NVA and VC troop withdrawal from the sanctuaries or face expulsion by force. Nevertheless, Prince Sihanouk was reluctant to take further action against the communists without some assurance of support from a major military power, namely the United States of America. For fear of becoming directly involved in the Vietnam War without substantial military support, Sihanouk held fast to proclaiming Cambodia a neutral nation.

The former French colony stood alone and unprotected. The Army of Cambodia was ill-equipped and lacked sufficient training to face the battle-hardened communist troops in a showdown. Not wanting to alienate the communists or the United States, Cambodia continued walking a tight rope under the prince.

The communist military headquarters, so-named Central Office of South Vietnam (COSVN) by allied commanders, was located in one of the border sanctuaries. At first, allied military leaders thought COSVN was located in Laos until aerial reconnaissance photos showed the location to be in Base Area 353 of the "Fish Hook," a hook-shaped piece of Cambodia that protrudes eastward into South Vietnam northwest of Saigon.

Information provided by a Chieu Hoi (open arms) defector corroborated the location of COSVN. Regardless, no overt military ground action was taken against COSVN or other sanctuaries because U. S. self-imposed war restrictions limited the use of American ground troops to within the borders of South Vietnam.

With permission from the White House in Washington D. C., top secret B-52 bombing raids on the Cambodian sanctuaries with the code name "Operation Menu" started on 18 March 1969. More B-52 attacks followed during the month. The U. S. bombing strikes helped motivate the Cambodians to finalize military plans to rid the eastern provinces of the unwanted communists.

In April, Cambodian ground forces were dispatched to the eastern provinces to roust out the NVA and VC. In May, air attacks against communist positions were conducted by the Cambodian Air Force using Soviet MiG jets and Cambodia's major seaport at Sihanoukville on the Gulf of Thailand was officially closed to the communists. Previously, military equipment and supplies for the NVA and VC were shipped to Sihanoukville from Red China and Eastern European Soviet-bloc countries to be transported overland across Cambodia to the communist sanctuaries.

Cambodian armed forces were unsuccessful in driving out the communist troops in spite of continued USAF B-52 arc light strikes during April and May. Anti-communist factions in the Royal Cambodian Government voiced impatience with the failure to reinstate sovereignty over the nation's eastern provinces.

In an effort to appease the government's anti-communist right wing, Lieutenant General Lon Nol was appointed Prime Minister by Prince Sihanouk in August of 1969.

Lon Nol and his supporters firmly believed the Cambodian Army could regain control of eastern provinces. Somewhat naive as to the comparative strength of communist forces and those of the Cambodian Army, Lon Nol proceeded to take matters into his own hands.

On 18 March 1970, when Prince Sihanouk was visiting Russian leaders in Moscow, Prime Minister Lon Nol and Deputy Prime Minister Prince Sisowath Sirik Matak took control of the government in a National Assembly vote; thus, ousting Prince Sihanouk and his monarchy. With pro-western Lon Nol and Sisowath Sirik Matak in power, the United States and South Vietnam had a new ally to help fight the communists.

Through the end of March and all of April 1970, U.S. and South Vietnamese armed forces expanded covert operations in Cambodia. In April, Air America planes flew war supplies to Phnom Penh, capital city of Cambodia. Over three thousand Cambodian military officers and soldiers returned to Phnom Penh and their homeland from South Vietnam where they had received training from U.S. Special Forces.

On April 30, 1970, United States and South Vietnamese ground forces invaded Cambodia along the South Vietnam border to attack and destroy the communist sanctuaries Over 30,000 U.S. ground troops were involved in the invasion. AC-119 Shadow gunships were fragged to provide night support for American forces after the initial surge. U. S. President Richard Nixon called the invasion an "incursion" and set a withdrawal deadline of 30 June 70 for U.S. ground troops. American troops were also restricted from advancing more than thirty kilometers (eighteen miles) into Cambodia.

The invasion of Cambodia came as a surprise to Lon Nol and his government. Neither the United States nor South Vietnam had bothered to consult or forewarn Lon Nol. American government leaders justified the action as a means of protecting American forces stationed in South Vietnam while U. S. troop withdrawals and Vietnamization of the war progressed. Vietnamization meant South Vietnam would eventually take sole responsibility for the war effort against the communists.

Cambodian confidence in their new government headed by General Lon Nol grew tremendously after the American incursion. The war against the communists became very popular as thousands of men and women volunteered for the Force Armee Nationale Khmere (FANK) swelling its ranks to an all-time high of 150,000 troops. Still, the Cambodian Army was outnumbered by communist forces.

Enemy actions in South Vietnam dropped dramatically because of the highly successful invasion of Cambodia. With their sanctuary camps and supply depots either captured or destroyed, NVA and VC troops moved westward toward the Mekong River and Phnom Penh, deeper into Cambodia taking control of the countryside along the way.

U. S. ground troops were withdrawn from Cambodia by the established deadline of June 30th. By the end of July, communist forces had defeated most of the Cambodian Army in the border region taking control of provinces east of the Mekong River. The northeastern provinces of Rattanakiri, Mondulkiri, and Stung Treng were the first to fall under complete control of communists troops.

To the shock of Cambodians, Angkor, the ancient shrines of the Khmere civilization in northwest Cambodia, soon fell under the control of the NVA. In the Parrot's Beak, Svay Rieng, a scant sixty-five miles west of Saigon, was soon lost to communist troops followed by the large French-owned rubber plantations north of Cambodia's Phnom Penh to Saigon Highway 1. The VC took control of Kratie making the provincial capital city headquarters for the South Vietnamese National Liberation Front. Sixteen of the nineteen province capitals in Cambodia had been or were under attack by communist forces.

Cambodian Army garrisons found themselves isolated from main government forces while many were completely surrounded by enemy troops. The nation had turned into a huge battlefield. A state of crisis existed within the country. Lon Nol's pro-western doctrine made the new Cambodian government and its army the primary military target for the communists.

Safe passage on Cambodian roads, waterways and railways became nearly impossible. Roadblocks, mines, and ambushes were common. The NVA, VC, and Khmer Rouge (Cambodian communists) controlled the countryside day and night. The indestructible Ho Chi Minh Trail with its array of roads and paths resumed full operation as troops, equipment and supplies flowed from North Vietnam through Laos into Cambodia. With the Cambodian deep-water seaport of Kompong Som effectively closed to the communists by Lon Nol in March, the Mekong

River and its tributaries from Laos became critically important to the North Vietnamese as a strategic route to re-supply communist troops in Cambodia.

The Vietnam War had fully engulfed Cambodia. The country was desperately fighting to survive the onslaught of communist forces. North Vietnam had shown its intent to keep its forces in Cambodia to not only regain sanctuaries along the border but to topple the new Cambodian government. Hopes of a negotiated settlement to end hostilities vanished as the Paris peace talks dragged to a deadlock.

Increasingly distressed, the Cambodian government looked to the United States for support and air strikes to help defend government-controlled cities and to support Cambodian ground troops. Close-air support twenty-four hours a day was needed and requested.

The White House and subsequently the 7th Air Force responded to Lon Nol's request by secretly assigning the task of providing round-the-clock direct air support for Cambodia to the 17th Special Operations Squadron C Flight with its five Shadow gunships stationed at Tan Son Nhut Air Base.

EIGHT

The Cambodia Incursion

D uring April and May 1970, command changes came at squadron level when Lt. Col. William Reeter replaced Lt. Col. James Roach as 17th SOS Operations Officer, and Major Robert L. Hintzen became the Squadron Executive Officer, replacing Major Robert Mems who was assigned a position in the 14th SOW. Captain George L. Schenck, Jr. replaced Captain Robert Thompson as the Squadron Maintenance Officer. MSgt James E. Manker replaced MSgt Nelson Horner as the Squadron First Sergeant.

On 10 April, Lt. Col. Alfred I. Flynn replaced Lt. Col. William Reeter as A Flight Commander. Three days later, Captain Frank C. Watson replaced Major Francis A. Nealon as Administrative Officer. On 15 May, Major Richard S. Ribinski replaced Lt. Col. Charles "Chuck" James as Flight Operations Officer. Captain Maly and MSgt Lewis remained as A Flight Maintenance Officer and First Sergeant, respectively.

The B Squadron concept was dropped at Phan Rang and the B Flight concept reinstated. Following were the squadron/flight positions at Phan Rang: Lt. Col. Don Clark, 17th SOS Squadron Commander; Lt. Col. Bill Reeter, 17th Squadron/B Flight Operations Officer; Lt. Col. Samuel A. Martin, B Flight Commander; Captain George L. Schenck, Jr., Squadron/B Flight Maintenance Officer; MSgt James E. Manker, First Sergeant.

The FOL at Tan Son Nhut experienced no changes in command with Lt. Col. White as C Flight Commander, Major Boschian as Ops Officer, Major Stoner as Administrative Officer, and MSgt Weber as First Sergeant.

Shortages of maintenance personnel and flight engineers hampered operations from mid-May into June for all three FOLs due to increased numbers of men completing their tours of duty and returning to the states. Total assigned maintenance personnel dropped to 70% with one Chief Master Sergeant, one Technical Sergeant, and thirteen Staff Sergeants to act as line chiefs, maintenance expeditors, dock chiefs, shift chiefs, and crew chiefs.[1]

A significant portion of available man-hours at all three 17th SOS FOLs was expended on engine changes and propeller regulator changes due to failures prior to normal life-time expectancy. Soon the supply of replacement engines in-country was critically low. For a brief period at Tan Son Nhut during late May and early June, replacement engines were required at an alarming rate when rebuilt engines from the States failed well before engine life expectancy and many times during initial test flights. Normal C Fight test hops to check-out newly installed engines were flown to and over the South China Sea near Vung Tau, but test hops soon became extremely adventurous for test pilots and flight engineers. Pilot distrust of the Texas rebuilt R-3350 engines grew with each engine failure. After experiencing repeated failures with rebuilt engines, test flights were restricted to fly over the airbase until the quality of rebuilt engines showed significant improvement and reliability. Thereafter, test hops resumed to Vung Tau. The 14th SOW assisted 17th maintenance with personnel during the shortage of manpower and the crisis of engine failures and propeller regulator changes. Additional personnel for the 17th SOS were in the Vietnam pipeline to arrive in-country by mid-June.

During April, Shadows based at Tan Son Nhut started flying more missions along the South Vietnam border with Cambodia to support operations of American and allied troops probing the border regions around the high infiltration routes in the Parrot's Beak and Dog's Head. The border was indecipherable especially at night, flying at 2,500 to 3,500 feet AGL.

On 29 April 1970, ARVN troops launched attacks across the border from III and IV Corps into Cambodia in Operation Toan Thang 43, meaning "Total Victory" in English. The Parrot's Beak from which NVA and VC units operated from for years was attacked by approximately 48,000 ARVN troops accompanied by U.S. Advisors. The border area was nicknamed "Parrot's Beak" because the outline of the border resembled a parrot's beak on maps. As the crow flies, the beak of the parrot was a scant thirty-five miles due west from the heart of Saigon.

A South Vietnamese tank column thundered down Route 1 to join up with Cambodian troops at the town of Svay Rieng, Cambodia. By mutual agreement the ARVN advance stopped at the edge of Svay Rieng located in the Parrot's Beak fifty-five miles west-northwest of Saigon. Upon the arrival of another armored column and additional foot soldiers, the ARVN moved forward to engage NVA/VC troops who provided stiff resistance before retreating and melting away farther into Cambodia.

On 1 May 1970, Task Force Shoemaker of "Operation Rockcrusher" (aka Toan Thang 43) pushed across the border into Cambodia at the Fish Hook after USAF SAC B-52 bombers, 7th AF fighter/bombers, and U.S. Army artillery units softened the area for invasion forces. Two 15,000-pound bombs were dropped from C-130 cargo planes to create helicopter landing zones. Thousands of allied soldiers drove into Cambodia sixty-five miles north of Saigon. American armored cavalry and infantry foot soldiers methodically advanced across the border on muddy roads, and across muddy fields and swollen streams created by heavy thunderstorms the previous day and evening to attack. American forces raced toward the COSVN and other strategic enemy base camps. U.S. and South Vietnamese forces combined for the dual objectives: 1. shore up the weak Cambodian army struggling with North Vietnam Army units, and 2. destroy enemy forces and supplies long cached in numerous border base camps. Seventh Air Force provided special assets for the attack including two flareships from Cam Ranh Bay, four AC-119K Stinger gunships from Phan Rang, ten extra alert sorties, aerial tanker support, and nighttime forward air controllers.[2]

On 2 May, U.S. ground units continued forward progress in the Fish Hook. At 1125, airborne radar reported a northward bound NVA convoy trying to escape from the Fish Hook toward Cambodia Route 7. An AC-

119 gunship was ordered to find and destroy the convoy. The Shadow searched but could not locate the convoy.

On 8 May 1970, Delta Company, 2nd Battalion, 12th Cavalry operations pushed into Cambodia amid heavy NVA resistance while finding large caches of enemy weapons and ammunition. A captured NVA soldier, who confessed with an M-16 under his nose, that the NVA were massing for a major counter-attack on the American's perimeter even providing direction and distance to the northwest, was a Godsend. With that vital information, U.S. Army Captain James F. Johnson "directed USAF Spooky (Shadow), which zigzagged above all night, firing the 6,000 rounds-a-minute bursts so close to the perimeter at times that they could hear the rounds hitting the ground before they heard the report of the weapon. As Johnson began to doze off as the night wore on, he was reassured each time he jerked awake to hear the high-pitched wail of the miniguns and see solid red lines of their tracers."[3]

Once MACV commander, General Abrams, allocated close-air support (CAS) sorties, subordinate ground commanders decided where to use the strikes. During the incursion, two major considerations were how long it would take planes to get to the border and how long they could stay there. CAS from fighter/bombers at Bien Hoa could be over the Fish Hook in seven minutes, while A-1s took about twenty minutes. Jets from Binh Thuy in the Mekong Delta took fifteen minutes to reach the Fish Hook. Once on station, the planes could normally stay for half an hour while packing napalm or 5,000/7,500 pound bombs. Fixed-wing gunships like Shadow gunships from Tan Son Nhut could get to the border within twenty minutes and stay on station for four to five hours.

Flying close air support (CAS) for American troops during nighttime were fixed-wing gunships, USAF AC-119G (Shadow), and AC-119K (Stinger) gunships. VNAF AC-47 gunships provided night CAS for ARVN troops in Cambodia. They were particularly effective against NVA supply columns and infantry attacks. The gunships were fortunate in several regards. First, in May 1970 the air defense guns moved out of North Vietnam in 1969 and early 1970 were primarily located in southern Laos and northeastern Cambodia. Secondly, these (anti-aircraft) weapons were aimed optically rather than by radar; thus the gunships could operate at night at acceptable levels of risk. Fortunately for low flying aircraft like the Shadow, Soviet Union SA-7 (Strella) infrared heat-seeking, shoulder-fired surface-to-air missiles were still a year or so away from introduction into the Southeast Asia War. As the gunship crews knew too well, if the enemy was in range of the gunship's weapons, the gunship might well be in range of enemy ground weapons.

Most NVA/VC troops and support personnel quickly fled their Cambodian base camps along the border and retreated farther into Cambodia to avoid the blitzkrieg of American tanks, armored personnel carriers (APCs), and infantry. A rearguard of enemy troops stayed and fought, trying to slow the invasion with defensive action. U.S. helicopter gunships struck enemy that stood to fight the onslaught and chased those who retreated from the action.

Monsoon rains came soon. Tanks from the 11th Armored Cavalry Regiment slogged their way westward. They crashed through dense jungles to crush enemy troops in bunkers and trench lines. By early June, both day and night covert missions were flown in Cambodia by AC-119 Shadow gunships based at Tan Son Nhut.

Flying night CAPs over American troops in Cambodia during June, Shadows contacted U.S ground units for situation reports and to let the GIs on the ground know that a Shadow gunship was overhead to provide illumination or fire support. As a Shadow copilot, I got the sitrep from a GI that all was quiet. I then asked him if there was anything they needed. The GI answered, "Tell my 'highers' to send more water and body bags."

President Nixon's administration strategists had gambled. They figured these heavily supplied North Vietnamese bases inside Cambodia were critical to the safe withdrawal of American forces in Vietnam and to give more time for the Improvement and Modernization (I & M) of Vietnam armed forces called Vietnamization of the war. A successful offensive against the safe havens of enemy troops would cripple Hanoi's war machine for months.

The Cambodian Incursion created more anti-war opposition and demonstrations in CONUS. Anyone in the U.S. who listened to TV and radio news broadcasts or read newspapers and magazines was fully aware of the debacle at Kent State University in Ohio where four students were accidentally killed by National Guardsmen during an anti-war demonstration. This tragedy spurred more and much larger demonstrations against the war in various locations such as Washington, D.C. and New York City. But nothing was reported about the brave American soldiers and airmen who died during the incursion.

Anti-war protests and demonstrations against the Cambodian Incursion had little, if no effect on U. S. ground, air, or riverine forces fighting in Southeast Asia. The American GI (Government Issue) in SEA continued the fight against communist armed forces. GIs were fighting for the lives of fellow-Americans and foreign allies as well as their own lives. In the 17th SOS, reaction to anti-war demonstrations at home was to fight the enemy even harder in support of American and allied ground forces.

When Richard Nixon assumed the Office of 37th President of the United States of America in 1969, previously initiated efforts by the Johnson Administration were already underway to improve the military forces of South Vietnam. Now with Nixon in office, trying to keep his presidential campaign pledge to end the war and bring about "Peace with Honor" in Vietnam, Vietnamization of the war and American troop withdrawals became a top priority.

***

Operation Freedom Deal

Areas of Operation and Rules of Engagement for U.S. air support and strikes in Cambodia changed as time passed since initial thrusts of U.S. and ARVN ground troops into Cambodia. By mid-May 1970, Operation Freedom Deal, an aerial interdiction campaign, was initiated to maintain surveillance of enemy activity and to slow down enemy road and river travel in northeastern Cambodia bounded by the borders of South Vietnam and Laos and a line 200 meters west of the Mekong River and Route 13 between Kratie and Snoul. The campaign authorized the use of U.S. tactical warplanes against enemy forces in northeastern Cambodia as needed to protect American forces stationed in Vietnam. For close air support in Freedom Deal areas of Cambodia, approval of attacks came from military headquarters at the U.S. Military Assistant Command, South Vietnam's Joint General Staff, and the Cambodian armed forces.[4]

***

Weeks prior to the Cambodian Incursion, main force NVA regiments and VC units moved westward from border sanctuaries toward the Mekong River, Phnom Penh, and deeper into the northeastern provinces of Cambodia to avoid a major confrontation with invading U.S. and ARVN ground forces. Consequently, the uprooted NVA/VC troops had to contend with the Cambodian Army (FANK) stationed in northeastern provinces of the country, now under control of the new pro-western government and its leader Lon Nol.

On 5-6 May 1970, NVA and VC troops captured the Mekong River city of Kratie (Kracheh) and the FANK ordnance depot located there. Supplies seized at the depot partially offset losses in eastern Cambodia sanctuary depots along the RVN border. Then, two NVA/VC battalions headed north to the Mekong River city of Stoeng Treng to launch a night attack on 14 May. By 18 May, Stoeng Treng was captured, giving the communist troops control of all major LOCs north of Kratie.

To further weaken FANK control in northern and northeastern Cambodia, the NVA/VC increased pressure on the three strategic garrison towns of Lomphat, Bakiev, and Labansiek. Lomphat and Bakiev were first attacked on 14 May and thereafter. Under constant attack, defenders of Lomphat were forced to withdraw to Labansiek on 31 May, leaving Labansiek and Bakiev as the only significant towns in northeastern Cambodia under control of government troops.

Enemy forces advanced to and probed the area south of Phnom Penh near Phum Banam in May. Located approximately halfway between Kratie and Phnom Penh, Kampong Cham (KPC), the capital city of Kampong Cham Province was probed by enemy troops in early May. On 11-12 May, the enemy captured Tonle Bet located across the Mekong from Kampong Cham city. FANK troops at KPC were reinforced by the government on the same day. Kampong Cham was attacked again on 15 May. The attack was repulsed and FANK troops remained in control of the city. Meanwhile, other FANK troops retook Tonle Bet on the same day. Regardless, FANK families in KPC were evacuated the next day. On 18 May, the FANK announced that enemy forces had withdrawn from KPC.

Svay Rieng located on Highway 1 in extreme southeastern Cambodia and Prey Veng located about halfway between Svay Rieng and Phnom Penh repulsed enemy attacks on 26 and 28 May, respectively. Enemy forces soon made their presence known west of the Mekong in the vicinity of Kampong Thom (KPT) located on Route 6. In gaining control of KPT, the enemy could seek the aid of 150,000 Vietnamese living in the food-rich Tonle Sap area while blocking the Route 6 supply line into north-western Cambodia. On 30 May, KPT reported increased enemy forces surrounding the city and that the enemy had effectively blocked LOCs with Phnom Penh. The next day, enemy mortars rained down on the capital city of Kompong Thom Province.

***

From day five of the Cambodia Incursion, AC-119G Shadow gunships had been flying night support missions for U.S. ground forces operating in Cambodia. Daylight missions were not required of Shadows until the need for aerial support of a Cambodian Army relief convoy traveling on Route 6 to Kompong Thom came under attack. 17th SOS C Flight was called to launch a gunship to find and provide fire support for the convoy. The unknown status of enemy anti-aircraft guns available to communist troops in Cambodia was of major concern for the Shadow crew, especially during broad daylight.

Accordingly, the first daylight Shadow gunship mission in Cambodia was flown in May by a C Flight crew. First Lieutenant Dennis Davis was the aircraft commander and Captain Hank Alau was the navigator on the Shadow crew. Alau wrote,

> We had already flown the early mission, pulled strip alert, and completed our duty at 0600 hours. The ops officer called our aircraft commander, Lt Denny Davis and asked if our crew could fly another mission. There was actually another crew available and our flight commander, Lt. Col. White had tried to send them on the mission. The available crew consisted of flight evaluators and instructors who were scheduled to fly a daylight firepower demonstration for the Army. Thus, TUOC declined to

send the instructor crew after deciding there were too many valuable people on board. Lt. Col. White's response was, "What the hell is this, a suicide mission?" Consequently, this mission caused our crew to adopt the name "The Expendables."

We broke ground at 1000 hours (at Tan Son Nhut Air Base) and headed for Kompong Thom for the first daylight mission into Cambodia. Some of the "Expendable" crewmembers were AC 1/Lt Davis, CP 1/Lt Bob Mundle, NAV Capt Hank Alau, NOS 1/Lt Rodney B. Sizemore, FE MSgt Bill Abels, and Gunner TSgt Paden. (Names of the IO and other gunner cannot be located.)

About 15 minutes after arriving onsite we got instructions from a Rustic FAC directing us south to the town of Skoun. When we got there we found a column of Kompong Thom-bound relief forces pinned down by enemy fire. It was a relief column like I had never seen before, consisting of civilian buses and trucks and no military vehicles. Cloud cover forced us down to 1,500 feet where we were easily able to provide significant support. MSgt Abels had our engines leaned out so well and milked for all they were worth. As a result we were airborne an amazing six hours. When we landed at Tan Son Nhut, the number one engine quit as we turned off the runway onto the taxiway.

Lt. Col. White met us in the revetment and told us that they all thought we had crashed and were getting ready to launch a SAR effort. Once inside C Flight Ops, we were met and debriefed by a MACV intelligence officer who was interested in the relief column progress, capability, and leadership. This was the first and only time we received this kind of debriefing. When the Intel officer left, he made a cryptic statement to the effect, "Yeah, these are the guys we trained and left, never to be heard from again." This led us to suspect that this was not your ordinary intelligence officer."[5]

Shadow aircraft commander Lt. Davis added to the story:

> Because the convoy was in "dire straits" to say the least, we
> stayed on target past bingo fuel. Aircraft commander screw-
> up! We encountered bad weather en route back to Tan Son
> Nhut, so I decided to try landing at Bien Hoa, but they were
> below minimums; therefore we were committed to landing at
> Tan Son Nhut (aka TACAN Channel 102). TSN was right at
> minimums in heavy rain and our fuel was so critical, I asked
> for a bail-out heading in case I failed to get the aircraft on the
> ground. Of course, we made a safe landing.
>
> Our flight commander, Lt. Col. White was standing out in
> the rain next to the revetments when we were parked. I guess
> he didn't think he would see us again. He didn't realize he was
> dealing with a bunch of crazy lieutenants and one captain. My
> FE, Sgt Abels asked if he could "stick the fuel tanks" and I
> replied that I didn't care but I didn't want to know the result.
> At the Intel debriefing, the "intelligence" officers had no clue
> as to what we would encounter on the mission. The mission
> briefing we got the next day in preparation for another daylight
> flight in Cambodia was the same information from our de-
> briefing from the first mission."[6]

***

The initial objective of Operation Freedom Deal was solely interdiction,
but it soon became obvious that some direct air support for Cambodian
ground troops was vital to save government outpost garrisons. With the
evacuation of and withdrawal of government troops from Lomphat on 31
May, this situation became clear at Labansiek and Bakiev, the last FANK
strongholds in the northeastern provinces of Cambodia. Both towns denied the enemy use of critical portions of Routes 19 and 194.

Operation Freedom Deal was modified on 7 June from strictly striking
enemy lines of communication to striking enemy ground forces attacking
FANK garrisons in or near major cities in northeastern Cambodia. USAF
missions were classified top secret as Nixon administration officials reit-

erated that the U.S. would not provide air support for ARVN operations beyond the thirty kilometer limit of the Cambodian Incursion. Thus, support for FANK forces was technically okay.

Additional sorties were concurrently fragged by 7th Air Force on 7 June for the northeastern Cambodia government controlled towns of Labansiek and Bakiev. From 13 June to 20 June, the two towns became primary interdiction areas for U.S. air strikes.

During the first week of June, Labansiek was attacked on numerous occasions while enemy activity increased around Bakiev. As heavy ground action continued after 13 June, USAF fighters under FAC control began attacking known enemy locations (KELs) around the two towns. Fixed-wing gunships operating alone without FAC control also attacked enemy units threatening the towns. But, because of troop losses and supply/reinforcement problems, the Cambodian government decided to evacuate the two northeastern strongholds. Evacuations began on 23 June under continuous USAF fighter cover. Primary evacuation aircraft were USAF C-7 Caribous and C-123 Providers. An ARVN relief column also arrived on 23 June. More than 7,000 Cambodian refugees were eventually resettled in RVN. The Cambodian government withdrawal left the northeastern provinces in total control of the NVA/VC.[7]

Another key city under enemy attack was Siem Reap, located on Route 6 in northwestern Cambodia. Shadow gunships defended the city against attacks by NVA and Khmer Rouge forces on 8 and 10 June. By the middle of the month, enemy troops occupied the ancient city of Angkor Wat to the northeast of the city. Although Siem Reap was not seriously threatened during the latter part of June, periodic airstrikes helped drive away enemy units in outlying areas.

After the evacuation of Cambodian soldiers and their families from northeastern providences, 7th Air Force initiated Operation Freedom Action, an air operation separate from Freedom Deal as authorized by JCS on June 17. Freedom Action authorized 7th Air Force Commander, General Brown thru General Abrams, to intervene with American aircraft in any battle throughout the country of Cambodia where enemy victories would pose a military or psychological threat to the Lon Nol government. B-52 bombers could be used in Freedom Action just as in Freedom Deal.

Due to the expansion and intensity of NVA attacks throughout Cambodia CAS became priority over interdiction missions for USAF aircraft. Under Freedom Action Rules of Engagement, NVA, VC, and Khmer Rouge forces could be attacked by U.S. aircraft all across Cambodia.[8]

USAF aircraft flew their first strikes under Freedom Action on 20 June. On that date alone, 16 sorties struck enemy positions in the vicinity of Kompong Thom. KPT had been under enemy pressure since 4 June when a force of at least regimental size attacked the city. Although the city had been reinforced, fighting continued for the next week. As the month progressed, the situation at KPT became more tenuous.

Reinforcement convoys were unable to reach KPT because of enemy ambushes on Route 6; therefore on 15-16 June, VNAF helicopters airlifted additional Cambodian troops to Kompong Thom as enemy forces moved within .7 kilometers of the city center. By 20 June, it was feared the city might fall when MACV directed 7th AF to provide direct air support for the city defenders. Consequently, two AC-119G Shadow gunship sorties, two UC-123 flareship sorties, and six fighter sorties were flown in support of KPT on 20 June. By the end of June, approximately twelve more Shadow gunship sorties, forty-six tactical air sorties, and eighty-two fighter sorties were flown in support of KPT.

Tactical aircraft like the AC-119 gunship could attack enemy targets at any time provided the Cambodian ground commander approved the attack via direct radio contact with the Shadow. Working with Hotel 303 Major Oum, commander at KPT, Shadow gunships were instrumental in defending the city from being overrun. Defenders of Kompong Thom were, according to Lon Nol, the principal benefactors as American airmen saved from death or capture the besieged province capital.[9]

All U.S. airmen flying CAS were always mindful of enemy anti-aircraft fire and the risk of being shot down. If that should happen, American flyers could rely on USAF Sea & Air Rescue (SAR) units stationed in Thailand to save them from capture, torture, imprisonment, or execution by the enemy. USAF SAR missions were permitted in all of Cambodia and were authorized to return ground fire received while conducting rescue operations. ARVN helicopters were another possibility for rescue. And after time, CIA-operated Air America aircraft were observed on the ground at remote locations by Shadow gunship crews during day missions. Knowing that Air America was capable of rescuing downed airmen as proven elsewhere, Shadows had a back-up "ace in the hole" for rescue.

It was initially thought that sufficient numbers of French-speaking VNAF FACs qualified to direct U.S. air strikes would be available to communicate with the Cambodians, but that was not the case. Also in short supply were FANK Liaison Officers who could speak English. Thus, there existed a language barrier between U.S. aircraft and Cambodian ground contacts. It became necessary to enlist USAF officers and airmen who were fluent in French to act as airborne interpreters. Although 7th AF was able to fill this need from SEA resources, many of the interpreters were not on flying status and none had attended appropriate survival schools, therefore, waivers for flying status were quickly granted.

Radio procedures were also established for communication between USAF, VNAF, and Cambodian Air Force aircraft. A common radio frequency was also established for initial contact between Cambodian ground commanders and allied aircraft. Because of increased enemy activities and attacks on Cambodia government installations and LOCs, targets identified for USAF aircraft by the ground commanders were considered validated and aerial strikes ensued.

Operation Freedom Action would end on 29 June with the withdrawal of U.S. ground forces from Cambodia. With the inclusion of the Cooper-Church resolution into the defense appropriations bill for fiscal year 1971, U. S. ground troops and/or military advisers were banned from Cambodia and Laos. But, U. S. air operations in Cambodia and Laos were omitted in the resolution; thereby, legitimizing continued American air support for the Cambodians. Thus, the inaugural period of USAF air support for Cambodians during the Cambodia Incursion was only the beginning of a prolonged aerial campaign to keep pressure on the enemy and to insure that a new allied government survived. With the fast approaching deadline date of 1 July 1970 for U.S. ground forces to be withdrawn from Cambodian soil, a sustained U. S. air operations plan to support the fledgling Cambodia government of Lon Nol was deemed essential for continued withdrawal of American troops from Vietnam and Vietnamization of the Vietnam War.

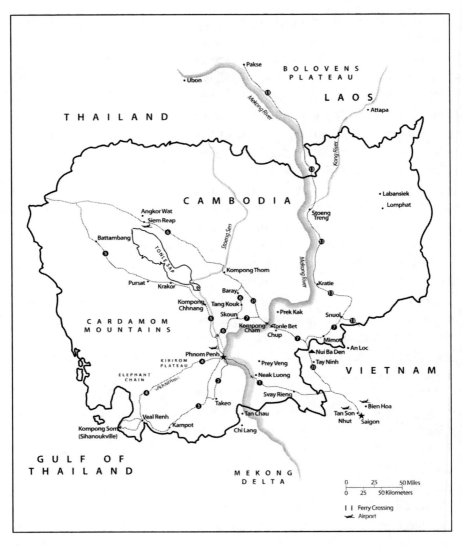

Republic of Cambodia.

NINE

Secret Shadows Cover Cambodia

While American and ARVN ground forces continued raiding enemy base camps and supply depots in Cambodia during June, plans were underway by the White House and 7th Air Force to conduct a sustained secret U. S. aerial campaign in Cambodia to support the Lon Nol government. Reconnaissance flights over enemy-held territory, interdiction of enemy LOCs, and radio contact with Cambodian ground forces while providing direct air support as needed, were critical to a successful ending to the Cambodian Incursion at the end of June 1970.

For the 17th Special Operations Squadron, prolonged and expanded Shadow gunship operations in Cambodia were forthcoming. Normal changes in the squadron occurred in leadership positions during June and would continue during July and August due to personnel completing duty tours in Vietnam. At headquarters 17th SOS, Lt. Col. Edward A. Elbert, Jr. became Squadron Commander, replacing Lt. Col. Don Clark who was transferred to the 14th SOW. Lt. Col. Alfred I. Flynn replaced Lt. Col. Reeter as Squadron Operations Officer, Lt. Col. John M. Fear replaced Lt. Col. Wilson as Squadron Navigator, and Major Thomas V. Soltys replaced Major Hintzen as Squadron Executive Officer.

Squadron maintenance manning markedly improved during the quarterly report, but a shortage of supervisory manpower still plagued the unit. This temporary problem was alleviated by training unqualified people to fill vacant slots. An influx of qualified supervisors soon solved the problem. Flight engineers were still undermanned at 75% during June and July, but by the first of September manning was at 91%. Pilot and navigator positions were over manned. During August, over manning reached a high of 141% for pilots and 125% for navigators; consequently in September, thirty to forty day rollbacks on tours of duty were given to a number of lucky pilots and navigators.

Newly assigned command positions at 17th SOS FOLs included: A Flight Commander Lt. Col. Bill R. Whitsell replaced Lt. Col. Flynn; Maj Phillip E. J. Lee replaced Capt Frank C. Watson as Administrative Officer; TSgt Jay A. Collars replaced MSgt Lewis as First Sergeant. In B Flight at Phan Rang, Lt. Col. Flynn was assigned as Flight Commander and Operations Officer, Maj Marice F. Golden was assigned Assistant Flight Operations Officer. Maj. Charles Meier was Squadron/Flight Administrative Officer, Capt George Schenck was Squadron/Flight Maintenance Officer, and MSgt Manker was Squadron First Sergeant.

Lt. Col. Tom A. Teal replaced Lt. Col. Harry A. White, Jr. as C Flight Commander in June. Upon his August arrival, Lt. Col. William "Bill" Gregory became Operations Officer. Maj Earl J. Farney replaced Maj Richard L. Stoner as Administrative Officer while also assigned as Maintenance Officer and Flight Crew Navigator. MSgt Clarence B. Weber was First Sergeant.

At the beginning of June, the seventeen AC-119G gunships of the 17th SOS were deployed as follows: A Flight at Phu Cat—five; B Flight at Phan Rang—six plus one gunship in phase; C Flight at Tan Son Nhut—five. A Flight at Phu Cat was primarily responsible for RVN Military Regions (Corps) I & II; B Flight was charged to cover II and III Corps; while C Flight covered III and IV Corps. The primary mission of the 17th SOS at the start of June was to seek out and destroy by delivery of airborne armament forces hostile to the interests of free world forces in South Vietnam. The squadron's secondary missions included: 1) To aid in base defense. 2) To aid in all combat missions where flare and searchlight illumination are required. 3) To conduct in-theater training missions for new crews being indoctrinated upon arrival. Squadron strength included 114 officers and 202 airmen for a total of 316 personnel.[1]

***

Nicknamed by C Flight personnel as "The Personal Guns of 7th Air Force Headquarters" based at Tan Son Nhut, the Flight of five AC-119G Shadow gunships were the only U.S. Air Force armed combat aircraft stationed at the sprawling airport located on the northwestern edge of Saigon. The reason behind the nickname was that Headquarters 7th Air Force would directly call C Flight operations on the telephone to launch an Alpha Alert C Flight gunship crew to respond to allied troops-in-contact with enemy forces.

C Flight of the 17th SOS was comprised of approximately forty officers, forty enlisted/noncommissioned officers, and approximately thirty ground maintenance personnel. Six combat crews were fully manned with eight crewmembers each and two partial crews were available but needed gunners and illuminator operators to complete each crew. The shortage of gunners would remain a problem for schedulers throughout the year. The constant turnover of personnel, required in-country training, scheduling R&R and Leave, and working around duty-not-including flight (DNIF) due to injuries or sickness plus the status of operational ready aircraft challenged the best of schedulers.

C Flight had been flying night sorties and a few day sorties over Cambodia during the Incursion. In the battle for the Fish Hook area alone, the U. S. Air Force flew 172 missions of which Shadows had their share. Supporting American ground troops was one thing but then supporting the Cambodian Army was another. Flying interdiction missions (aka armed reconnaissance) and gathering intelligence from English-speaking Cambodian ground commanders became SOP. The greatest problem for Shadow crews in providing direct fire support and gathering information was communicating with Cambodians on the ground who could not speak English. This problem continued until it became obvious that interpreters were needed onboard the gunship. The language barrier between American Shadows and Khmer Army Commanders necessitated recruitment and use of interpreters to accomplish direct support missions.

The original mission of the AC-119G Shadow gunship was to fly and fight in South Vietnam only at night with the motto "Deny Him the Dark." Nevertheless, with the Cambodia Incursion and impending aerial campaign for continued support of the Lon Nol government in Cambodia, things rapidly changed for the 17th SOS, especially for C Flight based at Tan Son Nhut. Daylight sorties became more common and the number of fragged sorties increased with time as the need for direct air support from Shadow gunships also increased. For C Flight aircrews, it was a call to action that sure beat sitting on alert for TIC scrambles or waiting for fragged "Shadow Box" night missions over South Vietnam. A Shadow sortie was a scheduled mission for one gunship, fragged by higher authority scheduling at 14th Special Operations Wing located at Phan Rang Air Base. Shadows usually called a sortie, a mission.

With the impending withdrawal of American ground troops from Cambodia by the end of June, the need to provide the new government of Lon Nol in Cambodia and Cambodian armed forces with air support to ward off attacks by NVA and Khmer Rouge forces became obvious to U.S. leaders. The need for intelligence as well as direct air support of the Cambodian Army resulted in a Nixon White House directive to form a Top Secret Special Task Force of Forward Air Controllers (FACs) called "Rustic" on 19 June.[2]

Consequently, Rustic FACs flying O-2s during nighttime and OV-10s during daytime soon provided round-the-clock coverage for Cambodia. The Task Force mission of Rustic FACs was classified Top Secret as would be the case for Shadow missions in Cambodia. In late June, Rustic FACs joined Shadow gunships in aerial support for the Province Capital of Kompong Thom that was under attack. A meeting of commanding officers of Rustic FACs and representatives from the 7th AF, 14th SOW, 17th SOS, and C Flight soon followed to coordinate Rustic and Shadow efforts over Cambodia.

On a Sunday afternoon in late June, 17th SOS C Flight Commander, Lt. Col. Tom Teal was sitting and smoking his pipe at his office desk in the Shadow Operations building located on the Tan Son Nhut flight line when C Flight's mission was drastically changed. Teal wrote in his memoir, "My secure phone rang and the DCO (Deputy Commander of Operations) of the 14th SOW said that our mission was to provide Shadow gunship coverage over Cambodia day and night, twenty-four hours a day. Stress to all your people that this is a highly classified [secret] mission and no radio or communications of any kind will mention Cambodia. Now how many sorties a day will it take to keep coverage over Cambodia? I said initially six sorties a day should be suggested to Seventh AF with Shadows flying 4.5 hours which we have been doing. That would leave a thirty minute gap between sorties over Cambodia but could be made up as necessary by launching the next sortie thirty minutes early. For six sorties a day we will require five more aircraft with seven more crews, and assorted maintenance and parts. The DCO said that he would pass that information to Seventh AF and the DCM [Deputy Commander of Maintenance] will be in touch. The DCM called and said he agreed with the ten aircraft for six per day or thirteen for eight sorties per day. Then our detailed planning started."[3]

To avoid any undue attention to increased Shadow operations, Tan Son Nhut Air Base scheduled bus routes were still used to transport C Flight enlisted aircrew personnel housed off base at the Merlin Hotel to and from Shadow Ops. With "around-the-clock" sorties fragged every day, Teal scheduled sortie takeoff times and support schedules to coincide with the existing bus schedule. Additional ground vehicles were added to the Flight as needed to meet the schedule and future mission requirements.

To insure that an AC-119 gunship would make scheduled take-off times, a back-up crew on stand-by status that was scheduled to take-off three hours later was required to be in their aircraft, engines running if necessary, to take off if the primary aircraft could not make the scheduled take-off time. If the back-up crew had to launch early, the primary crew became the back-up crew and would assume alert status until the next scheduled launch time in three hours. Confusing? Not for Shadows of C Flight.

***

Of top priority was the need to find and reserve appropriate housing for incoming personnel and parking spots for additional aircraft. Captain Jose Cachuela was assigned to handle the logistics. Barracks rooms were located and assigned for expected incoming personnel. Additional revetted parking spots close to Shadow Ops for five to eight additional AC-119 gunships were easily secured because C Flight operations was located near the runway and because the Flight was the only shooting outfit at Tan Son Nhut. The operations building for C Flight was adequate to accommodate additional flying helmets, parachutes, survival vests, life preservers, and guns of additional aircrews. The exact start time for flying around the clock in Cambodia depended on the arrival time of aircrews and aircraft with maintenance personnel and appropriate equipment and spare parts. Plans orchestrated by Teal only required necessary operations orders from 7th AF with the number of daily sorties required and rules of engagement. Rules of Engagement such as areas of operations, communications, call signs, clearance to fire, were being coordinated by headquarters of the 17th SOS, 14th SOW, and 7th AF.

By the end of June, 17th SOS operations at Tan Son Nhut FOL C Flight started growing with the addition of two Shadow gunships and crews from Phu Cat and two AC-119K Stinger gunships with three complete crews sent from Da Nang, temporarily loaned by the 18th SOS to fill in the required number of sorties in Cambodia. With four additional gunships at Tan Son Nhut for interdiction missions against enemy infiltration routes on the Mekong River and the Ho Chi Minh Trail, C Flight Shadows could concentrate more on directly supporting the Cambodian Army.

Operational Order 538-69 from 7th Air Force Headquarters listed the priority of combat missions for C Flight and the 17th Special Operations Squadron Gunship III (AC-119) Priorities:

1. Close fire support of friendly troops in contact.
2. Close fire support of U. S. and friendly military installations including forts and outposts.

3. Close fire support of strategic hamlets, villages and district towns.

4. Pre-planned armed recce and interdiction of hostile areas and infiltration routes.

5. Search and Rescue support.

6. Night and day armed escort for road and close off-shore convoys.

7. Illumination for night fighter strikes.

8. Harassment and Interdiction.

17th SOS C Flight Commander Teal wrote: "With Seventh Air Force's operations order in hand and flight, maintenance crews, and aircraft in place, we began the treadmill of flying around the clock over Cambodia in early July 1970 with six sorties a day. The sorties were increased to eight sorties daily in August. We were given call signs and frequencies of several different locations in country which put us in contact with each location commander. [Radio call signs for Cambodian ground contacts was 'Hotel' followed by two or three digits or a name.] Example: Hotel 303 was the call sign for the commander at Kompong Thom (KPT), Major Oum, who had the authority of a troops-in-contact commander and who could direct us to any part of his territory and fire at his designated target or targets. Most of our first few months were spent working for Hotel 303 and preventing his town from being overrun by the bad guys. We sure shot up the old saw mill area on almost every mission there as well as other locations. We definitely saved KPT from being taken."[4]

***

Freedom Action lasted until 30 June when American ground troops withdrew from Cambodia. Thereafter, Freedom Deal Rules of Engagement were reinstated in original areas of operation with the additional expansion to southern Cambodia. Between air interdiction, close air support, and logistical functions, airpower had played a significant role in the Cambodian Incursion. B-52s conducted 643 Arc Light strikes along the Cambodian border during May and June. In making a major

Fighting C Flight Commander Lt. Col. Tom Teal at his desk on which sits a statuette of Apsara, the beautiful Cambodian ballet dancer. The statuette was presented to the 17th SOS by visiting Cambodian officers on behalf of the Cambodia government in deep appreciation for the air support provided by Shadows.

effort to provide CAS to American ground forces in Cambodia, USAF planes flew 5,189 fragged sorties and 1,675 scrambled sorties in addition to 193 gunship and 44 flareship sorties. The VNAF flew 2,691 strike sorties and 184 gunship sorties in support of ARVN troops.[5] Between 5 May and 30 June 1970; AC-119 gunships flew 178 sorties, fired 1,412,028 rounds, and dropped 1,463 flares in support of U.S. ground troops operations in Cambodia.[6]

American losses in Cambodia Operation Rockcrusher totaled 284 men killed in action, 2,339 wounded in action, and thirteen missing in action. For their actions, the Cambodian Incursion proved to exceed initial expectations of the campaign. Major General George Casey declared the operation was the most successful in the history of the USA 1st Air Cavalry Division. During the two month Incursion, the NVA and VC had been defeated and driven from their Cambodia border sanctuaries while losing their training camps, staging areas, and war supplies to attack South Vietnam. U.S. and ARVN forces killed 11,349 enemy troops while capturing 2,328 soldiers during the sixty-day offensive into Cambodia.[7]

There were no doubts among allied forces; the Cambodian Incursion was a major success. Because of the Incursion and subsequent ARVN ground actions and USAF/VNAF aerial actions to hunt down and destroy the enemy during months thereafter brought about the beginning of somewhat tranquility over most of South Vietnam. There were no attacks at Tan Son Nhut or Saigon or other major cities. Only a few USAF bases in South Vietnam would experience enemy attacks for the remainder of the year. The Republic of Vietnam took pleasure in the absence of fighting and turmoil in their homeland. Their armed forces, the ARVN and VNAF were taking the war to the NVA and VC enemy in Cambodia.

Shortly before and during the USA and ARVN raids on Cambodian sanctuaries, main force NVA and VC units retreated and dispersed throughout Cambodia, establishing their headquarters near Kratie, while Khmer Rouge (KR) forces moved into Kampong Thom Province. Consequently, since mid-June, the province capital city of Kompong Thom (KPT) had become a major objective to capture by NVA and KR troops because of the city's strategic location on major supply routes to Thailand and Laos. The Tenth Brigade of the Cambodian Army successfully defended the city against the onslaught of attacks in spite of shortages in war materials and supplies. Ammunition and troop reinforcements were desperately needed. KPT became isolated, a city under siege surrounded by thousands of enemy troops. Consequently, Rustic FACs and Shadow gunships became the aerial guardians of Kompong Thom.

In early July 1970, the Eleventh Brigade of the Cambodian Army was dispatched from Phnom Penh to reinforce the Tenth Brigade at Kompong Thom. The relief convoy slowly motored up Route 6 (from Phnom Penh), eventually past Skoun to within twenty miles south of KPT, but was forced to retreat back to Skoun because of an enemy-destroyed bridge on Route 6 to KPT.[8]

Shadow navigator Major Earl Farney recorded on tape, as required for all Shadow missions, missions he flew in support of a Cambodian relief convoy, radio call sign "303 Cambodian Troop," on Route 6 to KPT. Farney wrote:

> The trucks started out at the very end of June from Phnom Penh to relieve the siege of Kompong Thom. The Cambodian convoys were something else; school buses, Pepsi Cola trucks, hop-tacs, anything that rolled. We flew cover for days. Progress up Route 6 was hardly noticeable. The convoy got as far as Phum Khley, twenty miles short of destination KPT. A bridge was either washed-out or destroyed by enemy just short of the town, with no prospect of getting it fixed. So the hapless convoy turned about and headed south toward the capital. Then it happened. Ambush! And the Shadows were there to save the convoy. Exasperating; it was weeks before 303 pulled safely into Phnom Penh.[9]

Finally, to relieve the beleaguered 10th Brigade defenders at KPT, South Vietnamese helicopters were used to airlift the 11th Brigade directly from Phnom Penh to KPT. AC-119 Shadow gunships of C Flight flew overhead cover for this daytime airlift as Rustic FACs operated as on-site air controllers. With reinforcements in place, enemy forces withdrew to fight another day or night.

Lt. Col. Tom Teal wrote, "We [Shadows] must have done a good job there [KPT] because we were soon sent to various other locations all over Cambodia either for troops-in-contact or for interdiction of hostile supplies entering Kompong Som on the Gulf of Siam, road routes over most of Cambodia or locations on the Mekong River such as Kompong Cham. We at times flew missions patrolling the Mekong from Saigon to Phnom Penh and beyond towards the headwaters of that great river."

During this critical time of unknowns, 17th SOS C Flight validated the versatility of AC-119 Shadow gunships. Shadows flew armed reconnaissance interdiction missions while providing protection for road and aerial convoys and direct fire support/night illumination for Cambodian troops fighting enemy forces. Under extremely vulnerable combat conditions of flying low and slow over enemy troops and enemy-held territory especially during daylight, Shadow gunship crews proved to be fearless aerial warriors.

Flying at firing altitudes from 1,500 to 3,500 feet AGL in the face of enemy forces during daytime was dangerous. Shadow crews were at first extremely apprehensive about their vulnerability to unknown capabilities of enemy anti-aircraft guns during day missions. In broad daylight, enemy gunners could clearly see their target; a big black target flying slowly in circles right above them. At least flying at night, the Shadow could hide in the darkness of night skies that provided a shield against visual detection by enemy gunners, but daytime offered no hiding places.

Enemy forces were consolidating throughout Cambodia after evacuating Vietnam border sanctuaries to conduct operations against the Cambodian Army. Their strength and capabilities were uncertain, especially when it came to anti-aircraft guns. Fortunately, the air space over Cambodia would prove lightly defended by communist ground forces for various reasons. The fluid action of enemy troops restricted their capability to transport and utilize heavy anti-aircraft artillery (AAA).

Enemy anti-aircraft guns predominantly encountered by Shadow gunships ranged from 12.7mm to .30 caliber and .51 caliber machine guns. The maximum effective range of these guns was 3,500 feet. The most effective range for Shadow gunship 7.62mm miniguns was at or below 3,500 feet. Thus, gun duels between Shadows and enemy gunners became common. Enemy gunners scored several hits on the AC-119 gunships, but couldn't shoot down the black bird. In most encounters, enemy gun sites were either silenced or destroyed by the Shadow. This gave Shadow crewmembers needed confidence to counteract normal uneasiness associated with flying a combat aircraft during daylight that was originally designated for nighttime operations. Persistent caution to overconfidence in the minds of many Shadow air crewmen was when the enemy would deploy heavier anti-aircraft weapons in Cambodia.

As enemy gunners became more cautious about firing at the black gun plane for fear of getting blasted, 17th SOS C Flight Shadow and Stinger aircrews became more confident in looking for targets and trouble in Cambodia and usually found them and thrived on them. Life and death encounters between AC-119 gunship crews and enemy ground troops became more and more common during the aerial campaign in Cambodia. TIC situations in particular brought out the best in American airmen when friendly troops on the ground depended on fire support from the sky to survive.

Shadows risked their lives to save the lives of Cambodians and South Vietnamese. An American on the ground was something special. If a GIs life was at stake, Shadow crews would virtually lapse into frenzy. They'd go through hell and back to save one U.S. grunt. Army Rescue choppers called "Dust Off" made Shadow gunships look like pikers. Shadows had witnessed Army aviators repeatedly descend into waves of enemy crossfire and near-zero visibility to pull out U.S. wounded. It was unbelievable what heroic acts took place.

Secrecy of Shadow missions in Cambodia was upheld by all involved. Mission reports were safeguarded until handed over to HQ 7th AF by C Flight CO, Lt. Col. Teal. Teal wrote, "The communications and other security precautions were so well observed by the Shadow and Stinger crews, and the few higher headquarters personnel who knew, that the news media never got a whiff of the operations in Cambodia. I know that as a Shadow commander I was required to get up at 4:00 a.m. each morning, review the Flight's combat report from the previous day, then hand carry that report to a colonel in 7th AF operations. That went on for over forty consecutive days until I took a break."[10]

Command and control of U.S. air operations in Southeast Asia came under the Commander of Military Assistance Command, Vietnam (COMUSMACV), General Creighton Abrams and his Air Deputy 7th AF Commander General George S. Brown. Orders were issued by the 7th AF Commander thru his Deputy Chief of Staff for Operations to the Director of Combat Operations (DCO). From the DCO, 7th AF orders and frags were issued for the 14th SOW, 17th SOS, and the Airborne Battlefield Command and Control Center (ABCCC).[11]

Rules of engagement (ROEs) included Cambodian verification of and authorization for attacking targets identified within enemy-controlled areas absent non-combatants. USAF 14th SOW psy-ops aircraft broadcasted over loudspeakers and dropped leaflets to warn Cambodian civilians of imminent attacks and/or to not travel during nighttime. Any traffic on roads and waterways during darkness were subject to attack from the air.

Flying armed reconnaissance missions in northern and northeastern Cambodia, Shadows closely shadowed the Mekong River and Route 13, stalking these two major enemy infiltration routes in enemy-held territory. No clearances were required for Shadows to fire on unsuspecting enemy road vehicles, river boats, or troops.

Unbeknownst to Shadow and Stinger aircrews of C Flight at the time was that they had become part of 7th AF Operation Commando Hunt IV which interdicted enemy infiltration routes in Laos and northern and northeastern Cambodia from May thru October 1970. The region had become controlled by communist forces; thus called "Indian Country" by American Flyers. Later in November when the northwestern monsoon dry season started, Shadows would become a part of Operation Commando Hunt V that would last through May 1971.

As in South Vietnam, a USAF forward air controller (FAC) directed most air strikes, except for B-52 Arc Light strikes and nighttime sorties assigned to Shadow gunships. USAF B-52 bombers dropped bombs on designated targets upon receiving a signal from Combat Skyspot ground radar operators. Air Force AC-119 and AC-130 gunships were also exempt from using a FAC while operating in special operations areas if approved by Cambodian officers. Thus, targets that Shadow gunships fired on were either approved by an English speaking Cambodian ground commander or by "Agate," the radio call sign for 7th AF In-Country/Cambodian Command Center (TACC) located at Tan Son Nhut, or by "Pawnee Target," the radio call sign of the Direct Air Support Center (DASC) located at Pleiku or by a USAF FAC flying as on-scene commander at target location.

In the fall of 1970, airborne command and control centers (ABCCC) aboard EC-121 aircraft with the radio call sign "Ramrod" would clear Shadow for firing on targets if there was no contact with a ground commander or FAC. Later in the year, Shadows would be turned loose in designated free fire zones on interdiction routes whereby anyone or anything that moved or was suspected enemy could be attacked. VHF, UHF, and FM radios aboard the Shadow were used in communications with ground and air contacts.

French interpreters became an integral part of the Shadow crew on night missions. Many Cambodian ground commanders spoke only Cambodian (Khmer) and French. Having been a French Colony, French was the second language of educated Cambodians, specifically military officers. Without direct Cambodian radio ground contacts who spoke English, even broken-English, Shadow gunships and FACs like Rustic flying in Cambodia were at a loss not knowing the Khmer language. Rustic did have some Cambodians made available to fly with them. Consequently, French-speaking GIs in Southeast Asia were recruited to fly with FACs and the AC-119 gunships in Cambodia.

No one in C Flight could speak, let alone understand the Khmer language of Cambodia. Only one C Flight member knew how to speak French; Captain Sandy Shaw. During this time period in July after U.S. troops had withdrawn from Cambodia, I flew as copilot for Captain Shaw. For me, Captain Shaw was a character out of "Terry and the Pirates." His head of lengthy, wavy hair, long side burns, and handle-bar mustache defied air force regulations but not his expertise at flying and firing the Shadow gunship. I didn't understand a French word between Sandy and the Cambodians. I did my copilot job of maintaining the altitude (pitch) of the gunship in the firing circle while continually monitoring onboard radios, both engine instruments, airspeed indicator, and angle of bank. Of course, I kept an eye out the starboard side of the aircraft for anti-aircraft fire. Captain Shaw was cool under combat. He made many Cambodians very happy with his accurate fire and his French.

***

Humor does occur in war zones. During a visit to South Vietnam, U.S. Vice-President Spiro Agnew was in Saigon and a participant in an impromptu awards ceremony at Tan Son Nhut Air Base for Americans receiving the Vietnamese Cross of Gallantry for combat action in Vietnam. In addition to Agnew, high ranking USAF and VNAF officers were in attendance. Agnew would pin medals on recipients. Captain Shaw was scheduled to receive the Cross at the ceremony, unbeknownst to Shaw or anybody in C Flight until a few hours before the ceremony began. Scrambling and unable to find the whereabouts of Shaw, C Flight ops decided to send an imposter with Shaw's name tag firmly affixed to the chest of the imposter's 1505 uniform to the ceremony. The ceremony concluded without a hitch and the imposter proudly wore the medal back to Shadow ops. Where was Sandy? He was on R&R!

***

Seventh Air Force scrambled to find French-speaking American servicemen stationed in Vietnam. When found, screened, and provided with proper security clearance, the volunteer interpreters became important crewmembers on FACs and gunships flying in Cambodia. These men were dedicated American servicemen who put supporting the war effort above any personal satisfaction. One of the most popular French interpreters to fly with Shadows of C Flight was USAF SSgt Rene Pommerelle. Pommerelle was an AF security policeman at Phu Cat AB prior to joining C Flight. He, like other interpreters, showed unrelenting efforts and bravery while flying combat missions as often as flight duty permitted. Interpreters like Pommerelle facilitated air to ground attacks while gathering valuable intelligence. Pommerelle would eventually be awarded the Distinguished Flying Cross with oak leaf cluster for his dedicated service in Shadow gunships.

Freedom Deal ROEs for Cambodia stressed the protection of cultural, historic, and artistic properties throughout the country. A list of cultural sites had been issued along with restricted areas prohibiting air strikes within 1,000 meters. Aircraft were instructed to withdraw from these sites even if anti-aircraft fire was encountered. Photographs of each area were taken by 7th AF reconnaissance units and reproduced for distribution to all FACs, gunship units, tactical air units, and headquarters concerned with the operations in Cambodia.[12]

To help protect Cambodian national shrines, pagodas, and buildings and to avoid accidental attacks on friendly ground troops and civilians, English-speaking Cambodian officers were used to verify targets from the Tactical Air Control Center (TACC) Radio Call Sign "AGATE" located at Tan Son Nhut and the Direct Air Support Center (DASC) located at Pleiku.

One of the most, if not the most cherished treasures of Khmer civilization and cultural sites was Angkor Wat, a twelfth century Hindu temple complex located in northwestern Cambodia near the city of Siem Reap. Ruins at Angkor Wat consisted of ancient pyramids, temples, and towers surrounded by a giant wall and water moat covering an area nearly one square mile. The complex was close to Angkor, the capital of the Khmer Empire from the ninth to the fifteenth century. Also located nearby was the thirteenth century Hindu temple area of Angkor Thom. These two national and world treasures were in sad condition. Both the jungle and the ground war being fought to push occupying communist forces from the temples threatened the relics. Protected from air attack, the ruins protected the refugees of NVA/KR troops. The ground commander at Siem Reap utilized the fire power of Shadow gunships around the temples, the jungle areas and the roads near the temples. Nonetheless, Shadows were not allowed to shoot within the temple complexes even when they took ground fire from enemy troops occupying the complexes.

***

Radio transmissions between Shadow gunships flying in Cambodia and the tactical air control center "Agate" in Vietnam were encrypted (aka "ciphered" or scrambled) to avoid transmissions being intercepted by enemy radio. NVA Intel listened to Shadow unencrypted transmissions over VHF and UHF radios and sometimes impersonated 'friendly' ground contacts requesting Shadow gunships to fire on positions that were actually Cambodian Army positions. It was not unusual for NVA radio operators to speak better English than did the Cambodians or South Vietnamese ground contacts. It was a strange feeling for Shadow pilots and navigators to talk directly with the enemy.

All Shadow gunship radio transmissions and intercom communications were recorded on cassette tapes on every combat mission. The Shadow navigator was responsible for operating the Sony cassette tape recorder and changing tapes as needed from engines startup to engines shutdown. Many mission tapes were copied by Shadow crewmen for personal reasons. Rumors circulated among C Flight members that some original mission tapes found their way to the Oval Office in Washington, DC.

President Nixon's announcement about U.S. air support in Cambodia was stated under the guise of strictly interdiction missions in explicit areas of operation. Justification for aggressive use of U.S. air power in Cambodia stemmed from the fact that aerial support served well as a substitute for American ground troop involvement on the ground. The use of U.S. air power in Cambodia might (and did) help prevent enemy attacks on American forces stationed in Vietnam.

In actuality, interdiction mission reports were altered to also include tactical air strikes. Seventh Air Force would provide direct CAS in addition to interdiction provided the distinction between interdiction missions and tactical air strikes for the Cambodians were not acknowledged on paper. Thus, close-air support for the Cambodians became aerial interdiction and the two were tallied under interdiction missions in reports of all attack sorties flown by U.S. warplanes in Cambodia.

Seventh Air Force used secure means of communication to report strikes outside normal operating areas of Cambodia and consequently generated a cover target to be listed in routine reports. Not until February 1971, when the same aircraft was reported downed at two different locations, did the Department of Defense become aware of the cover story.[13]

In July 1970, Cambodian requests for U.S. air support around Battambang in northwestern Cambodia and the Kirirom Plateau, west of Phnom Penh were rejected by 7th Air Force. But, the threat of enemy attacks at Siem Reap located near the northern shore of Tonle Sap, prompted the use of USAF Shadow gunships and flare ships. Also in July, 7th AF received permission to attack enemy traffic on sections of Route 12 between Siem Reap and Kompong Thom.

On 12 July, 7th AF received permission to expand the extended interdiction zone to include areas bounded by Routes 75, 155, 1543, and Prek Kompong Spean. Thus U.S. air operations were excluded from the Parrot's Beak. Regardless of Freedom Deal expansions, North Vietnamese and Cambodian Khmer Rouge forces continued their advance into all regions of Cambodia. Aerial and ground reconnaissance reported increased enemy traffic on trails, roads, highways, and waterways hauling supplies to communist armed forces forming around Kompong Thom. American air crews and Salem House patrols from MACV Studies & Observation Group (SOG) witnessed enemy troop movements and concentrations. SOG patrols were American-led South Vietnamese patrols which included ethnic Cambodians on ground reconnaissance missions up to fifty kilometers within Cambodia. Salem House probes might travel on foot or be inserted by U.S. or ARVN helicopters. Area of operations expanded westward throughout 1970 from the South Vietnam border.

Shadow Navigator/NOS Captain Robert Safreno wrote about supporting a (Salem) road watch team that was in deep trouble.

We were summoned to go as quick as we could to the Tri-border area of South Vietnam, Cambodia, and Laos. A road watch team was in trouble there and supposed to be completely surrounded by VC. We arrived in the area a short time later, but could not see anything going on. We made radio contact with the road watch team, but could hardly hear them as they were whispering into their radios. They stated that they were completely surrounded and asked us to shoot around them. As we could not see where they were we asked them for some kind of light. What they did was to put the blue strobe light into their cap and pointed it up at the gunship. I picked them up on the NOS and was the only one that could see the light. The pilot looked through his gunsight at my cross hairs and saw where I was looking. He then moved a couple hundred meters out from that point and started shooting in our firing circle. The road watch team got on their radios and said, "That's it, keep it up." His voice was now getting louder. He then asked us to move our shooting in a certain direction. As we were shooting and moving as he indicated, he kept saying, "That's it, great shooting keep it up, keep it moving." We could hear shooting noises down there and asked him what it was. He said, "That's your bullets hitting in front of us. Keep shooting, you're blowing a hole for us to escape." We finished up and left the area. Unfortunately we never did find out what happened to the road watch team.

By the end of 1970, Salem teams without American advisors were operating inside Cambodia up to fifty kilometers west of the Vietnam border and south of the Laotian border to the Gulf of Thailand. Salem House teams and U.S. air reconnaissance aircraft observed porters, bicycles, and ox carts hauling war supplies from Laos to communist transshipment areas in northern jungles of Cambodia to be transferred to trucks for transport down Route 12. USAF forward aircraft controllers observed the movement of supplies with infrared night observation devices (night scopes).[14]

For the month of July, C Flight operations officer, Lt. Col. William Gregory reported to HQ 17th SOS that the Flight flew twenty-three sorties in RVN Corps III and fifty-eight sorties in Cambodia (Corps V) without any ground or air aborts. The Flight was only fragged for sixty sorties in RVN Corps III and IV during the month, thus indicating that twenty-one sorties were scrambled during the month as the direct result of enemy actions.

At the end of July, expansion of Freedom Deal continued. Generals Abrams and Brown determined that if the government of Lon Nol was to survive, U.S. air power was required. Consequently a five-day air campaign was conducted to sustain Cambodian forces west of Phnom Penh on the Kirirom Plateau. This campaign failed to stop the communist advance toward Route 4 which linked Phnom Penh and Cambodia's major seaport Kompong Som (formerly Sihanoukville). U.S. tactical air strikes would continue until September 1970 when communist forces drove Lon Nol forces from the Kirirom Plateau.[15]

By 31 July 1970, two more AC-119K Stinger gunships with three complete combat aircrews were temporarily deployed to Tan Son Nhut to augment 17th SOS C Flight operations in Cambodia. It became obvious that 7th Air Force plans for the aerial campaign in Cambodia hinged on the employment and effectiveness of AC-119 gunships.

TEN

Fighting C Flight

The Vietnam ground war had definitely shifted from in-country South Vietnam to out-country Cambodia since the Cambodia Incursion. The whole Cambodian operation had been a shot in the arm for the South Vietnamese forces. For the first time in the war, South Vietnamese armed forces were finally unleashed from their borders to pursue, track down, and confront their communist enemies. ARVN infantry, artillery, and armor units poured into eastern Cambodia after American ground forces withdrew at the end of June. ARVN helicopters and VNAF planes like the A-1 and AC-47 followed and supported ARVN forces to attack the NVA and VC with vengeance. ARVN troops advanced farther and farther into Cambodia, pursuing NVA and VC forces while indirectly supporting the Cambodian Army (FARK).

The Cambodia operation was a solid success; quick and decisive. Things were looking up. Charlie's sanctuaries and logistics pipeline along the South Vietnam border had been broken and his troops had scattered throughout Cambodia.

Despite the fact that Shadows of Saigon had been flying night missions and some day missions during and following the Cambodia Incursion, the commitment to task 17th SOS C Flight for continual night and day aerial interdiction (aka armed reconnaissance) missions over Cambodia officially began on 1 August; thereby, fulfilling round-the-clock air support for embattled Lon Nol government troops. FOL C Flight based at Tan Son Nhut became the hub for 17th SOS operations in Cambodia (aka V Corps). The number of AC-119 Shadow and Stinger gunships and crews assigned to C Flight steadily increased during July for the all-out 24/7 effort of aerial support for allied ground forces fighting communist armed forces in Cambodia. The first AC-119K Stinger gunship mission to Cambodia from Tan Son Nhut was flown on the night of 2 August 1970.

The reported busiest airport in the world at the time, Saigon's Tan Son Nhut Airport, became a beehive of activity for AC-119 gunship operations. Morale for Shadowmen went sky high as "flyin' and fightin'" became SOP. The "Shadows Lair" flight line building for C Flight Ops and Maintenance became an armed command post. To improve communications with Shadows flying to and from Cambodia, C Flight traded two M-16 rifles to the U.S. Army for a UHF radio. Flight frequency selected for the new Shadow Ops base radio was Channel 69. Thereafter, Shadow navigators called in aircraft performance shortly after take-off before leaving "Company" freq. Upon crossing the Cambodia fence on the way back to TSN, the Shadow Nav called Ops to report estimated time of arrival and aircraft maintenance and regeneration needs for the gunship upon landing. Maintenance operations were hectic with three more Shadow gunships and two Stinger gunships requiring regular attention let alone major problems. The eventual arrival of more qualified maintenance personnel helped alleviate the strain on C Flight maintenance.

***

Seventh Air Force gave first mission priority to support TICs. Next was convoy escort and then armed reconnaissance. On many occasions, the Shadows supported friendly units under night attack. Assaults were frequently broken when the gunship appeared overhead. The Cambodian ground commanders and radio operators quickly learned the names "Shadow," "Rustic," "Spike," "Sundog," and other American aircraft radio call signs. From Kompong Cham to Siem Reap, from Kratie to

Kompong Som (formerly Sihanoukville), American aircraft knew the Cambodian radio call signs with the prefix "Hotel" followed by numbers or letters.

Providing twenty-four-hour coverage of Cambodia over enemy controlled territory had really put Shadow crewmen lives past the frontlines, if there ever were frontlines in the war. Flying the big, slow, black airplane in daylight really made an easy target for communist gunners, especially when flying close to the ground in order for the pilot to see where to shoot. The monsoon wet season that started in June created major problems with all the clouds and rain over the AO. Hits on the aircraft taken from enemy .51 caliber machine guns became more common. Shadows were lucky that nobody onboard the gunships had been hit. Most hits were taken in the booms and tail section. Enemy gunners had not yet learned to lead their target more.

The demand of twenty-four-hour air interdiction missions in Cambodia soon created problems with in-country aircrew training and checkout for the 17th SOS.[1] Aircraft maintenance problems became minor after additional maintenance personnel and equipment were sent to bolster C Flight capabilities at TSN. Thereafter, the old "flying boxcar" turned attack gunship soared like an eagle searching for prey. Having competent and dedicated ground crews to keep the warbird airworthy and operationally ready for combat was reassuring to Shadow flight crews.

New scenarios in pre-flight and post-flight procedures evolved for AC-119 Shadow aircrews at TSN now on the rotating sortie schedule of providing twenty-four-hour coverage of Cambodia. Typical for a fragged sortie to Cambodia in August 1970 follows:

> Four AC-119 Shadow gunships were parked in four of the five steel-reinforced concrete revetments next to the pale green one-story Shadow's Lair. Three additional Shadow and two Stinger gunships were parked in revetments across the taxi-ways from the Shadow Operations building that fronted the main taxi-way leading directly to end of runway 25 left, the primary runway used for take-offs at TSN. Runway 25 right

was also used for take-offs but primarily for landings when 25 left was active. Revetments helped protect airplanes from sustaining damage from enemy mortar and rocket attacks.

Shadow gunship crew #1 scheduled for the one o'clock (1300 hours) afternoon takeoff time to Cambodia, assembled in Shadow Ops at ten-hundred (1000) hours to prepare for assuming alert status at eleven o'clock to replace gunship crew #3 who currently was on alert, ready to launch at a moment's notice while having already prepared for their scheduled take-off time of 1100 hours. Gunship crew #3 had arrived at Shadow Ops at 0700 hours and assumed alert at 0800 hours. Crew #3 would replace Shadow gunship crew #5 that launched at 0800 hours and was presently flying over Cambodia.

With the assigned number of sorties for C Flight now fragged for eight every twenty-four hours, the "merry-go-round" of missions was in high gear. Missions of gunships overlapped one another by two hours since the average mission was scheduled for five hours in duration from take-off to landing. Time from take-off at Tan Son Nhut to the Cambodia border normally ranged between thirty and forty-five minutes, depending on mission profile. When crew #3 launched at 1100 hours, crew #1 assumed alert status, ready to launch in case needed. By the time gunship crew #3 checked into the AO to replace gunship crew #5, crew #5 would be close to or would have reached Bingo fuel and headed toward homebase at Tan Son Nhut under normal circumstances. When gunship crew #5 landed at TSN, crew #1 was prepared for their launch time of 1300 hours. Crew after crew followed the scheduled launch times unless an emergency situation warranted the immediate launch of the alert crew.

Many things had to be accomplished before a Shadow crew would be ready to assume alert. After checking-in at Shadow Operations, the aircraft commander pilot and the (table) navigator headed to 7th AF headquarters for mission briefing. Driving one of C Flight's Air Force blue, Dodge double-cab pickup trucks with the Shadow's emblem stenciled in white on the doors, the driver closely followed the yellow painted driving lanes across the airport tarmac, watching out for taxiing airplanes, helicopters and land vehicles, sharing the tarmac. Past the flight line guard post, the street ran straight to 7th Air Force Headquarters.

Entering the nerve-center for 7th Air Force operations in Southeast Asia, an atmosphere of deadly serious business prevailed as headquarters personnel moved about with hushed voices lost in the vastness of operations. The center of command and control had lots of stars and birds; i.e., generals and colonels. Much if not most of the latest information that 7th AF Intel knew about the real-time situation in Cambodia came from mission debriefings of Shadow crews and/or Rustic FACs.

At one briefing at HQ 7th AF, an Intelligence (Intel) Officer, carrying a rolled map, met the Shadow pilot and navigator and pointed to a small briefing room. Unrolling the map on the table, he proceeded to brief the two Shadowmen:

> Looks like you guys may be busy again today. Mission reports filed by Shadows since you flew yesterday indicate a major effort by the enemy to hold the area around Skoun to control this intersection of Highways 6 and 7 and stop the relief column to KPT. They have ambushed and blocked the Cambodian advance toward the intersection. It's been reported there are two or three enemy battalions concentrated in the area. That could mean over thirty-five hundred enemy troops in the area. Since your last mission yesterday over Skoun, anti-aircraft guns are still there even though a number of sites have been reported destroyed. Every Shadow has reported taking ground fire since your last mission. If weather permits, maybe Rustic can direct some fast-movers to bomb their positions. You know what the weather has been like out there. Shadows have had a tough time getting the job done with all the rain and low clouds. Fast movers wouldn't be able to find the target. You're the best weapon we have to help the Cambodians. Do you have any questions? [Pause] If not, Good Luck!

On the way back to Shadow Ops, the Shadow aircraft commander and navigator stopped at Tan Son Nhut Base Operations to check the weather forecast for the AO. The forecast could have been on tape because it was the same as yesterday. Overcast skies with low, ragged cloud bottoms and rain that meant limited visibility with an eye out for the possible development of severe thunderstorms which could result in high winds with extreme gusts causing even more dangerous flying conditions. No surprise; it was the monsoon wet season.

Forecasting the weather at Tan Son Nhut had reached a new level of sophistication with the use of meteorological satellites. Weather satellite imagery provided forecasters with photographs of atmospheric conditions which proved reliable in forecasting unpredictable weather patterns of the monsoon season in Southeast Asia that ran from June thru October. Weathermen at Tan Son Nhut knew that Shadow gunships and FACs relied on good weather conditions at low altitudes to accomplish their mission and used the new technology to forewarn low flying warplanes like the AC-119 gunships, O-2, and OV-10 FACs of potential hazardous weather conditions.

Weather briefings were just a reminder that if the aircraft didn't kill the crew and if enemy guns didn't shoot them down; then the weather could very well get the job done. Shadow gunships had no weather radar. For that matter, Shadows had no onboard radar at all. Flying combat in Cambodia was strictly visual flight rules (VFR). There was no radar control center in Cambodia to keep aircraft separated or to warn aircraft in the AO of severe storms. TACAN radial and DME distance information was critical for aircraft location in the AO. Knowing the direction and distance from a TACAN station within range was most helpful in navigation. Many, many Shadow missions in Cambodia exceeded the maximum range of TACAN stations in South Vietnam and Thailand, causing the table navigator to strictly rely on maps. Maps were always used by the navigator to keep the Shadow pilot informed of the current flying location and to positively identify targets. Flares and the night observation scope were used to see ground targets in the dark of night. Otherwise, radio communications with FACs and FANK ground commanders was the vital element to conducting aerial operations in Cambodia. At least the terrain around Skoun was flat and Shadow gunships during this time in the Cambodia Air Campaign didn't have to worry about flying into the side of a mountain.

Upon returning to Shadow Ops, the pilot and navigator performed their pre-flight inspections of the aircraft before briefing the crew. Sometimes, 7th AF Intel officers and base weather personnel briefed gunship crews at Shadow Operations. Thus, the whole crew knew what was taking place in the AO and what weather conditions might be encountered. This saved the pilot and navigator time briefing their crew on mission profile.

All eight Shadow crewmembers performed pre-flight inspections of the gunship before assuming alert status. The pilots checked aircraft structure and controls. The table navigator checked the firing control computer system and the NOS checked the observation scope. The gunship had been filled with avgas from fuel trucks and ammunition and flares from munitions trucks under direction of the flight engineer, gunners, and the illuminator operator. The gunship had twenty-two self-sealing bladder tanks in the wings. Bladders were filled with reticulated polyurethane foam to suppress explosions. The two gunners completed inspections of the four miniguns, having already loaded sixty cans of ammo weighing sixty-six pounds each. Depending on take-off weight limits under existing weather conditions, Shadows carried 27,000 to 30,000 rounds of 7.62 millimeter bullets onboard to Cambodia.

AC-119 Shadow gunship miniguns fired 7.62mm ammunition consisting of ball and tracer rounds intended for use against personnel or material targets. Every fifth round shot from the minigun was a red tracer round. To make Shadow's firepower more potent against enemy reinforced bunkers, anti-aircraft gun sites, armored sampans, and road vehicles, C Flight received a small amount of 7.62mm high explosive incendiary (HEI) ammunition to test during August. The 7.62mm HEI ammunition was designed for use against light land and water vehicles because of its fragmentation and incendiary effects. Like fighter aircraft, Shadows at times mixed loads of HEI ammunition with standard ball and tracer ammunition. The ammunition worked so well, more HEI ammo was requested by the 17th SOS from 7th Air Force and PACAF. Shadow pilots reported that firing HEI gave them better accuracy because they could see bullets impact on targets.

But, because the miniguns fired at such high rates, some HEI ammo actually exploded in minigun barrels. Shadow gunner TSgt. Norman J. Evans was hit in the eye by fragments from HEI bullet explosions during firing. Evans flew his next mission with an eye patch. Again a shortage of gunners existed in C Flight and personal injuries did not always exclude personnel from flying combat missions.

Cans of ammo were securely strapped down to the airframe since ammo can racks had been removed to lessen aircraft weight. The IO checked the white spot light and the twenty-four flares loaded into the flare launcher.

If something on the aircraft was found not operational or not flightworthy between preflight inspections or engine run-ups checks just prior to taking the active runway for takeoff, it was either immediately fixed by ground maintenance or by the crew's flight engineer. If not fixable prior to the scheduled mission launch time, another CR gunship would be assigned to the crew in order to make the scheduled takeoff time.

With satisfactory preflight inspections completed, the crew returned to the Shadow Ops building to assume alert until their scheduled takeoff time unless scrambled for some reason. While on alert status, crewmen joked around, checked personal equipment, played cards, wrote letters, read and re-read letters from home, watched AFVN television, or played pool and table tennis (both a pool table and a Ping-Pong table were in the Shadow Ops briefing/recreation room). Some finished-off mess hall flight lunches. Some had leftovers in the white boxes from the chow hall, filled with cold fried chicken or sandwiches, apples, cookies, and milk or juice to take along for snacking during the mission. It wasn't long before the gunship crew returning from the AO had landed with news from the front, telling the latest about the Skoun situation. Some reports were matter of fact, others were downright scary.

With their replacement crew arriving at Shadows Ops to prepare for assuming alert, Shadow crew #1 started the ritual of getting ready for another combat mission. Approximately forty-five minutes before their scheduled takeoff time of 1300 hours, crewmembers gradually drifted to the personal equipment room and began to "saddle-up" with flight gear before heading to the gunship. The time had come to don survival vests which contained plastic water flasks and two survival radios. Each man checked his water flask and double-checked battery power on his two survival radios. Parachutes were examined before pulling over the shoulders the heavy weight of "God Forbid," a chance for life after flight. Smith & Weston .38 caliber revolvers were checked-out and loaded with bullets, then holstered in survival vests. Some crewmembers wore a gun belt to holster revolvers in place of stashing the revolver into an inside chest pocket of the survival vest. Extra bullets for the .38 "pea-shooter" were stored in slots on the gun belt. Some crewmen carried U. S. Army Kabar knives with seven inch blades on their gun belts. The two Shadow gunners checked-out two M-16 rifles and numerous ammo clips which would be stowed in the gunship cargo area (gun deck) just in case of bailout or landing in enemy-held territory. Flying helmets and flight gloves were essentials for combat. The navigators checked-out two metal ammunition cans filled with maps of the AO and lugged them with help toward the door of Shadow Ops.

Sitting alert in the comfort of the air-conditioned Shadow Lair within the safe confines of Tan Son Nhut Air Base was about to end. The time had come for crew #1 to mount the monster and leave the security of friendly environs for the dangers of hostile territory. The takeoff time of 1300 hours was nearing. The time had come to fly and fight in another battleground of Cambodia.

Action was still hot and heavy in the area around NVA-held Skoun which blocked FANK relief columns from reaching Kompong Thom north on Route 6. The radio contact at Skoun was still Hotel 44. On their flight path to relieve Shadow crew #3 still flying over Skoun, Shadow crew #1 was instructed via radio to get current sit-reps from Hotel Prey Veng and Hotel KPC at Kampong Cham. If either FANK location needed immediate help, crew #1 would report the situation, using encrypted radio transmissions to the combat control center Agate, to scramble the alert gunship at TSN. The primary mission of Shadow crew #1 was to replace Shadow gunship crew #3 on station over Skoun and provide continued fire support for the Cambodians.

***

Shadow gunships clawed their way into the sticky air every three hours around the clock. Tracking the 310 degree TACAN radial of Channel 102 from Tan Son Nhut, Shadows flew over Chu Chi, Tay Ninh, past the 986 meters high Black Virgin Mountain (Nui Bai Den) to the "dog face" direct to Kampong Cham. The "dog face" was that portion of the Vietnam-Cambodian border shaped like a dog's head. It was located thirty miles northeast of Tay Ninh. References such as "dog face," "fish hook," and "parrot's beak" were frequently used in air traffic nomenclature to expedite clearance of gunship actions from clearing authority.

Shadow navigator Maj. Earl Farney stated, "At first, we had some problems with artillery clearances. It was a sporty course from Tan Son Nhut to the 'fence' which frequently meant costly time delays. Then, we met with the Army and resolved the situation. Artillery clearances were granted to the Cambodian border prior to takeoff."[2]

The flight schedule for C Flight aircrews moved forward by three hours each week so crews weren't strapped with flying the same time of day or night. For example: flight crew #1 scheduled for the 1300 hours takeoff time would fly that time slot for five or six days straight before getting a day or two off the flying schedule. After the day or two off, the crew was scheduled for the 1600 hours takeoff time for the next five or six days before getting another day or two off, etc. Eight crews were required to meet the eight fragged sorties for C Flight in a twenty-four-hour period. To compensate for crewmen on leave, R&R, or DNIF and to afford aircrews a day or two off the flight schedule, a minimum of twelve aircrews were needed to fully man the rotating flight schedule.

If aircraft aborts occurred on the ground, the aircrew transferred to another combat ready (CR) gunship to meet the scheduled takeoff time. If crews aborted flights shortly after becoming airborne, the Shadow upon landing would transfer to another CR gunship and takeoff again for the AO. If aborted aircraft caused a shortage of CR gunships, the gunship and crew returning and landing from their mission in the AO might be and sometimes were "turned-around" for another mission in Cambodia with the same crew and aircraft after refueling and rearming. In many cases due to periodic shortages of flight engineers, gunners, or IOs, individual crewmembers on the returning crew were required to fly "back-to-back" missions. The required crew rest period of eight hours between flights was summarily waived.

If the scheduled gunship could not replace the gunship in the AO, many times the gunship in the AO flew to Ubon Royal Thai Air Force Base, Thailand for regeneration (i.e., refuel and rearm before flying "back-to-back" missions). USAF units were stationed at Ubon which was located approximately fifty miles north of the Cambodian border and forty miles west of the Laotian border. As a result, the all-out effort to have a Shadow ever-present overhead in Cambodia was accomplished.

Shadow pilots were forbidden to land, unless a dire emergency, in Cambodia due to the secrecy of missions. At this time, no one knew that U.S. planes were used to support the Cambodian Army. Foreign and American war correspondents were on the ground in Cambodia, especially in and around Phnom Penh, snooping and gathering information for reports on the fighting. There were only two runways in Cambodia that the AC-119 gunship could safely land. Runway 5/23 at Pochenong Airport, located approximately four miles west of Phnom Penh, provided 9800 feet of asphalt, and runway 5/23 at Siem Reap Airport, located about six miles south of the city of Siem Reap just off Route 6, had 8000 feet of concrete surface. Nevertheless, Phnom Penh's Pochenong Airport was designated by Shadow navigators in pre-strike briefings as the primary emergency airfield in case of an emergency landing in Cambodia.

In a joint effort by French and Cambodian governments years prior to open hostilities in Cambodia, the Siem Reap Airport was constructed to handle commercial jetliners transporting tourists visiting the ancient ruins of Angkor. The nearby ruins at Angkor Thom encompassed a wall-enclosed four square mile area of temples and shrines that were being restored by French and Cambodian archeologists. The temples at Thom were considered by many to be world architectural wonders. The NVA had taken sanctuary in Wat shortly after the Cambodian Incursion, knowing full-well the ruins were priceless relics, thus immune to aerial attack.

***

On 20 August as requested by 7th AF Commander General George Brown, Kampong Chhnang was added to the list of threatened Cambodian cities approved for all out U.S. air support thus far provided at Kompong Cham and Kompong Thom. Kompong Chhnang was located on Highway 5 at the southern tip of the Tonle Sap.

U.S. air "interdiction" missions in Cambodia had hence evolved from the original Freedom Deal during May 1970 with two extensions of operating areas, and Freedom Deal Alpha. The last interdiction plan encompassed areas from Cambodia Route 7 to the Laotian Border and extended to approximately 75 miles west of the Mekong.[3]

VNAF AC-47 gunships effectively supported the ARVN in Cambodia during nighttime. AC-119 gunships flying in Cambodia were not always aware of AC-47 gunship operations or presence in the darkness of night because the VNAF operated on different radio frequencies and also flew blacked-out just like Shadow gunships.

Flying a mission blacked-out (no lights) on a dark moonless night in the vicinity of Kompong Cham during which our crew was totally surprised to see steady streams of red tracers, at our altitude not a mile away, race earthward from an unseen source. We knew there was no other AC-119 gunship flying in our AO and there was no airborne USAF Rustic FAC at the time; therefore without visual confirmation or radio contact with the source of fire, we assumed the source of the red streams of fire was a VNAF AC-47 gunship. We quickly departed the area. If it were not for the red line of tracers, we would not have known that another aircraft was operating in our area. This fact raised major concern over possible mid-air collisions at nighttime with VNAF aircraft. Our experience was reported during mission debriefings, but nothing resulted as VNAF and USAF gunships continued nighttime operations without any radio communication whatsoever.

Shadow gunships reported "crossing the fence" between South Vietnam and Cambodia to the airborne command and control center "Ramrod" and checking in with the Shadow gunship flying in and out of the AO to get a sit-rep and weather conditions in the AO. The replacement Shadow would immediately ask, "Are there any Rustics in the AO?" If the answer was, "Affirmative," the Rustic FAC call number and radio frequency were recorded and soon dialed-in. If the answer was, "Negative," Shadows would still call Rustic Alpha Control to make sure there were no Rustics flying in the AO or Rustics on their way into to AO.

FACs with the radio call sign of Rustic flew OV-10 aircraft during daytime and O-2 aircraft during nighttime out of Bien Hoa Air Base, RVN to direct tactical air operations in Cambodia, the new V Corps of the Vietnam War. USAF FAC aircraft were on-site commanders for air strikes and there to identify targets while protecting friendly troops from USAF attack aircraft. Rustic FACs checked on ground commanders of Cambodian garrisons to gather intelligence and for situation reports as did Shadows. When aerial fire support for the Cambodians was needed, the FAC would radio requests for strike aircraft (i.e., "fast movers" like A-37s, F-100s, and F-4s or "slow movers" like AC-119 gunships). Shadows and Rustics teamed together to provide effective close-air support for the Cambodians. Rustics were instrumental in finding enemy targets for AC-119 gunships and receiving pre-approval for firing on targets for Shadow gunships upon arrival in the target area. Even so, for the most part, Shadows worked independently of FACs and worked directly with Cambodian ground commanders.

***

17th SOS combat crews and personnel constantly changed because air crewmembers and ground maintenance personnel had completed their tour of duty in Vietnam, having reached their DEROS to return home stateside. Others were temporarily relieved of duty having earned leave from duty (normally five to seven days), or rest and recuperation (R&R) for seven days, or designated DNIF by a flight surgeon due to sickness or injury. Fortunately for many Shadow aircrews at Tan Son Nhut, aircrew members remained somewhat stable which promoted camaraderie and mission-driven teamwork critical in successful accomplishment of combat missions. An experienced crew that consistently flew and worked together as a team under combat conditions soon created a close brotherhood of flying warriors.

Every soul assigned to C Flight from lieutenant colonels to airmen first class, whether flight or ground crew took pride in the 17th SOS FOL of Shadows at Tan Son Nhut and pushed hard to meet the grueling schedule to cover Cambodia. Aircrews became hardened to the steady diet of flying and fighting. C Flight personnel met themselves coming and going to the flightline for another mission to Cambodia. Shadow gunships met one another flying into or departing the AO. Occasionally, two Shadow gunships worked the same target at the same time. Ground maintenance crews and support personnel worked twelve-hour shifts both night and day to keep the gunships operational and combat ready. Tiresome and wearisome tasks proved exhausting and stressful. And yet, every man realized they were a crucial component to the success of the Flight and its assigned secret mission. With personnel upholding high spirits of special operations warriors, the Flight had become a close-knit and proud USAF flying fraternity of gunship brothers. Before long, C Flight became known as "Fighting C Flight" of the 17th Special Operations Squadron.

***

Fighting C Flight Administrative Officer and Navigator Earl Farney wrote about reporting mission results in Cambodia: "At first, we seldom got accurate data on numbers of enemy killed or wounded by Shadow attacks on enemy troops. The enemy offensives were too fluid and usually conducted during nighttime. Friendly forces were reluctant to sweep nighttime battle areas before daylight and by then, the enemy had either carried or dragged away their dead and wounded."[4]

Fighting C Flight commander Lt. Col. Teal wrote,

> We had been flying for several months [in Cambodia[but
> the only Battle Damage Assessment [BDA] we received was
> of course from the crew reports. We really wondered how ef-
> fective we were in our role as a gunship unit and higher
> headquarters must have had questions also. All of a sudden,
> the Cambodian ground commanders started including a pre-
> liminary number of enemy killed by that sortie as well as tar-
> gets fired on. Later, their final report to 7th AF would reflect
> the actual number of enemy verified killed. At commander's
> call, I mentioned that we now knew that the gunship's sorties
> had been and were becoming more effective. I quoted from a
> recent BDA report that a single sortie had a body count of
> over 240 attackers killed by air (KBA).[5]

***

AC-119 gunships concentrated their firepower within a sixty-mile radius
of Kampong Cham (KPC), strategically located forty-one miles northeast
of the Cambodian capital city of Phnom Penh. Numerous sorties extended
from KPC along Route 6 to Kampong Thom, and Route 7 to Skoun. Occasionally, Route 5 south from Kampong Chhnang, and Route 4 west from
Phnom Penh were subject of concentrated enemy interest. The plan of the
Reds was simple; strangle Phnom Penh and the Cambodian province capitals by controlling the countryside, waterways, and highways.

Armed reconnaissance missions of Shadows in Cambodia focused on
river sampans and road vehicles. Shadows soon found out that Charlie
armored his bamboo fleet of sampans and road vehicles. High Explosive
Incendiary (HEI) 7.62mm ammunition fired by Shadow gunships
proved to be extremely effective in severely damaging or destroying
enemy armored boats and highway vehicles.

***

On 20 August 1970, the Lon Nol government initiated a military campaign called Operation Chenla Dey Teuk (aka Chenla I). Operational

objectives were to relieve the Cambodian Army brigades at Kompong Thom and to secure its rice producing region surrounding the province capital city. The campaign would ultimately last from September through most of December 1970. The months of November and December would prove the effectiveness of AC-119 Shadow gunships in defending a city (Kompong Thom) under siege.

Critical to success of the campaign was the town Skoun, located at the intersection of Routes 6 and 7, some thirty-five miles north of Phnom Penh. Route 6 to Kompong Thom had to be cleared of occupying NVA troops so the town could to be used as a staging area for Chenla I. Upon Cambodian and 7th Air Force agreement, clearance to destroy the pagoda housing the NVA artillery gun on Route 6 was granted and the pagoda was demolished by bombs and napalm delivered by USAF F-100 Sabre fighter/bombers under the direction of a Rustic FAC. With the roadblock eliminated, Skoun was summarily cleared of enemy troops and the relief column of Cambodian government forces moved forward up Route 6 toward KPT.[6]

During August 1970, representatives from the Rustic FACs and the 17th SOS met at Bien Hoa AB, RVN, to establish better coordination and procedures for joint operations. Common intelligence estimated that the enemy activity level would be at a high sustained level. With this as a basic premise, Lt. Col. Jim Lester, Rustic Operations Officer, requested a maximum usage of daylight sorties (for AC-119 gunships) as could be sustained from resources available. A schedule with two daylight and four night sorties was agreed upon.

Procedures were established for a random flow of aircraft with unmated contacting Rustic Alpha for target areas. A new concept was initiated mating FAC and 17th/18th SOS aircraft as a hunter-killer team on selected interdiction missions. 18th Stinger gunships were fragged as a separate sortie in a night truck/sampan joint hunter-killer mission. In a like manner, a hunter-killer team of Shadows and Rustic FACs were used day and night when enemy activity permitted mating. The primary mission for Shadow was defense of ground units and close-air support.[7] After the meeting at Bien Hoa, Rustic FACs and Shadow gunships worked "hand in glove" providing aerial support for the Cambodians.

Fighting C Flight Commander Teal wrote,

The longer we flew over Cambodia, the more complicated
the missions became. Working troops in contact makes it
easy to get clearance to fire from the ground commander, but
our areas of operations were now getting free fire clearance
for designated areas and stretches of lines of communication
outside of those areas. What this meant was that 7th AF and
the Cambodian representatives were designating areas that
were completely in enemy hands and targets of opportunity,
such as sampans, could be shot at will because of the pre-ap-
proved status. To make sure that the crews had accurate and
up-to-date information for these free fire zones, I had classified folders assembled with appropriate maps marked, the
latest messages included and other important information
generally pertaining to the missions. I had installed a large
map that covered the wall in my office. This map was used
for each crew to brief me or Lt. Col. Bill Gregory, Flight operations officer, on the free fire zones and other parts of their
mission. It worked. I do not remember any reports of firing
mistakes outside the areas. Major Earl Farney, a navigator
who was our Det. Admin. Officer, took care of this time con-
suming chore as well as flying and overseeing all the paper
work for the unit. Everything he did was outstanding and
very much appreciated by me.[8]

ELEVEN

Guardian Strikers

S eventh Air Force Aerial Interdiction Campaigns to interrupt the flow of NVA troops and supplies down the Ho Chi Minh Trail from North Vietnam through southern Laos and eastern Cambodia started during the northeast monsoon dry season of 1968-69 with the operation code name "Commando Hunt." Commando Hunt I began 15 November 1968 and ended in April 1969. Each of the following six campaigns lasted approximately six months during each wet and dry monsoon season.

Seventh Air Force designated the southwest monsoon (wet) season Commando Hunt II and subsequently designated even-numbered Commando Hunt Campaigns IV and VI for the rainy southwest monsoon season and designated odd-numbered Campaigns III, V, and VII for the northeast monsoon dry season. The last Commando Hunt VII ended in April 1972.

The interdiction campaigns had two major objectives: 1) To reduce the enemy's logistical flow by substantially increasing the time needed to move supplies from North Vietnam to South Vietnam and 2) To destroy trucks and supply caches along the roads, pathways, and waterways and in enemy truck parks and storage areas along the trail.

Air Commando propeller-driven AT-28, A-26, A-1E aircraft and fighter/bomber jets like the F-4, F-100, and F-105 were used against truck traffic on the Trail during the time period of Hunt I thru Hunt III. It soon became evident that risking a multi-million dollar jet aircraft to destroy one truck was ludicrous. In addition to requiring a FAC to mark targets, fighter jets flying at speeds exceeding 200 knots proved to be much less accurate than slower propeller-driven attack planes in hitting small targets like a truck.

Propeller-driven AC-47 gunships flying low and slow in firing orbits over the Trail proved effective but increased losses of the aircraft to enemy anti-aircraft fire proved that the Spooky gunship was too vulnerable for anti-aircraft guns located in Laos. In early 1969, AC-119G Shadow gunships of the 71st SOS also flew missions on the Trail, but were soon relieved of that duty because of vulnerability to enemy anti-aircraft guns. Armed with latest sensor technology and the firepower to orbit at higher altitudes, aerial interdiction success of AC-130 and AC-119K fixed-wing gunships opened command level jet-focused eyes to see that the Spectre and Stinger gunships were much more effective on the Trail, and thus became the dominant aerial interdiction attack force in the war against the Ho Chi Minh Trail.

As Commando Hunt operations proved successful, North Vietnam responded by placing larger numbers of anti-aircraft artillery (AAA) weapons (e.g., 23mm, 37mm, and 57mm guns) along the Ho Chi Minh Trail in Laos. By 1970, enemy triple-A sites on the Trail had increased to a point wherein the sites became targets for U.S. fighter/bombers to attack, while protecting USAF Spectre and Stinger gunships working the Trail.

After Cambodia Prince Sihanouk was ousted from power in March 1970, the Lon Nol government closed the country's major seaport at Sihanoukville and renamed it Kompong Som. The so-called "Sihanouk Trail" from the seaport overland route through Cambodia to supply arms and ammunition to NVA/VC sanctuaries located on the eastern border with South Vietnam no longer existed. No longer could North Vietnam rely on the seaport to receive ocean freighters from Eastern Soviet Bloc countries hauling war supplies for their troops.

Practically all the weapons and ammunition used by NVA/VC forces in South Vietnam military regions 2, 3, and 4 from 1966 to 1970 had been shipped through Sihanoukville. Much of the food and other consumables for communist forces in Cambodia had been purchased from the Cambodian economy and transported into South Vietnam and southern Laos.

Due to the loss of Sihanoukville seaport and the "Sihanouk Trail," North Vietnam was forced to expand supply routes from the north, making the most of their existing Ho Chi Minh network of roads, trails and waterways in southern Laos and northeastern Cambodia to supply NVA, VC, and Khmer Rouge armed forces. The Mekong River and its tributary Kong River soon became a major supply route from southern Laos into the heart of Cambodia.[1]

***

17th SOS Shadow gunships became involved in Operation Commando Hunt IV (May through October 1970) during and after the Cambodian Incursion even though C Flight's primary mission was to provide CAS for American and allied troops in Cambodia. During the Cambodia Incursion, Operation Freedom Deal had started on 30 May to provide continuous USAF aerial interdiction in Cambodia within the area limited to forty-eight kilometers between the South Vietnam border and the Mekong River. Thus, the 17th SOS was conducting missions in Cambodia under Operation Freedom Deal rules of engagement.

With the build-up of AC-119 gunships that included Stinger gunships from DaNang assigned to C Flight to augment operations in August, Shadow gunships were freed to support Cambodia Army units against enemy attacks while the more potent AC-119K Stinger gunships on loan from the 18th SOS prowled the highways, back roads, rivers, and waterways of eastern Cambodia and the southern tip of Laos for enemy traffic.

If not engaged with first priority missions of troops-in-contact, defending population centers, or capping road or river convoys, Shadows searched day and night for enemy activity on the Mekong River and its tributaries and Cambodia Routes 7 and 13 and their feeder roads from Kampong Cham to Stoeng Treng and many times points farther north into the Bolovens Plateau of southern Laos. Shadows and Stingers conducting armed recon attacked anything that moved on the waterways and roads of enemy-controlled northeastern Cambodia from ships, ferries, motor boats, barges, junks, and all sizes of sampans to trucks, cars, motorcycles, and ox carts.

17th SOS C Flight gunships continually roamed the skies day and night over Cambodia from 1 August 1970 forward. The limits of Operation Freedom Deal were soon extended westward past the Mekong River. Shadow and Stinger gunships, Rustic FACs, and various tactical aircraft were continually providing direct air support for Cambodian ground forces or conducting armed recon. These secret missions were officially denied by the U.S. and false coordinates were given in official reports to hide their existence. U.S. Department of Defense records would later show that out of more than 8,000 combat sorties flown in Cambodia between July 1970 and February 1971, approximately 40% were flown outside the authorized Freedom Deal boundaries. Shadows could definitely claim their share of the 40%.

***

General Lucius D. Clay, Jr. replaced General George Brown at the end of August 1970 as 7th Air Force Commander and Deputy for Air Operations in SEA to MACV Commander, General Creighton Abrams. General Clay proceeded to wage the most aggressive U.S. and VNAF air campaign in Cambodia within the limits of available intelligence and control facilities while conforming to the rules of engagement as specified in the original Freedom Deal. Neither fighters nor bombers could attack until Cambodian authorities had verified targets. As long as populated areas were avoided, B-52 arc light strikes and tactical aircraft strikes could be employed under Freedom Deal Extension, bounded on the north by Route 13, on the west by a line 200 meters beyond the Mekong River, on the south by Route 7, and on the east by the South Vietnam border. Actually, U.S. air strikes could be conducted beyond the Mekong and Route 7, if determined that air intervention was necessary to save an important town or military position that was in danger of being overrun by enemy troops.

Subsequently, U.S. air operations in Cambodia were soon conducted outside the enlarged region of Freedom Deal. U.S. air strikes were made available at all times in defense of provincial capital Kompong Thom located approximately seventy-five miles west of the Mekong on Route 6. The road was the major transportation lifeline on which life sustaining rice was transported from the Tonle Sap agriculture region to the nation's capital city of Phnom Penh and the provincial capital Kompong Cham. Both cities (Kompong Thom and Kompong Cham) were in serious trouble and were under attack by concentrations of NVA and Khmer Rouge troops. Cambodian officers gave approval to intervene at both cities.[2]

The deteriorating situation of the besieged FANK garrison at Kompong Thom necessitated a resupply and reinforcement attempt with a combined land and riverine operation. The riverine operation departed Phnom Penh on 7 September 1970 via the Tonle Sap River to Kampong Chhnang, thence via the Tonle Sap through the Stung Sen River to Kompong Thom. The land (road) convoy departed Skoun on the same date and proceeded toward Kompong Thom via Route 6.

Seventh Air Force command scheduled units to provide readily available twenty-four-hour protection to assist the relief forces (for KPT). This included the coordination of a dedicated schedule of gunships and Rustic FACs to insure maximum coverage for the road and riverine operation. Expanded ROE authorized the aircraft commander of AC-119 Shadow gunships to immediately fire to protect the convoys with target validation from FANK ground commanders. The added commitment increased the number of sorties flown by Shadow gunships to eight per day with scheduled four hour missions and three hour alert periods.[3]

One day during the KPT resupply and reinforcement operation, I was copilot on a C Flight Shadow diverted from an armed recce mission to provide cover for an aerial convoy of helicopters flying from Phnom Penh to Kompong Thom. It was a very special convoy of choppers because Lon Nol was a passenger on one of the helicopters. Highly concerned with the situation at KPT, he wanted to visit FANK troops defending the province capital city. The trip was quick and uneventful but our Shadow was there overhead, flying armed escort for the string of choppers, ready just in case the helicopters experienced difficulties along the flight route.

Things calmed down around Kampong Thom after the city had been successfully reinforced and resupplied by the combined land and riverine operation. The Cambodians had safely traveled Route 6 from Skoun to KPT and the river convoy safely reached KPT via planned water routes. Shadows and Rustics had provided continual air cover and support for both convoys.

Simultaneous to the KPT relief operations, combat action heated up around Siem Reap and Angkor Wat in northwestern Cambodia. A large communist force had attacked the City of Siem Reap from their Angkor Wat sanctuary. Communist forces, NVA in particular, had taken sanctuary in Angkor Wat shortly after the Cambodia Invasion in May, knowing the ruins were priceless relics of the ancient Khmer Empire; thus protected from air attack. The airport at Siem Reap was still under control of Cambodian Forces; which was good news for Shadows. Besides Pochenong Airport at Phnom Penh, Siem Reap Airport was the only other airport in Cambodia that Shadows could safely use for an emergency landing.

Two Shadow gunships had helped drive away initial night attacks by communist forces from Siem Reap. The radio call sign for Siem Reap was Hotel Juliet. The city's defenders, consisting of the Cambodian Army's 12th Infantry Brigade numbering between three and five thousand soldiers plus a Special Brigade composed of former Khmer Serei Resistance Forces, had held firm. Communist forces withdrew to the cover of Angkor Wat, regrouping for another assault on the city.

The enemy had concentrated troops around Siem Reap to capture the city and surrounding area which included the northern spans of Tonle Sap. The Tonle Sap, meaning Great Lake, provided the whole region with an abundance of fresh water fish. It all made sense. Fish from the Great Lake region and rice from the central basin of Cambodia's agriculture would feed an army.[4]

On 6 September 1970, Fighting C Flight Major Bill Gericke was the navigator on Shadow 81 that departed Tan Son Nhut for yet another mission to Siem Reap, located on Route 6 a few miles from the Tonle Sap, and 143 miles northwest of Phnom Penh. This sortie indicated some of the complexities of fighting an air war in the hinterlands of Cambodia.

Major William Gericke recorded the following in his diary:

> We were briefed well in advance to go to Siem Reap. That's the village near the northwest end of the Tonle Sap Lake. All was quiet when we arrived on scene. Hotel Juliet wanted us to shoot in an area about five clicks southeast of town. All we could see was yoked oxen, several bicycles, a couple of carts, and a few field workers. They could have been part of the 150 Viet Cong [that] Juliet said are there, but we still didn't shoot. We did fire north of town between Siem Reap and Angkor Wat. [I] took several pictures of Angkor Wat. We reconned a couple of more points for Juliet and spotted the fall of two rounds of 105mm. The rounds lobbed into the old Air France Hotel just west outside of Angkor Wat. Juliet got on a talking jag; a political speech. He hates Vietnamese and French. Claims the Communists are selling the Angkor Wat antiques in Hong Kong. He talked about peace and independence and thinks a republic is coming. He invited us to visit, and said he needed breakfast. We reconned the Tonle Sap Lake for TACC on the way home. [We] fired 25,000 rounds.[5]

The following dialogue on 6 September 1970 between Hotel Juliet and Shadow 81 aircraft commander Major Bill Ware was transcribed from the tape recording of the mission by Shadow 81 navigator Major Bill Gericke:

Hotel Juliet: To all Shadows, Rustics, Spikes, I'd like to inform your commanders. We came to Siem Reap over three months ago. This place is very dangerous. So when we came down here, [it's] never quiet. Always contact by the VC. If no contact with Shadow and Rustic, we cannot stand. My folk are Cambodian descent. It is important that your government help my folk. Please call another Shadow to come and help us. When we came here from Kompong Cham, we had over 100 wounded and 15 killed. I used to be a guide at Angkor Wat and talked to your people from the states. But now I am a soldier. I'm not very high class; just a lowly soldier. You copy?

Major Ware: Roger, you're a very good soldier.

Hotel Juliet: Roger, roger. I'd like to join you in the aircraft, but I cannot. I am happy now because you are here, but my stomach is empty. When I am talking to you, it's like talking to my folk, and I'm so happy to think you'll help us.

Major Ware: Roger, we will help you as long as we can.

Over the gunship intercom, Major Ware said, "That poor guy is really hurting. Makes you wish we could really help them."

Shadow 81 Navigator Major Gericke commented, "Yes, he just wanted someone to talk to; the poor son of a gun. These Cambodians seem to have a lot more sincerity than anyone else."

"You said it! I like working with them," said Major Ware.

Fighting C Flight Shadow Major Earl Farney stated the general feelings of all Shadowmen when he wrote, "We (Shadows) really liked the friendliness and openness of the Cambodians that we worked with over the radios during intense combat conditions and during intelligence gathering of ground situation reports. Feelings of kindred soon developed between us and those Cambodians we conversed with over the radio in providing aerial support. We were glad to fight for them. We suspected their war effort against the more powerful communist forces was futile without full pledged commitment from the U.S., but we much admired their resolve to live under a new government and new leadership that meant freedom from the previous monarchy form of government. They really didn't want war, but realized war was the only way to resolve their issues with communist troops."[6]

***

With Angkor Wat occupied by NVA troops, scrimmages between the NVA and Cambodian troops occurred in the area. After one Angkor Wat temple was hit by 82mm mortars, the fear of further damage or destruction of the temple compound prompted Cambodia Vice-Premier Sisowath Sirik Matak to broadcast appeals for international control of the temple compound. His efforts were unsuccessful and Angkor Wat remained in communist hands. NVA troops knew they were safe from airstrikes within the confines of Angkor Wat. All U.S. FACs and gunships were ordered to not fire into the ancient city of temples even if they took ground fire from the area. Of course the enemy fired at any aircraft flying at low levels over the moat-enclosed city.

***

Lieutentant Colonel Teal stated the following:

> We got so busy in Cambodia on different targets that we needed at times more fire power and five Stinger gunships became part of our operations. I remember going on one of the first Stinger missions sent to Kompong Cham. It was a daylight mission with the target/s of big ships tied up at the wharfs. What a sight to see the two twenty mm Gatling guns pouring rounds into the troop carriers and supply ships. We never saw the big one sink but it did show a decided list when we left. The Stinger pilot looked like an old west gunfighter with dark eyes spaced wide apart and a thin mustache above his lip. I know this! He was the best shooter I had seen in Shadow, Stinger, or Spectre gunships. I was an amateur shooter compared to this young captain. I am sorry that I don't remember his name. There was a less gung ho Stinger crew who took off and was back on the ground in about forty-five minutes. I met the aircraft. He said he could not get through the storm clouds to get to Cambodia. I told the pilot to get his crew onboard, take off and try again to get safely

through the clouds. You are expected to keep trying until your sortie time is up or you have to return to base because of fuel. Incidentally, we had additional 17th SOS Shadow aircraft and crews join us from time to time in our coverage of Cambodia.[7]

***

By August, the Cambodians only controlled small defended areas of the country like province capital cities, towns, villages, and in some cases merely government buildings, schools, pagodas, temples, or shrines. Otherwise, Charlie owned the countryside. So it wasn't unusual for Shadow to be flying cover along the Mekong from pagoda to temple. Hotel 26 was the radio call sign for the Cambodian Army commander located seventeen miles north of Phnom Penh on the eastern banks of the Mekong. One night in late August, Hotel 26 was in serious trouble. The tactical air support control center (radio call sign Agate) for Cambodia was aware of the situation, having already requested airstrikes and a follow-on Shadow gunship in support of Hotel 26.

Hotel 26 was holed-up in a pagoda. He was taking incoming mortars from the riverbank, fifty meters west and from a barn, thirty meters east of his location. There was also sporadic incoming from a bridge to the northeast.

Shadow 83 had been diverted from a similar situation with Hotel 407, a few miles upriver. Eight-three was now overhead of Hotel 26's location. With 3,200 pounds of avgas remaining, 3 ½ cans of ammunition (5,250 rounds) and eight flares still onboard; Shadow 83 could support Hotel 26 for a short time before RTB. Aircraft Commander Major Don Fraker eased down to firing altitude, coaxed in some rudder, and rolled into a left pylon turn. Transcribed from tape recorded communications onboard Shadow 83 and between Shadow 83 and Hotel 26 follows after Fraker ordered, "Launch another flare now":

Comment made over Shadow intercom: "Hotel 407 was the same way."
Another comment over intercom: "Check the tracers. Eleven o'clock."

Shadow NOS: "I don't see anything."

Shadow NAV: "There, level on the horizon."

Comment over intercom: "There's quite a wind down there. Watch the flares drift."

At that time, Hotel 407 reported taking incoming again. Hotel 26 had big problems with the barn, a long metallic building. It was ringed with palm trees. Charlie was lobbing mortars from the barn onto the pagoda. Major Fraker opened fire on high rate and red tracers bounced off the rooftop. It looked like the 4th of July.

"SHAD-DOE, this is Hotel 26."

"Roger 26. Go ahead."

"Now I would like to inform you that my commander, who would like to inform you and your chief of the base. He speak English very free so he told me to inform you. This place is very dangerous. It is important that Shadow and Rustic is coming to help us. Otherwise, we cannot stand. You copy?"

"Yes 26, we copy."

"This evening around five o'clock my second in command was wounded. Many, many VC. So I would like you to call another Shad-doe."

"Do not worry, 26. It has been requested."

"Alright, you say that from 28, 29 and today on the 33, we cannot eat. We have very little food and cannot sleep. My commander cannot sleep because he is worried. Please help us. Four or five hundred VC. You copy?"

"Roger 26. We copy."

The Shadow crew was silent. Only the growling sound of miniguns being fired was heard. Shadow 83 circled and fired, time after time. The enemy ground fire stopped. Hotel 26 was quiet. He must have fallen asleep. One last calculation of the fuel onboard and Shadow 83 departed the area for Saigon. The crew was dead tired, mentally debilitated. Eyes were moist and you know why. Charlie had waited. Time was on his side. Two days later, Shadow 83 swung south to raise Hotel 26. Circling above, repeated attempts to raise Hotel 26 on the radio were tried. Circling the pagoda, Hotel 26 never answered Shadow's call. All was silent. Only the ripples of the muddy Mekong moved.

***

As Freedom Deal and U.S. air operations expanded throughout Cambodia, control and coordination of aircraft flying in Cambodian airspace became a major problem in view of the fact that not all aircraft flying in the country were American. A fully equipped airborne command post was needed to replace the EC-47D that previously had provided radio relays between U.S. aircraft operating in Cambodia and command centers located in South Vietnam.

C-130s based at Udorn RTAFB, Thailand were also used as Airborne Battlefield Command and Control Centers (ABCCC) to coordinate USAF combat operations in Laos. In the Steel Tiger region of southern Laos, the ABCCC daytime radio call sign was "Hillsboro" and "Moonbeam" for nighttime. In the Barrel Roll region of northern Laos, the ABCCC call sign for daytime was "Cricket" and for nighttime, "Alley Cat."

In September 1970, four Lockheed EC-121D aircraft with radar platforms were recalled to Korat Air Base, Thailand to help control and coordinate air traffic in Cambodia.[8] Radio communication and air traffic separation were paramount. To better coordinate the air effort in Cambodia, the EC-121 was employed as an extension of TACC (U) on 2 September 1970. The Airborne Command and Control Center (TACC-A) was used by Shadow and Stinger gunships for aircraft separation, air strike coordination, and as an expeditious means to obtain firing clearance. Previous firing clearances were obtained from Pawnee Target on HF radio and Rustic Alpha on UHF, VHF, or FM radios through Agate, the 7th AF In-Country/Cambodian Command Center (TACO).

On 13 September 1970, 7th AF Commander General Clay presented plaques with mounted .38 caliber CHICOM pistols to the commanders of the 17th SOS and the 18th SOS, in appreciation of the efforts and success of AC-119 gunships for effectively disrupting the flow of supplies to enemy units and the destruction of enemy staging areas from supported units in Cambodia.

Also on 13 September, Colonel A.F. Eaton replaced Colonel William Fairbrother as commander of the 14th Special Operations Wing. Lt. Col. Edward A. Elbert was commander of the 17th SOS. The FANK ground commander at Kompong Thom, Major Oum (radio call sign "Hotel

303"), credited 17th SOS Shadow gunships for playing a prominent role in relieving the province capital from the enemy's siege. Thus the AC-119 gunship had proven itself a formidable weapon system, capable of performing its mission with no loss of force.

On 22 and 23 September, a relief convoy on Route 6 south of Kompong Cham stalled. Psyop EC-47s of the 9th SOS B Flight stationed at Bien Hoa flew numerous missions in the area, dropping millions of attack warning leaflets and Hoi Chanhs (aka Chieu Hoi) safe conduct leaflets for enemy troops to desert their cause. The imminent danger of battle was broadcast over speakers to civilians along the route.

During the three months of July, August, and September 1970, Cambodian airspace proved to be a permissive environment for daylight gunship sorties at established firing altitudes of 4,500 feet ("D" altitude), 3,500 feet ("C" altitude), and 2,500 feet ("B" altitude). "A" firing altitude of 1,500 feet was not considered operationally safe. With the maximum effective range of Shadow and Stinger 7.62mm miniguns at 3,500 feet and the maximum effective range of NVA 12.7mm and .51 caliber anti-aircraft machine guns at 3,250 feet, battle sites often became a stand-off between the gunship and enemy anti-aircraft gunners.

By the end of September, the force of AC-119G Shadow gunships assigned to C Flight at Tan Son Nhut totaled eight as two Shadow gunships remained stationed with A Flight at Phu Cat, and six gunships were deployed with B Flight at Phan Rang plus one gunship in phase. While the Cambodian operation at Tan Son Nhut had expanded, the elements of the 17th SOS at Phan Rang and Phu Cat continued to provide complete support for Free World Forces in South Vietnam. Statistical information for the 17th Special Operations Squadron quarterly report submitted to 14th SOW for the months of July, August, and September 1970 included:

	July	August	September	Total
Combat Sorties	252	295	369	916
Missions Fragged	186	186	307*	579
Combat Hours	821.3	1247.0	1058.4	3126.7
Rounds Expended	2,216,900	3,259,927	2,392,010	7,912,937

Flares	2165	2915	1813	6893
KBA (Confirmed)	77	46	332	455
KBA (Estimated)	200-300	520	758	1487-1587
Vehicles Destroyed	0	0	5	5
Vehicles Damaged	0	18	17	35
Sampans Destroyed	48	6	5	59
Sampans Damaged	0	25	17	42
Secondaries	15	23	35	85
Buildings Destroyed	0	1	3	4
Buildings Damaged	0	2	149	151
Mortars	0	2	7	9
AAA Sites	0	0	2	2
TICs	53	40	35	128

*50 of the fragged missions were flown by AC-119K aircraft loaned to the 17th SOS for the AI (aerial interdiction) mission operated by C Flight.

***

During the quarter, the AC-119K Stinger aircraft from the 18th SOS loaned to the 17th SOS to supplement the operations of C Flight in Cambodia reported the following statistics:

	July	August	September	Total
Combat Sorties	0	50	76	126
Flying Hours	0	180	315	495
Rounds Exp. (7.62)	0	263,700	239,267	502,967
Rounds Exp. (20mm)	0	93,973	116,745	210,718
KBA	0	200	163	363
Vehicles Destroyed	0	0	22	22
Vehicles Damaged	0	12	1	13
Sampans Destroyed	0	27	8	35
Sampans Damaged	0	22	15	37
River Boats Destroyed	0	5	12	17
River Boats Damaged	0	17	1	18
Buildings Destroyed	0	1	10	11
Buildings Damaged	0	32	7	39
Secondaries	0	18	26	44

Statistical information shows the impact of the Shadow and Stinger gunship build-up at Tan Son Nhut to start providing Cambodia with twenty-four-hour air support in August 1970. Thirty-nine enemy AAA reactions in Cambodia were reported by 17th SOS during the three month period. Two Shadow gunships sustained hits; one of which was during daylight action. One was hit by small arms fire during July and the other Shadow was hit by anti-aircraft fire in August. No casualties were reported.

During August and September, the FOL C Flight at Tan Son Nhut was able, with the help of AC-119K Stinger gunships, to fulfill the assigned task of round-the-clock interdiction coverage of NVA and VC supply routes. Flying interdiction missions, Shadow was able to react to enemy supply movements in almost any part of Cambodia. The combined efforts of Shadow and Stinger gunships undoubtedly saved a number of friendly positions from capture or destruction by enemy troops.

From 1 August to 30 September, 17th SOS C Flight AC-119G Shadow gunships flew 325 sorties and 18th SOS AC-119K Stinger gunships flew 126 sorties from Tan Son Nhut providing round-the-clock air support for Cambodia. As recorded in the 14th SOW History for the quarter, "The 17th SOS has been able to provide continuous and timely support of Cambodian units during all of the reporting period and have amassed an amazing total of kills. The 17th SOS has been especially effective in saving a number of Cambodian provincial capitals from capture by the enemy. Cambodia has proved to be a permissive environment for fixed-wing gunships on both daylight and night sorties."[9]

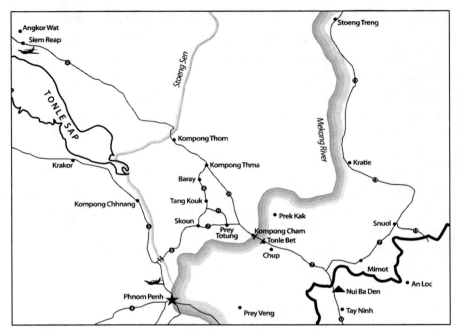

Central Cambodia.

TWELVE

Fearless Fliers

O n 1 October 1970, three AC-119G Shadow gunships and aircrews from Phu Cat A Flight of the 17th SOS were transferred PCS to C Flight at Tan Son Nhut to support the all-out gunship effort in Cambodia. On 10 October 70, an additional three Shadow gunships and aircrews from Phan Rang B Flight moved PCS to C Flight at Tan Son Nhut to replace TDY 18th SOS Stinger gunships and crews, moving back to their PCS bases. The last mission flown from Tan Son Nhut by these TDY Stinger crews was 11 October 1970.[1]

At various times during the Air Campaign in Cambodia, Fighting C Flight had up to 15 AC-119 gunships assigned to the Flight. Shadow gunships were the mainstay, but at times when Shadow gunships were needed elsewhere, AC-119K Stinger gunships were sent TDY to Tan Son Nhut to augment the fleet of gunships needed for continual coverage of Cambodia.

On the first day of October 1970, an O-2 Rustic FAC was shot down by an NVA 12.7mm anti-aircraft machine gun, killing both pilots.[2] This loss struck home at Fighting C Flight operations and in the minds of Shadow crews. Rustics were brothers-in-arms. Flying slow and too low in the face of enemy anti-aircraft guns could very well result in tragic death. The Shadows had been fortunate thus far in their day and night coverage of Cambodia. Regardless, during times of low cloud ceilings and/or inclement weather conditions, some Shadow pilots even flew below the minimum attack altitude of 1,500 feet AGL to fire on enemy forces during TICs, while knowing full well that the big black AC-119 gunship was an easy target for NVA anti-aircraft gunners especially during daytime.

Suppression of enemy ground fire during darkness of night was much easier than suppressing enemy ground fire during daylight. At nighttime, Shadows could see the streams of green or red tracer rounds fired by enemy gunners and mark their location for returning fire; whereas, during daylight missions when tracer bullets could not be seen, the pilot and his crew had difficulty finding locations of enemy gun sites firing at the gunship. Only the sounds of popcorn popping heard by crewmembers warned the Shadows that enemy bullets were extremely close to hitting the aircraft.

Shadow 28 Capt. Ralph Lefarth wrote,

> When I arrived in Vietnam, I heard how .51 caliber ground fire sounded like popcorn popping and I thought, "Yeah, sure." Well, it didn't take long before I found that to be very true. I remember flying over the Michelin Plantation one bright mid-morning when, "Pop, Pop, Pop." The 51 cal. was very close. We were at 3500 feet, flying straight and level going into central Cambodia. I immediately started evasive turns, when one of the crew in back called on the intercom wanting to go back and fly over the area to see if they would shoot at us again so we could shoot back. I ignored him. It would have been nearly impossible to find that gun in the daytime.[3]

Usually during daylight missions, radio calls from the Cambodian ground contacts alerted Shadow crews that enemy guns were shooting at the gunship. Again, Capt. Lefarth wrote,

On one occasion, we were working a target and our ground contact kept saying, "They are shooting at you, Shadow." I thought that was to get us to shoot faster, so when I heard a FAC in the area, I called him and asked him to come and see what was happening. In a few minutes the FAC called us and said, "Boy, are they having at you. Every time you fly over them, there are about eight 51 cal. sites shooting at you." The FAC then marked four sites with smoke rockets and gave general locations for the others. We then started firing on the gun sites.[4]

In the fluid action of Cambodia, NVA troops fought with small arms like AK-47 assault rifles, recoilless rifles, mortars, rocket-propelled grenades (RPGs) and heavy machine guns, primarily 12.7mm and .51 caliber machine guns. The NVA anti-aircraft versions of the 12.7mm machine gun proved to be deadly against low and slow flying aircraft.

Flying night missions over Cambodia became even more hazardous because other aircraft operating in the area of operation (AO) like the Shadows flew blacked-out (i.e., flying with all navigation and anti-collision lights off). Shadow pilots and navigators were responsible to safeguard their gunship from colliding with other aircraft flying in the AO through radio communication. Otherwise, avoidance of other aircraft was strictly visual. The Shadow's IO and AGs were responsible for scanning the skies to the rear of the gunship for other aircraft in addition to watching for anti-aircraft fire. There were no ground radar controllers to warn pilots of other aircraft flying over Cambodia and Laos; only the airborne command and control planes like the recently added ABCCC EC-121. Close calls were not that common but when they happened, only the Grace of God and Lady Luck saved the two aircraft from mid-air collisions. Radio communication between gunships working with FACs was critical.

Shadow pilot, Major John Windsor had an OV-10 fill his windscreen one night, enough so for Windsor to practically read the red glowing gauges of the FAC's cockpit instrument panel. The FAC had earlier reported to Windsor's Shadow that he was flying in another location. Both aircraft were flying blacked-out. A mental mistake on reporting location could have cost the lives of ten airmen, but fortunately did not. Captain Ralph Lefarth also reported a narrow miss with a FAC during a night mission. In such instances where the aircraft were already in radio contact, vulgar intercom and radio transmissions followed the incident from the Shadow pilot. Remember, all intercom and radio transmissions were recorded on tape by the Shadow navigator.

Avoidance of VNAF AC-47 gunships supporting ARVN troops in Cambodia was critical, especially during night missions. There was no radio communications between Shadow gunships and VNAF aircraft. Thus the sight of red streams of tracer bullets racing earthward in a dark sky from a blacked-out source was not uncommon. Without radio contact, Shadows assumed the source of fire was a VNAF AC-47 gunship.

Close-calls for Shadows were not only with FACs and occasional fast movers. Many Shadows flying in Cambodia experienced and reported close-calls with bombs falling through their position from B-52 Arc Light strikes. At Shadow pilot/navigator pre-mission intelligence briefings, scheduled B-52 strikes in Shadow's AO were covered if known at the time. Warnings of imminent B-52 strikes were supposed to be broadcast over Guard Channel (emergency radio channel) to alert aircraft flying in the strike area. But sometimes warnings were either not broadcast or missed by unsuspecting aircraft flying in the strike area. Sometimes, pre-mission briefed targets for B-52 strikes changed from primary to secondary targets located in AOs where Shadows and other special operations aircraft were flying. A number of Shadow crews reported utter shock when bombs fell through their location or bombs impacting the ground near their location. Fortunately, no Shadows or other allied aircraft were struck by B-52 bombs.

***

Southwestern monsoons created the wet season for Southeast Asia from June thru October. Commando Hunt IV was still underway. Shadows from Fightin' C Flight had joined the hunt throughout Cambodia and for the first time, B57G aircraft joined the hunt in the Steel Tiger region of Southern Laos on 18 October. Aircraft without weather radar onboard, like the AC-119G Shadow, relied heavily on "real time" weather reports from aircraft flying into or departing the AO.

Enemy troops usually attacked during nighttime and monsoon rains did not deter them from attacking government troops. As a result, Shadow missions were flown in all kinds of weather but flights were always called VFR. There were times when takeoff or landing was delayed because it was raining so hard that nobody could see outside the aircraft. On the ground or in flight, a hard blowing rain drenched the gunship's cargo area through the three open doorways and leaked into the cockpit around the side windows and overhead dome.

Accurate pre-mission weather briefings for Shadow gunships were critical during the wet season, especially for night missions. Flying blind without onboard weather radar, Shadows bounced and weaved their way through dark monsoon clouds, bursts of heavy downpours, strong gusty winds, and cracks of lightning bolts from thunderstorms to reach their AO. Pilots constantly transitioned from flying VFR to flying IFR (Instrument Flight Rules). Flying at 3,500 feet above the ground around, below, or through lines of monsoon thunderstorms was extremely hazardous flight conditions. There were nights that Shadow was the only aircraft flying over Cambodia, but in spite of severe weather, Shadow gunships fulfilled their assigned task of providing 24/7 air support for Cambodian government troops.

***

On 9 October, the Khmer Republic was established by the Cambodian National Assembly as the monarchy of Prince Sihanouk was officially abolished. Former Head of State and now President Lon Nol and the new Khmer Republic resolved to free the sovereign lands of Cambodia from the military occupation of communist forces of the People's Army of Vietnam (PAVN) (aka North Vietnam Army or NVA) and the National Liberation Federation (NLF) for the liberation of South Vietnam (aka Viet Cong or VC).

A new national Cambodian flag was designed and produced for the Khmer Republic. Shadows proudly wore the new Cambodian flag patches on party flight suits. Changes in the Cambodian military became more pro-western after years of French training and influence. Even the name of the Cambodian Air Force would be changed from Aviation National Khmere (AVNK) to Khmer Air Force (KAF).

***

At Phan Rang Headquarters 17th SOS, Major Stanley M. Maillet assumed the duties of Squadron Administrative Officer on 11 October when Major Charles Meier rotated back to the states. Captain Thomas H. Hughes replaced Captain George Schenck as Squadron Maintenance Officer in October when Captain Schenck was assigned to the 14th Field Maintenance Squadron (FMS). Squadron personnel manning in October stabilized at or near the 289 personnel authorized.

On 17 October, 7th Air Force approved VNAF Phase II aircrew training in AC-119G gunships by the 17th SOS at Phan Rang Air Base, RVN rather than at Lockbourne AFB, Ohio by the TAC. Over a month later on 30 November 70, VNAF/AFGP/7AF Joint Programmed Directive 71-106 was published. The major tasks included in the PAD for the 14th SOW was the responsibility for training and certifying 24 AC-119G VNAF aircrews (192 personnel) and 112 maintenance personnel under the Improvement and Modernization (I & M) plan for South Vietnam armed forces. Training for each class was scheduled to last approximately sixty days. Aircrew training would be in four increments. The first three crews would start training on 1 Feb 71 and the last seven crews would start training on 25 June 71. Lt. Col. William E. Cosner would be appointed 17th Special Operations Squadron Project Officer on 10 December 70. Through the I & M program, Vietnamization of the War would become reality while also benefiting Cambodia's new Khmer Republic.[5]

***

During the month of October, Shadow expenditures appreciably increased to a total of 2,280,018 rounds of 7.62mm. BDA also significantly increased. Phnom Penh official reports credited Shadow with over 1,400 KBA of the total 1559 KBA confirmed with another 300 KBA reported by another source but not confirmed at the time of the report. Reported antiaircraft reactions also increased during October to twenty-three.[6]

In Cambodia, the FANK were mainly fighting against an estimated three divisions of NVA troops. There were no U.S. ground troops or advisors to support the brave and courageous Cambodians defending their cities against ever-present communist attacks. With adequate air support from American FACs, fast movers, fixed-wing gunships and B-52s, the Khmer FANK needed and requested more weapons, ammunition, and equipment for their ground troops.

***

During the month of October 1970, the following 17th SOS Shadow flight crew members were awarded the Distinguished Flying Cross (DFC) on 5 October: Captain A. T. Shaw, Lt. Col. A.R. Savera, 1/Lt. Mankin, 1/Lt. S.J. Cooper, 1/Lt. R.W. Stidson, Maj. P.A. Diehl, Maj. S.T. Raczkowski, and Capt. T. W. Greisamer. On 6 October, the following were awarded the DFC: Major D.T. Olsen and TSgt C.E. Watson. On 9 October, 1/Lt. L.D. Davis was awarded the DFC. On 13 October: Captain A.W. Blackburn, 1/Lt. H.L. Lee, and 1/Lt. W.C. Lamont. On that date, SSgt B.W. Hodgkins was awarded the Air Force Commendation Medal (AFCM) and Maj. R.L. Hintsen, MSgt V.R. Raveling, and SSgt P.M. Feus were awarded DFCs. On 20 October, Capt. C. Black and 1/Lt. Noworth received the DFC and on 22 October, Capt. C. Strolla received the DFC.[7]

***

Seventh Air Force Operation Commando Hunt V—the third large MACV air interdiction campaign against North Vietnamese dry season efforts to resupply forces in South Vietnam, Cambodia, and Laos—actually began on 10 October, but officially started on 10 November 1970 when the dry northeast monsoon season started, in preparation for enemy resumption of full-scale activities in the month of November. Commando Hunt V would continue through 30 April 1971. New infiltration and supply routes into Cambodia for the NVA had been established through the Steel Tiger area of southern Laos. The objectives of the aerial interdiction campaign remained constant with previous three Commando Hunts: To reduce the flow of personnel and materials into the Republic of Vietnam and Cambodia and to make the enemy pay the price of losses in their efforts to dominate Southeast Asia. Full utilization of waterways and rivers in southern Laos and Cambodia to resupply troops was part of the plan for the PAVN.[8]

Thereafter, 7th Air Force increased the number of interdiction sorties for AC-119K and AC-130 fixed-wing gunships while concentrating efforts in the Steel Tiger region of Laos. The priority for AC-119K Stinger missions still remained close-air support for allied ground troops, therefore, an emergency radio call to divert to a TIC took precedence over hunting trucks. As part of Commando Hunt V, Shadow gunships from Fightin' C Flight flew armed reconnaissance missions day and night over the Mekong River and its tributaries northward from Kompong Cham to the Laotian border and on Cambodian Highway 13 and side roads from Snoul to Stoeng Treng. The Kong River flowing from southern Laos into the flat, swampy terrain of the Mekong at Stoeng Treng carried flotillas of sampans packed with supplies for communist troops in Cambodia.

During November, 7th AF authorized pre-cleared interdiction areas (i.e., free fire zones) to gunship operations within Freedom Deal in Cambodia due to the fluid operations and the fleeting nature of enemy targets and the delay in clearance that often enervated effective gunship interdiction and fire support. Henceforth, any road vehicles or watercraft in free fire zones were summarily attacked, resulting in damage, destruction, or sinking.[9]

***

By the middle of November, the number of 17th SOS AC-119G airborne weapons mechanics (aerial gunners) and flight engineers dropped below authorized strength level and continued to drop until a serious shortage was encountered. The shortage was alleviated by USAF sending airborne weapons mechanics with gunship experience and flight engineers with previous AC-119G experience TDY to the 17th SOS for periods of sixty-two to ninety days. Most, if not all of the TDY gunners and flight engineers, would not be home stateside for Christmas in 1970.

***

On 16 November, a force of 6,000 ARVN soldiers began a sweep in northeastern Cambodia that resulted in the capture of one of the largest caches of munitions and supplies ever found in Cambodia. Some 254 tons of .85mm ammunition, 11,150 gallons of gasoline, and ten tons of rice were confiscated by the ARVN. It was evident that supplies were stored for support of NVA attacks in South Vietnam during the current dry season.[10]

On 23 November 1970, Rustics lost their second aircraft over Cambodia. This time it was an OV-10 Bronco, call sign Rustic 02. Rustic 02 pilot Major Don Brooks was checking on a relief column westward-bound from Kompong Cham on Highway 7 to the site of a missing government convoy that had been ambushed and destroyed. The relief column had come under attack and requested air support. Major Brooks summoned Shadow 82, who was working with Rustic 12 in the AO, to fire on enemy mortar positions. While Shadow 82 attacked enemy positions, Rustic 02 orbited at approximately 3,000 feet and watched the gunship below in its firing circle. The relief column commander soon informed Rustic that he could hear a machine gun firing up at the aircraft when passing over a particular hamlet. Rustic 02 flew over the suspected enemy location but did not see anything. Ten minutes later, there was a loud explosion followed by severe vibrations within the Rustic Bronco. Fire erupted and the decision to bailout was made by Major Brooks. With "Mayday" calls completed, Brooks ordered his "backseater" Rustic Tango, SSgt Gil Bellefeuille, to eject. Brooks ejected immediately after Bellefeuille had ejected from the stricken aircraft. Both men landed in friendly territory and were rescued by VNAF helicopters based at Phnom Penh.[11]

Shadow 82 Aircraft Commander Capt. Bert B. Blanton narrated the downing of Rustic 02 as witnessed by him and his crew in the following letter submitted to Rustic Operations by 17th SOS "C" Flight/4485 on 24 November 1970:

Shadow 82 was working with Rustic 12 in the designated target area when Rustic 02 called for Shadow 82 to expend on a TIC at 1040 (hours). Shadow 82 was cleared to fire on target at 1100 (hours) by Rustic 02. Shadow 82 expended on target and was standing by while Rustic 02 checked on a 12.7mm site south of previous target reported active by the ground commander. Shadow 82 observed Rustic 02 check the suspected 12.7 site to the south. He proceeded to the north and crossed the highway and turned to a westerly heading. At 1120, Rustic 02 gave a Mayday call on guard saying, "Mayday, Mayday, Mayday. I am hit!" The OV-10 then turned to an easterly heading toward the friendly town losing altitude and trailing smoke. The aircraft appeared to be difficult to control. Then Rustic 02 made another transmission on guard stating, "We are on fire; we are bailing out." Shadow 82 observed two good parachutes. The aircraft made two circles and crashed two clicks southwest of the friendly town. The aircraft was completely destroyed. Shadow 82 pinpointed the positions of both the pilot (02) and the "backseater" on the ground. Made radio contact with 02 and relayed information to Rustic 12 who was now on the scene. Shadow 82 contacted Ethan and relayed information about the downed aircraft and requested "SAR" effort. Shadow 82 flew CAP over the downed-airmen and observed that they were in friendly hands at 1140. Shadow 82 observed two VNAF helicopters arriving on the scene. Shadow 82 and Rustic 12 helped coordinate the pickup of both airmen which was accomplished at 1152. The VNAF helicopters proceeded to a friendly city escorted by Rustic 12. Shadow 82 contacted Ethan relaying the successful pickup and the destination of the rescued personnel. The "SAR" effort was completed with everything under control. Shadow RTB'd at 1200 (hours).

Note: All times in the above narrative are TACAN (Tan Son Nhut Air Base) Ch 102 local.

***

The village of Prey Totung on Route 7 continued to be a hot spot for AC-119 gunships during November. The village had been under attack with control of the village changing hands several times. Time and time again, Shadows protected the town during hours of darkness against growing concentrations of NVA forces. Enemy anti-aircraft fire at Prey Totung became furious. When Shadows opened fire on enemy locations, barrages of enemy red tracers from .51 caliber and 7.62mm machine guns raced skyward toward the gunship. The battle for control of Routes 6, 7, 21, and 71 was ongoing with both friendly and enemy forces there in strength. The major battles for control of Prey Totung were yet to come.

***

During October and November, 17th SOS A Flight (Phu Cat) and B Flight (Phan Rang) continued to provide air support for friendly forces in South Vietnam while "beefed-up" FOL C Flight at Tan Son Nhut continued providing 24/7 air support for the Cambodians. Fighting C Flight was still totally committed to waging secret aerial war against communist troops in Cambodia.

17th SOS FOL C Flight gunship operations continued to expand in Cambodia. Operating from Saigon's Tan Son Nhut Airport, AC-119 Shadow and Stinger gunships sustained non-stop missions to interdict communist troop and supply lines while successfully fighting against communist ground forces of the NVA, VC, and the Khmer Rouge. The gunships were the chief aerial defenders of Cambodia's principal towns and cities of Prey Totung, Kompong Cham, Kompong Thom, Skoun, Siem Reap, Kompong Som, and Phnom Penh. Protection of these cities was crucial. All were control points for key highways in the lifeline of food, supplies, and ammunition for the Cambodian government armed forces.

The covert mission of AC-119 gunships in the Cambodian Aerial Campaign following the Incursion had worked and the operation was still unknown by outsiders. Fighting C Flight Commander Teal stated in his memoir, "I got a call from my contact at 7th AF. He told me that he was sending a mixed group of officers from Military Assistance Command Vietnam (MACV) for a briefing on our mission. I was to brief them completely and to answer any questions they asked. To put it mildly, they were astounded that we were running the type and number of missions daily and that we had been over Cambodia for months and they did not know about it. Obviously, we had held our cards close to our chest, and that's a big well done, Shadows and Stingers."

***

Cambodia and Laos were drying out from monsoon rains and flooding evidenced by increased enemy traffic. The addition of three Shadow gunships and crews from Alpha Flight at Phu Cat and three Shadow gunships and crews from Bravo Flight at Phan Rang helped C Flight meet the eight fragged missions per day after TDY Stingers moved back to their PCS stations. Day and night, more Hunter-Killer Teams consisting of an OV-10 or O-2 Rustic FAC and Shadow gunships stalked enemy infiltration routes into Cambodia from southern Laos.

The 14th SOW Gunship Operations Office at Phan Rang continued coordinating Fragmentary Orders for 17th SOS Shadow FOLs as directed by Headquarters 7th Air Force at Tan Son Nhut. Fragged sorties were scheduled missions for one aircraft; thus, Shadows persisted in calling a sortie, a mission.

Troops-in-contact scrambles, turn-arounds, diversions, check rides, test flights, phase inspections at Phan Rang, and corrosion control flights to Kadena Air Base at Okinawa added pressure on the squadron to maintain maximum combat status of operational ready gunships and crews. To complicate matters, air and ground crewmembers if approved, took seven days leave or seven days rest and recuperation (R & R) from duty schedules during their twelve month tours. Also adding to complications for manning combat crews were those airmen classified DNIF for various injuries or health reasons. New personnel (FNGs) reported for duty and in-country training to replace those with a DEROS. Personnel turnover proved to be a constant factor in change for the 17th SOS and for that matter for all U.S. military units in the war zone.

***

In Cambodia, holding government population centers and isolated troop garrisons under constant states of siege was proving to be effective strategy for communist forces that usually out-numbered Cambodian defenders. Six FANK Battalions of the 10th and 11th Infantry Brigades defended Kompong Thom. U.S. Air Force Intelligence reported at least five battalions of the NVA C-40 Division surrounding the capital city of Kompong Thom Province.

Flying at 3500 feet above the ground over Kampong Thom during midnight hours in November, Shadow 83 commenced firing on enemy mortar positions surrounding the province capital. Mortars and rockets were zeroed-in on the heart of the city. Fires and explosions erupted amid the buildings.

Aircraft commander, Major Don Fraker took guidance from the NOS through the computerized fire control system, set on fully automatic to pinpoint his minigun fire on the mortar sites. As Fraker fired on the mortar positions, two anti-aircraft guns simultaneously opened fire on the gunship. Red tracers from the .51 caliber machine guns streamed behind the Shadow's two tails. Fraker didn't flinch but stayed in the firing circle to continue firing on the mortar positions. Luckily, the enemy gunners again did not lead the gunship enough with their fire to hit the gunship.

The Shadow IO was half-in/half-out the open doorway of the aircraft, trying to spot the precise location of the anti-aircraft (AA) guns. The IO scanned the ground for tell-tale muzzle flashes. Spotting one enemy gun emplacement, the IO described the location to the NOS operator who immediately switched from locating mortar positions to finding the location of the enemy AA gun site on his scope. The NOS operator used the lower eyepiece on the scope which magnified ground targets four-power. This eyepiece was primarily used for night missions, utilizing any available moonlight or starlight in addition to the gunship's infrared light at nighttime.

The NOS operator enabled the Shadow to see in the dark of night, which confused the enemy and denied him the safe haven of darkness. On dark night missions, the pilot might never see the target with naked eyes but could fire and hit enemy targets thanks to the night infrared scope and the onboard fire control computer which enabled the cross hairs on the NOS to be shown on the pilot's gunsight. That was not the case now. The pilot, Fraker, could see the enemy AA gun emplacement targeted by the NOS operator and ordered the navigator to set the fire control computer to semiautomatic mode. He thought briefly of shooting from manual mode but didn't want to lose the enemy gun location. The NOS would keep him focused on the target.

A top eyepiece on the night observation scope, a three-power telescope could be used by the NOS but was normally used during daylight conditions to pinpoint a ground location for the Shadow pilot. NOS operators carried powerful binoculars for spotting targets during daylight conditions. Usually during daylight, the pilot could see targets and fired in manual mode without assistance from the NOS.

In automatic mode or semi-automatic mode of fire, the fire control computer provided a movable cross hair in the pilot's gunsight from information received from the night observation scope (NOS). The movable cross hair showed where the NOS aimed. In fully automatic mode, the computer would allow the guns to fire when the pilot pressed the trigger only when the fixed cross hair and the movable cross hair in the pilot's gunsight were within set coincidence or alignment. The coincidence, calibrated in milliradians from 0 to 70, was manually set on the computer by the navigator. The lower the setting; the smaller the fire zone, resulted in more accurate fire. With a setting of zero coincidence, the miniguns would not fire when the pilot pressed the trigger unless the fixed and the movable cross hairs were precisely superimposed. Smaller coincidence settings insured that only intended targets were hit. When friendly and enemy troops were in very close proximity to one another, an AC-119 gunship pilot would normally use the automatic mode to eliminate the chances of stray bullets hitting friendly troops.

In semi-automatic mode, the computer provided the movable cross hair in the pilot's gunsight, but did not require the pilot to perfectly align or superimpose the fixed cross hair with the movable cross hair to fire the guns when the trigger was pressed. The fire control computer also compensated for wind velocity and direction in automatic and semi-automatic modes.

Major Fraker's copilot (yours truly) was responsible for holding the firing altitude of 3500 feet by making minor adjustments with the control column. Fraker banked the gunship into a tight 35 degree firing circle to align the two cross hairs in his gunsight and pressed the trigger. A line of red tracers shot earthward, meeting a stream of red from the enemy gun. The enemy red faded behind the gunship's twin tails. Then more red lines of bullets shot past the right wing. Fraker kicked in rudder to keep the fixed cross hairs in his gunsight on the enemy gun position and pressed the trigger. Another G.E.MXU-470 minigun growled as thousands of 7.62 millimeter bullets rained down on the enemy gun, causing the enemy gunner to stop firing. The NOS reported over the aircraft intercom that the enemy gun was repeatedly hit. The Shadow gave away its precise location at night when the miniguns were fired. Red ribbons of tracers marked the path of bullets from their origin in the dark sky to the ground. That was usually the time when communist gunners opened fire on the Shadow. Many times, a duel between the Shadow pilot and the enemy anti-aircraft gunner resulted as lines of red tracers streaking earthward met and passed lines of red tracers shot skyward.

Still, the second enemy machine gun fired away at the gunship with its red tracers shooting by the nose of the aircraft. Fraker had the gun position in his sights and fired a barrage of bullets. Fire from the enemy gun ceased. Again the NOS reported direct hits on the gun site.

Enemy mortar and rocket fire into the city abruptly ended as exchanges of small arms fire between opposing ground forces became sporadic. A smoky calmness came over the city. Some buildings were still burning. The Shadow navigator conversed over the radio with Hotel

303. Major Oum stated the VC were retreating from their attack. He requested the Shadow shoot in the vicinity of the city sawmill where the attack had originated. The IO located the saw mill and Fraker raked the area with guns on high rate of fire until Winchester. Bingo fuel had been declared by the FE and Shadow 83 needed to head back to Saigon. There was another Shadow en route to KPT for CAP of the city. Major Oum was as usual extremely thankful for Shadow's support. He hoped to meet the Shadow crews sometime at some safe place.

Fortunately for Shadows, communist anti-aircraft gunners at KPT did not lead the gunship enough, especially at night, with their firing aim, resulting in red tracers streaming up behind the airplane. To add to confusing enemy AA gunners of Shadow's location during darkness, propellers on the aircraft were intentionally de-synchronized. The whopping sound of unsynchronized props created the condition similar to finding the location of a helicopter in the night sky. The nighttime blacked-out Shadow's airspeed was deceptively fast at 140 knots in the firing circle, especially on dark moonless nights with navigation and anti-collision lights turned-off. Occasionally, enemy gunners scored a "field goal" when their tracer bullets shot through the air space between the gunship's fuselage, booms, and horizontal stabilizer. The Shadow IO was responsible for calling field goals.

Government troops and civilians were acutely aware that communist forces controlled the countryside, most importantly Highway 6 and other back roads leading in and out of Kompong Thom, thus preventing the province capital from being fully reinforced with additional troops or resupplied on a regular basis. While talking on the radio with the ground commander, Major Oum, radio call sign Hotel 303 (aka Hotel KPT), Shadows learned early-on about the brave defenders and inhabitants of Kompong Thom. Due to the siege of the city by NVA troops and the shortage of food, they had resorted to killing animals in the city zoo for food. Still, Major Oum remained unyielding in the defense of KPT. His congenial radio demeanor during lulls in the fighting turned to all business when under attack.

No matter what the conditions were at KPT, Major Oum retained his sense of humor and high spirits while working with Shadows. He even joked about killing, butchering, and eating the oldest tiger at the city zoo while waiting for resupply convoys.

During a quiet daylight CAP of KPT, my Shadow talked to Major Oum about conditions in his city after surviving night after night of devastating attacks by the NVA. What could we Shadows bring them to help his troops to maintain their spirit to hold-off the NVA? After much joking, it was decided that the next day, Shadow would bring and drop recent issues of *Playboy* magazine to the troops at KPT.

Upon returning to TSN, the Shadow word went out, "Donate your *Playboys* for KPT." The next day, a Shadow air-dropped bundles of *Playboys* along with other magazines on KPT. According to Oum, his troops were ecstatic.

Shadows truly felt kindred to the Cambodians and their fight against communist troops. There was nothing Shadows would not do to help our new ally. After months of working closely with the ground commanders over radios, Shadows wondered what their new Cambodian brothers-in-arms looked like.

***

Kompong Cham (KPC), capital city of Kompong Cham Province was forty miles to the northeast of Phnom Penh. A major Mekong River port, KPC was located at a choke point in the river as it turned westward toward Phnom Penh. Route 7 ran west from KPC thru Prey Totung located at Route 71 junction and on westward to Skoun located at the junction with Route 6. There was no bridge across the Mekong River at KPC. Ferry boats were used to connect Route 7 on the northern shore of the Mekong with Route 7 on the southern shore of the river.

The riverport of KPC made an ideal debarkation point for the communist troops and supplies coming down the river from southern Laos. With KPC controlled by FANK troops, Charlie could offload on the southern banks of the Mekong and quickly hide in the nearby Chup rubber plantation to the southeast of the river. From there, Charlie could select the best infiltration routes into Military Regions III and IV of Vietnam. Or he could press on down the Mekong to Phnom Penh and surrounding areas. His fleet of various sizes of sampans was substantial and dedicated to its mission.

Shadow gunship crews soon developed a healthy respect for Charlie's "bamboo" fleet of watercraft navigating the Kong and Mekong, especially after many boats were modified with overhead protective covering to withstand aerial attacks. The infiltration route of men and materials was a professionally organized, effective logistics system. Boat after boat slyly inched their war downstream by the hundreds; so innocent looking with even women, children, and monks onboard. Sometimes it would take one of the "defenseless" pirogues to belch some .51 cal fire at the Shadow before receiving some "American religion" real fast. The rules of engagement had experienced somewhat of a traumatic evolution. They now followed logical rationale. The Mekong became part of Freedom Deal that included free fire zones which increased the effectiveness of the Shadow, especially during the darkness of night which Charlie preferred to operate.

Despite the patience and persistence of stealthy hunters finding and stalking prey to strike during water traffic interdiction, many times AC-119 Shadow gunship crews experienced limited success on sure targets and disappointment in their efforts when their warbird was diverted to a TIC priority. The gunship crew flew at maximum speed to reach allied troops-in-contact needing direct air support. It was very exasperating, but the Shadow's knew their top priority was TICs.

On 15 November, Shadow 83 took off at 1230 hours; a day sortie for Major Rodney B. Carter's crew. Carter was a gung-ho bachelor. He liked day sorties, so he could fire manually at the lousy VC. Great sport, watching them jump in the water and swim for shore. Get 'em before they hit the bush! But the rest of his crew was not always so adventuresome. They weren't completely sold on these day flights. The Shadow was meant to be a night bird. Daytime meant anything was an incongruent concept for the unconventional warfare conducted by fixed winged, side-firing, flying war machines.

Things happened fast as Carter drove the gunship in over "Cham" and checked-in with "Hotel KPC" on the radio. Weather was fair, but not what Shadows would call good. A low fog bank hovered over the Mekong. FANK troops at KPC were taking heavy mortar fire. Searching on his sensor, NOS operator Major Bill Gericke located one of the mortar sites. Shadow 83 reeled into a left pylon orbit and opened fire. Four enemy .51 cal machine guns belched lead at Carter's slow-flying blackbird but missed. Was it a Charlie trap for Shadow?

Carter blazed away on high rate of fire. He rocked the wings and kicked in some rudder to hit the targeted mortar site. While firing on and silencing the other mortar sites, the .50 caliber machine gunners again targeted Shadow 83.

Enemy tracers whizzed past the nose and wings of the aircraft. Sounds of popcorn popping were heard by crewmembers over the sound of the firing miniguns. This time, Charlie gunners shot with perfect lead angles at the black bulls-eye in the sky; then dead center. It was no time to gamble. Carter pulled off the target to check the damage. The bird had taken two hits. One impacted at the forward jamb of the night observation scope doorway, ricocheted, and exited the fuselage high right, leaving a two inch hole. A second round hit the tip of the right wing on the leading edge.

With the mortar attack on KPC stifled and without knowing more about possible damage to the gunship and knowing the obvious accuracy of the quadrangle of enemy anti-aircraft weapons, Carter peeled-off right and out of the firing circle and headed up the Mekong to check things out on the aircraft. With aircraft systems working normal and no further damage discovered, Carter and his crew continued up the Mekong on armed recon. Observing no targets on the river, Carter headed the aircraft back toward Tan Son Nhut at 1630 hours to rejuvenate for fighting another day. A surprising aspect told later by NOS Gericke was that he had just stepped away from the NOS doorway only moments before the .51 cal slug had torn through it.

***

Shadows escorted road convoys in Cambodia either alone or teamed-up with a FAC, usually a Rustic. When paired, the FAC searched for enemy possible ambush sites and preparations along the convoy's route while the AC-119G flew in a large elliptical orbit overhead. Cambodian ground commanders often upset convoy escort planning by scheduling their own convoys while failing to coordinate air cover support with higher authorities.

Without urgent calls to support a TIC, fragged Shadow sorties for interdiction/armed reconnaissance "seek and destroy" missions over Cambodia took on a life of their own. Checking in with various Cambodian ground commanders for a current sit-rep along the way was standard procedure. If all was quiet at KPC, KPT, and other government-controlled towns and cities, the Shadow flew northward from KPC above the Mekong and Route 13 that semi-paralleled the river, searching for sampans and road runners. Listening to music from AFVN radio in Saigon and eating flight lunches packed in white boxes from the TSN mess hall. For those who had finished eating their cold fried chicken, throwing chicken bones overboard broke the monotony of uneventful missions.

The Shadow NOS searched roads and waterways for movers or suspicious activities within the free fire zones. Using binoculars during daytime and the night scope during nighttime, the NOS was instrumental in finding enemy targets.

The month of November proved productive for Fighting C Flight, being credited for 460 enemy KBA and 127 enemy WBA. The Flight's BDA included four secondary explosions as a result of strikes. Factors contributing to lower numbers of KBA/WBA were new stricter ROE's, greater dispersion of enemy troops, and fewer FANK ground sweeps immediately following firing missions. Enemy AAA reactions decreased during the month to eleven. One Shadow gunship received two hits from .51 caliber machine gun fire.[12]

Following is additional data on Fighting C Flight's monthly report to HQ 17th SOS, using a new reporting BDA format initiated in November 1970:

Trucks Destroyed/Damaged: 3/18
Carts Destroyed/Damaged: 8/1
Two-Wheeled Vehicles Destroyed/Damaged: 24

Other Vehicles Destroyed/Damaged: 9
Sampans Destroyed/Damaged: 55/168
Motorboats/Launches/Ferries/Junks Destroyed/Damaged: 11/100

Enemy AAA Reactions

DAY	NIGHT	TWILIGHT
11 Nov–Shadow 84	4 Nov–Shadow 85	22 Nov–Shadow 81
15 Nov–Shadow 83 (2 Hits/.51cal.)	9 Nov–Shadow 80	
16 Nov–Shadow 82	20 Nov–Shadow 85	
18 Nov–Shadow 83	21 Nov–Shadow 87	
	24 Nov–Shadow 80	
	26 Nov–Shadow 87	

During a twenty-day span in November, Fightin' C Flight had flown 198 combat missions; thirty-eight more combat missions than fragged.

The following 17th SOS personnel and aircrew members were awarded decorations for achievements during the month of November: On 11 November, Maj. C.H. Meier, Jr. received the AFCM and 1/Lt. D.C. Riggs received the DFC. Captain C.W. Davis was awarded a DFC on 13 November. Other 17th SOS flight crew members receiving the DFC included: Technical Sergeant L.P. Burns on 5 November and on 20 November; Sgt J.B. Bradley, Capt. R.R. Twaddle, Capt. F.J. Gerner, SSgt J.A. Murdock III, SSgt M.P. Smith, 1/Lt. R.L. Cart, Jr., Sgt J. Goodson, TSgt E.J. McCormick, Sgt K.P. Stearn, SSgt R.M. Pommerelle (Interpreter), TSgt N.J. Evans, Capt. J.S. Craig, A1C O.V. York, 1/Lt. L.E. Fletcher, 1/Lt. R.B. Sizemore, 1/Lt. R.W. Mundle. On 22 November, 1/Lt. H.E. Laakman Jr., Capt. F.C. Watson, Maj. J.A. Lane, SSgt P.E. Petry, and Capt. K.M. Taylor received DFCs. Sgt J.M. Bryant, TSgt C.M. Liggon, A1C B.W. Bratt, and 1/Lt. J. Morales also received DFCs.[13]

***

Americans were not alone flying missions in support of the Cambodian Army. Many isolated FANK garrisons were fighting for shear survival against communist troops. For six weeks beginning on 1 Novem-

ber 1970, with Cambodian defenders barely holding on since summer
months against Khmer Rouge and NVA attacks, USAF AC-119 gunships flew 126 missions and fighter-bombers flew seventy-eight sorties
along with three bombing missions flown by B-52s in defense of the beleaguered garrison at KPC. The VNAF also supported KPC with 426
combat sorties in defending Kompong Cham during this time period. On
14 December, the South Vietnamese conducted a helicopter air operation to successfully replace the Cambodian garrison at KPC with an
ARVN infantry battalion and an artillery battery.[14]

THIRTEEN

Shadows Over Laos

During the first days of December, TICs between Royal Laotian forces defending Lima Sites (Landing Sites) against NVA/Pathet Lao troops on the Bolovens Plateau in southern Laos, resulted in the diversion of AC-119K Stinger gunships originally fragged for air interdiction missions over the Ho Chi Minh Trail. On 4 December 70, Stinger gunships of the 18th SOS based at DaNang began supporting friendly forces on the Bolovens Plateau when requested. On 7 December, the Stingers were released from Bolovens duty to resume air interdiction on the Ho Chi Minh Trail and the 17th SOS Shadow gunships were assigned the task of providing air support for Lima Sites on the Plateau. The 17th SOS was fragged by 7th AF for six nighttime missions over the Bolovens Plateau. At 1700 hours on 7 December 1970, three gunships and four aircrews stationed at Phan Rang flew to supplement A Flight at Phu Cat, the base of operations for this mission. Upon arrival, the aircraft were refueled and the 17th SOS began continuous all-night coverage of the Bolovens Plateau.

The deteriorating situation of Royal Laotian Army Lima Sites necessitated twenty-four-hour coverage of the Bolovens Plateau. The 17th undertook the nighttime support while tactical fighters from various squadrons provided daytime support. Laotian Air Force AC-47 gunships were also present in case of simultaneous attacks on separate Lima Sites. The Lima Sites were completely surrounded and each had most of its people concentrated in a small, but strong defensive perimeter. For example, Lima Site 22 (where most of the 17th SOS's effort was expended) had only one small outpost southeast of its location on 7 December. After five days of combat with continual air support, the Lima Site was able to place outposts outside their perimeters resulting in decreased incidents of hostile action. By 12 December, Lima Site 22 was able to situate six to eight large outposts outside of it perimeter. During the period 7-12 December, 17th SOS Shadows expended 333,375 rounds of 7.62mm ammo and 267 flares. BDA directly observed by Shadow crewmembers were five secondary explosions one of which was very large, four rocket positions and three mortar positions silenced, and two large fires.

On 11 December, the number of fragged missions was cut back from 6 to 5, one of which was a ground alert mission covering II and III Corps. From the 11th to the 19th of December, enemy activity on the Plateau remained relatively low compared with the first five days of the operation. On 14 December, the number of night sorties was reduced to four and on 16 December, the number of sorties was cut to three. On 19 December, the move of A Flight from Phu Cat to Phan Rang began and the crews and aircraft arrived on 20 December. However, early in the morning of 20 December, 7th AF decided to keep the operation over the Bolovens in effect and the aircraft and crews moved back to Phu Cat. The Bolovens Plateau operation continued from Phu Cat until 24 December when the operation was cancelled and the Shadow gunships from Phan Rang returned to home base. The final Shadow sortie from Phu Cat was flown on the 25 December 1970.

FOL A Flight at Phu Cat was previously scheduled to close down operations on 10 December with aircraft and aircrews transferred to Phan Rang B Flight, but with the outbreak of hostilities on the Bolovens Plateau, the move had to be delayed. With the cancellation of the Bolovens Plateau operation, on 25 December, the FOL A Flight at Phu Cat was closed and all personnel and aircraft were moved to Phan Rang to become part of B Flight. On 29 December, A Flight administrative and maintenance personnel moved to Phan Rang to complete the closing of Phu Cat FOL.

By 27 December, military intelligence indicated a very strong possibility of renewed enemy attacks of Lima Sites on the Bolovens Plateau. Therefore, 17th SOS B Flight was fragged for four missions a night into the area. Consequently, Shadow gunship missions out of Phan Rang resumed operations over the Plateau that would continue into January 1971.

December results of 17th SOS gunships flying forty-two sorties in support of Laotian Lima Sites on the Bolovens Plateau were as follows: fifty TICs, thirty-four KELs, four SELs, and sixteen CAP targets; 729,775 rounds of 7.62mm ammunition and 468 flares expended; two large secondaries, ten secondaries, two rocket and four mortar positions silenced; two large sustained fires, several small fires, and a large number of strikes on enemy positions with no results observed due to foliage or terrain.[1]

***

Meanwhile on 13 December 70, two AC-119K Stinger gunships and three aircrews from DaNang were deployed TDY to Tan Son Nhut to again augment Fighting C Flight Shadow operations in Cambodia. Primarily tasked with flying armed recon missions on enemy supply routes and lines of communication in northeastern Cambodia, the Stingers also helped defend friendly positions fighting against enemy attacks. The Stingers added greater punch to interdiction efforts against NVA supply routes, destroying enemy sampans, boats, buildings, bunkers, and road vehicles with their 20mm cannons. Supporting troops-in-contact, the Stinger's miniguns proved accurate and devastating to communist troops. These two TDY Stinger gunships and crews would be redeployed to DaNang on 25 January 71 and eventually stationed at Nahkon Phanom RTAFB, Thailand.

***

During a night mission on 6 December 70 while attacking enemy positions during a TIC, Shadow 59 (Major Don Fraker Aircraft Commander) received one hit from a .51 caliber machine gun. Damage to the aircraft was light; however, the copilot, 1/Lt. Donald Craig was hit in the leg by the bullet but received only superficial wounds. For this, Lt. Craig was awarded the Purple Heart on 26 March 1971.

***

On 12 December 1970, Cambodian ground forces stationed at the town of Prey Totung came under intense attacks from a large concentration of enemy units. Located on Route 7 midway between Kompong Cham and Skoun, Prey Totung controlled the communications and supplies of friendly forces and cities in the region. Hotel Prey Totung requested immediate Shadow gunship support. In response, over thirty-two gunship missions were flown in support of Prey Totung and surrounding area. Shadow gunships expended a total of 555,800 rounds of ammo on targets while launching 128 flares during the fifty-seven TICs and fifty-four KELs during the four day and nights of combat. (TIC, KEL, and SEL are not used in reporting missions in an official manner, for security reasons all missions are officially classified as Air Interdiction.) Seven gunships reported AAA reactions with one Shadow receiving a hit.[2]

During the four days and nights of fighting, Fighting C Flight gunships answered Hotel Prey Totung's request for fire power. Eleven 17th SOS aircrews and two 18th SOS aircrews flew sustained sorties from Tan Son Nhut in support of the Cambodian troops until enemy forces retired from battle and the town was secured on 15 December.

The Shadow and Stinger crews submitted for decorations during the battle at Prey Totung flew at least one sortie and in many cases two or more sorties. The following chronological list of outstanding combat missions flown by AC-119 gunships at Prey Totung was labeled "For Official Use Only" by Fighting C Flight navigators, Major John "Jack" Nicol and his assistant Captain Robert Safreno, who were assigned the additional duty of Flight Awards and Decorations Officers. From the list of brief mission descriptions, only one mission per crew was selected to be submitted to squadron headquarters for possible approval of awards or decorations.

AC-119G Shadow (*foreground*) flies wing position in formation with brother gunship AC-119K Stinger.

The day's date and take-off time are listed first (e.g., 12/0140) followed by the rank and name of the Aircraft Commander and the Shadow (SH) radio call sign number (e.g., SH-26). Channel (Ch) 102 is the TACAN station for Tan Son Nhut Air Base. Four of the sorties recommended for awards/decorations were Stinger (ST) gunship crews who were on temporary duty assignment with Fightin' C Flight at the time.

12/0140* – Captain William S. Cunningham and crew.
    Shadow (SH): 26 scrambled from Channel (Ch) 102 to support a besieged friendly village. Arrived on target at 0220, Rustic (FAC) 40 working target also called in air strikes. Friendlies receiving 12.7mm, Mortar, Small arms and 122mm Rocket fire. SH-26 expended all his ammunition took heavy 12.7mm and Rocket Propelled Grenade (RPG) fire. On target for 3.2 hours.

12/0326 – Captain Donald A. Rapuzzi, and crew.

SH-15 Scrambled from Ch-102 on the above target. When he arrived on scene there was hand to hand fighting in progress. He expended his ammunition right up to friendly positions. Troops-in-contact broken and he received heavy 12.7mm fire the whole time on target, 3.3 hours. Expended all his ammunition on the target. Ground commander confirmed 200 killed by air (KBA).

12/0636 – Captain Victor H. Heiner and crew.

SH-42 Scrambled from Ch-102 on same target. Rustic-18 and Rustic-12 marking targets for SH-42. SH-42 put down suppression fire on five targets and received moderate ground fire in return.

12/1008 – Major Donald D. Fraker and crew.

SH-28 was launched from Ch-102. He fired on target and broke a TIC. He also fired on a hostile supply concentration. SH-28 also struck many loaded small-motorized vehicles.

12/1354 – Captain Gary A. Totten and crew.

SH-71 launched from Ch-102 on target and fired on TIC. Pulled off for fighter strikes. Blade-02 was shot down, pilot ejected. SH-71 and SH-18 in area flying Combat Air Patrol (CAP). SH-71 pulled off target Returned to Base (RTB). Sh-18 continued to CAP.

12/1712 – Captain Bert H Blanton and crew.

SH-18 launched from Ch-102, on target, flew CAP, for Search and Rescue (SAR) effort on Blade-02. Pilot picked up in successful effort at 1813 hours. Air Strikes continued over above target. SH-18 CAP for strikes.

12/1950 – Jay R. Simmons and crew.

SH-66 launched from Ch-102, on target. Rustic 34 in area.

Fired on TIC, and known supplies and troop concentrations. Stopped the TIC.

12/2250 – Major Rodney B. Carter and crew.
SH-36 launched from Ch-102. There was a lull in activity and he flew CAP over the friendly position. SH-36 fired on suspected hostile locations and supply points and stopped TICs.

13/0152 – SH-16 Captain William S. Cunningham and crew.
Launched from Ch-102, on target, Rustic 38 in area. Fired on ground commander's direction all night. Drew intense 12.7mm fire from hostile force in bunkered positions around the town. Silenced two of the sites. Expended all ammunition. TIC still in progress when he returned to base.

13/0455 – Captain Jerry W. Marples and crew.
SH-27 launched from Ch-102, on target, Rustic 35 in area. Fired on TIC while receiving fire from 12.7mm sites surrounding the town. These enemy sites were well bunkered and threw up intense fire on SH-27. SH-27 pulled off target for air strikes.

13/0750 – Major Bautz and crew.
Stinger (ST)-81 launched from Ch-102, on target. Rustic 05 and Rustic 17 in the area along with SH-27. Fired on Rustic 05 direction and stopped TIC. ST 81 took ground fire, but stopped TIC in target area.

13/1029 – Lieutenant Colonel William B. Gregory, Jr. and crew.
SH-67, launched from Ch-102, on target. Working with Rustic 09 and Sundog 10. Expended on hostile supply line. Damaged seven motorized vehicles and two motorized sampans.

13/1350 – Major Donald D. Fraker and crew.
SH-80, launched from Ch-102, on target. Friendly troops in

town and out of ammunition. Fired on hostile positions and then broke a TIC. Flew air cover for airdrop of ammunition and supplies to friendly troops in the town.

13/1708 – Major Joe J. Jones and crew.
Stinger (ST)-17, launched from Ch-102, on target. Fired on mortar and 12.7mm positions that were active and bunkered in. Broke TIC and fired on supply lines of hostile force.

13/1955 – Captain Bert H. Blanton and crew.
SH-76, launched from Ch-102, on target. Fired on TIC and stopped it about 2200 hours. Remained over town on CAP, until returned to base.

13/2253 – Major Rodney B. Carter and crew.
SH-35, launched from Ch-102, on target. Rustic 34 in area. Town under heavy mortar attack, expended all of ammunition around town on targets and silenced the mortars.

14/0150 – Captain William S. Cunningham and crew.
SH-10, launched from Ch-102, on target. Fired on TIC and several bunkered antiaircraft sites. SH-10 took heavy automatic weapons fire and managed to silence one site.

14/0500 – Major Bautz and crew.
ST-59, launched from Ch-102, on target. Fired on two TICS' in target area. On target for 2.7 hours worked with Rustic-35.

14/0800 – Captain Marples and crew.
SH-73, launched from Ch-102, on target. Worked TIC's all through target area but was pulled off by Rustic-35 for (fighter/bomber) Air Strikes.

14/0945 – Lieutenant Colonel Gregory and crew.
SH-83, launched from Ch-102, on target. Flew CAP for

supply convoy, then was directed back to target area. Arrived over target and was pulled off for Air Strikes. SH-83, directed to the west of main target and fired on hostile positions.

14/1350 – Captain Heiner and crew.
SH-31, launched from Ch-102, on target. Pulled off target due to aircraft congestion. Allied aircraft all over the area. SH-31, cleared target and reconnoitered the area. Fired on hostile supply lines.

14/1701 – Major Jones and crew.
ST-94, launched from Ch-102, on target. No activity flew reconnaissance mission in area, then fired on hostile locations west of target.

14/1955 – Captain Walker and crew.
SH-39, launched from Ch-102, on target, directed on targets other than main target area as all was quiet over main target.

14/2255 – Captain Cunningham and crew.
SH-80, launched from Ch-102, on target, directed to fire on target and expended all ammunition during the three hours he remained on the target. SH-80 also took heavy automatic weapons fire from all around target town.

15/0155 – Major Carter and crew.
SH-65, launched from Ch-102, on target. Friendly town under heavy attack cleared to expend on hostile force. SH-65, took heavy automatic weapons fire from all around the town. Expended all ammunition during the 3.3 hours.

15/0510 – Captain Marples and crew.
SH-11, launched from Ch-102, on target. Fired on target, then directed to targets west of the main target area. In target area 3.5 hours.

15/0745 – Major Heiner and crew.

SH-81, launched from Ch-102, on target. Fired on clearance from Rustic-19. Hostile force had occupied part of the northern part of the town. They had set up antiaircraft positions in the building and SH-81 silenced them. Expended all ammunition on target.

15/1355 – Lieutenant Colonel Gregory and crew.

SH-85, launched from Ch-102, on target. Directed by Rustic-12 to cover airdrop of supplies. He protected the friendly forces until they gathered the supplies and also a helicopter pick up of friendly wounded. Fired on hostile force attempting to overrun the town and broke the attack. Hostile force pulled out of the area after four days.

Fighting C Flight Shadow Navigator/NOS operator Captain Robert Safreno, a member of Captain Bill Cunningham's crew, operated the NOS during Captain Cunningham's Shadow 26 mission on 12/0140.

Captain Safreno stated what happened during the first of four engagements at Prey Totung by his Shadow gunship crew:

> When we arrived on site, we could see activity on the ground. We contacted the ground commander and he informed us that they [the friendlies] were in the southwest corner of the town. The VC were in the rest of the town and firing on them. I located a machine gun site that was firing into the friendly positions. I put the crosshairs of the NOS on the site and gave consent to the pilot to shoot. He aligned the aircraft and started firing on the position. All hell broke loose; we immediately started getting a .51 cal shooting at us in our firing circle. There were six machine gun sites in our circle that opened up on us. They had us in what we called a "Shadow Trap."

As I looked into the NOS, trying to hold on the position, the streaks of light were coming up the barrel. I jumped back and I could see and hear the shells going by the left wing of the gunship. The noise was like popcorn popping on the stove. I backed up to the opposite side of the aircraft. I rethought my position. I was in aluminum aircraft and the bullets could go through any portion of it. So I forced myself to go back into the NOS and try to pinpoint the target again. I was having extreme problems trying to acquire the target and hold on to the NOS, as the streaks of tracer bullets were coming up the barrel straight at my eye.

All of a sudden the NOS went completely blank. If we were in sunlight, that might happen but not in the darkness of night. I asked the pilot, "What happened?" and our Flight Engineer stated that, "a big rocket just went by us and exploded." I immediately replied, "Let's get the hell out of here!" We broke the firing circle and regrouped. We called for extra reinforcements and resumed our attack. After expending all of our ammunition, we departed area, only to return for three more engagements at Prey Totung. After the four-day battle, the town was virtually destroyed, with the exception of where the friendly troops were located.[3]

It was estimated that at least 2,000 communist soldiers were killed during the four days and nights of fighting at Prey Totung, located forty-four miles northeast of Phnom Penh. A systematic body count was underway. A large portion of the estimated number of enemy killed was credited to strikes from U.S. fighter/bombers and gunships. Cambodian Paratroop Brigade Commander Lt. Col. Spey Yar claimed complete victory over communist forces. His paratroopers had led the resistance against wave after wave of enemy assaults on Cambodian positions.

Casualty numbers for the Cambodian forces was inconclusive. More than 100 wounded Cambodian soldiers were still waiting to be evacuated to Phnom Penh by helicopters

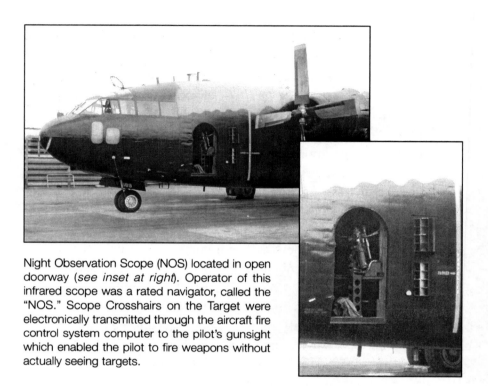

Night Observation Scope (NOS) located in open doorway (*see inset at right*). Operator of this infrared scope was a rated navigator, called the "NOS." Scope Crosshairs on the Target were electronically transmitted through the aircraft fire control system computer to the pilot's gunsight which enabled the pilot to fire weapons without actually seeing targets.

FOL Phu Cat Navigator/NOS Lt. Col. L.H. "Chris" Christopherson operating the Night Observation Scope. (*Courtesy of Bill Posey*)

***

As NVA attacks on Prey Totung were repulsed, Tang Kouk on Route 6 became the scene of furious fighting on 15 December. The ground radio operator Captain San Sok (aka SAM) with the radio call sign "Hotel 21" worked with Rustic FACs and Shadow gunships to fight-off an intense NVA attack. Tang Kouk was triangulated by three enemy 12.7mm machines guns inflicting heavy casualties on troops defending Tang Kouk while providing enhanced concentration of fire against aircraft. This tactic by NVA commanders worked well against the 360 degree firing orbit of the side-firing AC-119 gunships. Shadow pilots had to break-out of firing orbits to evade enemy fire, thus losing sight of enemy targets and enemy anti-aircraft gun positions. As a result, the on-scene Shadow gunship working targets for Hotel 21 was unable to locate the anti-aircraft gun positions.

To show the Shadow gun locations, the on-scene FAC, Rustic 21 (Major Richard Roberds) and IP Captain Mike Davenport (Rustic 17), flying an O-2, went "Christmas Tree" (i.e., turned on all his lights and dove earthward three different times), trolling for fire from the anti-aircraft guns to mark their location for the Shadow gunship. Intense gun fire resulted on each dive. Fortunately Rustic 21 was not hit as he turned out his lights and climbed to safety each time. The Shadow gunship finally located the enemy gun positions and commenced firing on their locations but had no success in silencing the weapons. Rustic then decided to request USAF fighter/bombers to attack the gun positions. With a flight of two F-100s launched and on the way to Tang Kouk, another Shadow gunship arrived on-scene and Rustic 21 repeated his Christmas Tree dives for the additional gunship to locate the enemy gun sites. Both gunships sprayed the enemy gun positions with thousands of 7.62mm bullets but still had no effect. This proved that the NVA gunners were most likely shielded by overhead protection in well-fortified bunkers. Upon the arrival of a Phan Rang-based two-ship flight of F-100s with the radio call sign of Blade, Rustic dove blacked out to mark the gun positions with smoke rockets. The F-100 Sabre jets wasted no time eliminating the three enemy guns with bombs. Blade flight followed their bombing runs with strafing of fleeing enemy troops up Route 6. Hotel 21 would live to see another day in Cambodia.[4]

Not long after, Lon Nol and the Cambodian government declared victory in Operation Chenla I, since the NVA had withdrawn and Route 6 was now open to relief convoys to KPT. Just as Lon Nol had over-estimated Cambodian military prowess in driving out North Vietnamese forces from sovereign territory in eastern provinces after his takeover, the reality that Route 6 was only temporarily open to government traffic and that road convoys to Kompong Thom were still in jeopardy. KPT was still under siege. The most dependable resupply route to the city was by riverine operations, using waterways from the Tonle Sap region during the wet season.

***

Cambodian air interdiction missions conducted on a 24/7 basis by Fighting C Flight during the months of October, November, and December of 1970 proved without a doubt to be highly successful. A total of 653 sorties were flown by Shadow gunships while TDY Stinger gunships assigned to C Flight helped out with sixty-six sorties in Cambodia. The Shadows were the primary air interdiction and deterrent force in Cambodia while credited with being the major factor in enabling FANK forces to successfully defend and maintain possession of population centers. Expenditures for the Shadows and Stingers during the three month period totaled 8,102,800 rounds of 7.62mm ammunition, 128,500 rounds of 20mm ammunition and 4,755 flares. The initial test results of 20mm API/HEI mixed ammunition expended by Stinger gunships in Cambodia were so favorable that it was decided to run similar tests in the Steel Tiger area of Laos.[5]

FOURTEEN

Recognition and Reports

A ir Bases from which Shadows operated offered various amenities to accommodate down-time of aircrew members and ground crew members. All bases obviously operated 24/7 in the war zone of South Vietnam. The most illustrious air base to be assigned was Tan Son Nhut Air Base (aka The Country Club). For 17th SOS personnel and even 18th SOS personnel assigned TDY to C Flight, the FOL was considered by many as a plush assignment, considering the state of war. Tan Son Nhut served as headquarters for 7th Air Force and MAC-V; thus, with the Republic of Vietnam's capital city, Saigon just outside the airport gates, the international gateway to the war zone was dubbed the busiest airport in the world.

When Fighting C Flight Shadow aircrews were not on alert status or flying missions or performing extra duties at Shadow Ops, there was time to sleep and rest. Off-duty time in the Shadow Flight was limited, but very precious and important. It was time to write letters home and to read letters from home or make tape recordings to send home or listen to tapes from home; a time to think about things like living. The batteries had to be recharged from the routine of fly, eat, and sleep. Physical activities like playing tennis, golf, handball, and basketball or just running helped keep flyers in good shape just in case of bailout and evading the enemy. Just relaxing in a safe environment was great. Reading or listening to music in the privacy of a barracks room helped calm the soul. Attending a movie at the base theater or a floor show at the club was part of getting away from the real world of war.

***

The drawdown of U.S. ground forces and relocation of USAF assets in Vietnam during 1970 opened and closed doors for remaining U.S. forces. The 45th Tactical Reconnaissance Squadron "Polkadot" detachment, consisting of sixteen RF-101C "Voodoo" jets and air crewmen departed Tan Son Nhut for Udorn RTAFB in Thailand by the time the detachment was inactivated in November 1970.[1] This was great news for Shadow officers of Fighting C Flight because the Voodoo's had vacated a private party hootch inside the fenced and guarded compound of air conditioned barracks reserved for flight officers such as Shadow pilots and navigators. The door was open!

Somehow, C Flight commander Lt. Col. Teal wrangled a deal with the base commander for the Shadows to inherit the "Voodoo" party hootch. Teal wrote,"...I made an appointment with the TSN base commander and asked for this place where off duty crewmembers could relax without going to the club with its dress code, etc. The base commander was reluctant to assign us such a place. I reminded him that Shadow was the only combat group on base that was firing real ammo at the enemy and flying around the clock, seven days a week and holidays. He said that he knew that, but did not want to set a precedent, etc. I must have been persistent in calls and visits to him because he relented and Shadow got its party hootch."[2]

Major Earl Farney wrote, "It was like heaven for Shadow men who dressed-up for the full-bird and star-laden officers club at Tan Son Nhut. We now had a private sanctuary right across the street from our barracks to unwind from combat missions at any hour of day or night and to socialize with other Shadow officers that we seldom got to see let alone know. Before the Shadow party hootch, Shadows gathered in individual barracks rooms or a commons area dayroom connecting two barracks, not fit for such anytime gatherings. Many Shadows slept while others were awake. A code of silence was respected within Shadow barracks. The hootch had couches and chairs, refrigerators and coolers for a cold beer anytime day or night. The hootch became the center for socializing of Shadow officers."[3]

Sight-seeing and dining-out in downtown Saigon and Cholon was convenient for those assigned to C Flight. The Flight continued their support through monetary and material donations that started in 1969 for the Thong Thain Hoc Orphanage in Saigon.

Periodic visits to the orphanage were made by Shadows to insure that monies and supplies for the orphanage were delivered and utilized for the benefit of the war orphans. The Flight continued support of the orphanage until departing Tan Son Nhut in 1971.

Upon Lt. Col. Teal's initiative, a dining-in/awards banquet was planned at the TSN Officer's Club for December. Teal stated, "After one of my Commander's Call at which I challenged C Flight to Make Shadow Proud, I overheard some officer crew members talking to each other and saying that the unit was doing a great job but who knew about it? I knew that we could not call in the reporters but there was a way to let the crews know that very important people knew about them and their missions. Seventh Air Force Vice-Commander Major General Earnest C. Hardin, Jr. who had flown as an observer almost monthly since June on Shadow missions over Cambodia was asked and accepted to be guest speaker at the dining-in. The pilots and crews who flew with General Hardin had nothing but respect for him."[4]

Accordingly, the upstairs room at the TSN O'Club was reserved and black Shadow party flight suits were designed and ordered at a decent price for Fighting C Flight Shadowmen for the occasion by Captain Jose Cachuela. Shadow 1 plaques were designed by Lt. Col. Teal and ordered to present to individuals outside the 17th SOS who had helped C Flight achieve success over Cambodia.

Unexpectedly, very special guests arrived at Tan Son Nhut just in time for the banquet. Shadowmen of Fighting C Flight would finally get

Cambodia officers visit Fighting C Flight at Tan Son Nhut in 1970
(*left to right*): Maj. Chak Bory, Lt. Tim Tang, Lt. Col. Tom Teal, Lt.
Col. Lieou Phin Oum, Capt. Nil, and Capt. Yarman.

to meet in-person some of the Cambodian ground commanders who
they had worked with for months over the radio while providing direct
air support. A five-man delegation of Cambodian officers led by recently promoted Lieutenant Colonel Lieou Phin Oum (Hotel 303) was
flown via a VNAF C-119 from Phnom Penh to Tan Son Nhut. Seventh
Air Force protocol asked if the Cambodians wished to see the 7th AF
Headquarters. They responded graciously and indicated they preferred
to go immediately to Shadow Operations on the flight line.

The Cambodians brought with them gifts from the Cambodian government for all Fighting C Flight officers in appreciation of dedicated air support by Shadows. In addition, the Khmer Republic (Cambodian govern-

Shadow Navigator Capt. James Craig (*left*) talks with 7th Air Force Vice-Commander General Earnest C. Hardin, Jr. at the fall 1970 Shadow Dining-In/Awards Banquet held at the Tan Son Nhut Officers Club.

ment) presented a statuette trophy to the 17th Special Operations Squadron in gratitude for the air support provided by AC-119 Shadow gunships.

Included in the five member delegation were Maj. Chak Bory (Hotel 302), Lt. Tim Tang, Capt. Nil, and Capt. Yarman. They stood before Lt. Col. Teal with tears in their eyes. Oum and Bory had directed endless hours of Shadow air cover of Kompong Thom during the fourteen-day siege of Kompong Thom. And still fresh on their minds was the fact that their troops and city residents had to butcher and eat animals from the zoo in order to survive.

Major Earl Farney recorded on cassette tape the event held in Shadow Ops. Major Bory in a chocked-up voice said, "Colonel Teal, I am having difficulty expressing myself. We of the Cambodian 10th Brigade wish to thank the Shadows for saving our lives...." His words broke and he could say no more. The usually tough Shadow crewmembers present got up and walked out. They didn't want anyone to see their tears. The GI Shadow walked tall, my friend; particularly this day. Every Shadow crew and staff man received a grateful gift from the surviving men of the 10th.

High ranking officers from the 14th SOW at Phan Rang also attended the banquet in addition to special guests from 7th AF HQ along with the Cambodian delegation. Two very pretty Vietnamese waitresses in tailored Shadow party suits (that fit oh-so-well) served dinner and drinks. After dinner, General Hardin gave a short talk addressing the importance of Shadow's mission followed by his pinning DFC and Air Medals approved in November for Fighting C Flight Shadow pilots and navigators while citations of each award was read aloud. Guests receiving the Shadow 1 plaques from Fighting C Flight were General Hardin, Lt. Col. Teal's "Contact Colonel" at 7th AF Headquarters, and Lt. Col. Oum.

During a short visit to the packed Shadow Party Hootch after the banquet, Lt. Col. Oum reconfirmed that *Playboy* magazines had been great morale boosters for his troops and he again thanked the Shadowmen for close-air support which saved Kompong Thom. Again, Maj. Farney recorded the event on tape. Maj. Bory spoke:

> I would like to salute all you gentlemen. I am so glad to be able to come over here. My dream has come true. I thought it was not possible. Thank you for all you have done for us. You always came in time when we needed help. On behalf of our commander and our families, we want to thank you. We are so happy to be able to see you. We were many; many months away from our families in Phnom Penh…I am short of words, sir. I can tell you, all you gentlemen; you not only came over our places to fight away the bad guys, you took care of us. You inquired every time you came over our position. Well, how is your situation, Hotel 302? Looks like you are going to stand; how is your ammunition, how many wounded? Oh, sir; we took some rounds from the south from

the "sawmill." Well Shadow, it's hard to express our opinion. Anytime you came over, one, two, three hour, we got some sleep. No fresh food, no cigarettes, very little anything. But you got the convoy through! I say once again our true thanks, and to all the people of the United States; you helped a peaceful people get their freedom back. I hope it lasts. Thank you and we salute you once again.[5]

Then Col. Oum spoke, "Major Bory's expression of gratitude was great. I wish to say thank you one more time."

After the Cambodian officers finished, a Shadow pilot, Lt. Fletcher, responded:

I was there in the beginning of June 1970 when Kompong Thom was first starting to be attacked by the Viet Cong. In those days, we were known as Shadow 75, 77, or 78. We only flew at night and I'm sure that many times you wondered what we looked like and what kind of an airplane we flew. Your call sign then was Cambodia Trooper 302 and Hotel Tonle. We'd shoot at the edge of the city limits and sometimes within the city. Almost always we shot at the "Chinese graveyard" and at the "sawmill." It seemed like the VC always launched an attack from these positions. As we started flying in the daytime, we could see Kompong Thom much better and it was such a beautiful city in the beginning, before the bombing started. We all admire Hotel 302 and 303 and all you Cambodians for the stamina and bravery you have shown in these months and in the months to come. We'd see mortars, rockets, and machine gun tracers. We'd see all that fire into Kompong Thom and wonder how you survived it, but after meeting you personally, we know how strong and wonderful Cambodian people really are. I hope we can always be friends and your country and my country can live in peace forever. Thank you."[6]

During the following days, all Cambodian delegation members were briefed on the capabilities of the Shadow and how to best utilize the gunship. Each Cambodian flew at least one combat mission on a Shadow gunship over Cambodia during their visit to Tan Son Nhut.

***

With Operation Chenla I concluded in mid-December, the ARVN launched another offensive in a series of Toan Thang operations with extensive sweeps of Chup Plantation in Cambodia. With air support of VNAF and USAF aircraft, the ARVN captured a number of large caches of petroleum, rice, ammunition, and heavy road repair equipment.[7]

For the month of December 1970, Fighting C Flight reported the following statistics to Headquarters 17th SOS for Shadow actions in Cambodia:

Killed By Air: 374 (Confirmed)
Wounded By Air: 13 (Confirmed)
Trucks Destroyed: 4   Trucks Damaged: 28
Carts Damaged: 2
Two-Wheel Vehicles Damaged or Destroyed: 36
Other Vehicles Damaged or Destroyed: 41
Sampans Destroyed: 7   Sampans Damaged: 149

Fighting C Flight Operations Officer Lt. Col. Bill Gregory summarized Flight operations for the months of July thru early December in a report submitted to 17th SOS Headquarters:

	Fragged	Flown	Air Aborts	Ground Aborts
July	60 (III&IV Corps)	23 (III Corps)	0	0
		58 (Cambodia 'V' Corps)		
Aug.	60 (III & IV Corps)	219 (Cambodia)	2	2
Sep.	228	231	1	1
Oct.	248	249	5	3
Nov.	240	245	7	-
Dec.	88	89	1	-

Note: All C Flight missions from September forward were flown in Cambodia.[8]

***

The command and control function in Cambodia at this time was exercised through the airborne extension of the TACC at 7th AF Headquarters, called TACCA. Two EC-121R aircraft from Korat Royal Thai Air Force Base (RTAFB) provided almost continuous coverage from pre-dawn to dusk. TACCA was unique in that there were representatives from Cambodia, Thailand, South Vietnam, and the U.S. onboard the aircraft. The Cambodian representative had authority to validate targets for Shadow strikes. As with the ABCCC in Laos, TACCA could order air strikes, but most often deferred the decision to TACC.[9]

***

Commander of the 17th SOS, Lt. Col. Ed Elbert, summarized his conclusions of squadron actions in the quarterly report covering October, November, and December 1970 to the 14th SOW:

> From the experience of "C" Flight, it is concluded that mating Shadow/Stinger aircraft with Rustic FACs in Cambodia has provided flexibility and increased target coverage. Combined with the expanded ROEs and the pre-cleared interdiction areas, timely and more effective strikes on enemy movements are possible. The use of an airborne command and control center has made the request and granting of clearances to fire much easier and timely. This has had the effect of shortening time between requesting clearance and getting the clearance [to expend], which makes support of friendly units much easier. With all the improvements in tactics, and command and control the flexibility of response and speed of response to enemy activity has been greatly increased.
>
> The operations of "A" and "B" Flights in Laos has proved the survivability of the AC-119G (Shadow) during night operations over that country. With proper routing and precautions, the G series 119 has been able to survive the crossing of the Ho Chi Minh Trail with minimal danger. The use of

AC-119G aircraft in support of Laotian ground forces has proven its worth. While the Shadow gunships were overhead, there was no friendly position that was overrun.

The prognosis for the next quarter, January thru March 1971, is continued operations by "C" Flight over Cambodia with "B" Flight covering the Bolovens Plateau in Laos and Military Regions II and III in South Vietnam."[10]

At the end of December, the 17th SOS reported personnel levels at ninety-nine officers and 174 airmen for a total of 273 men in the squadron. Sixteen AC-119G gunships were primary to the mission of the squadron with one AC-119G gunship as back-up during phase. Four 7.62mm machine guns per aircraft remained standard along with electronics of one fire control computer per aircraft, one fire central display per aircraft, Sony tape recorders series 500. A two million candlepower spotlight and flare launcher with the capacity for twenty-four U.S. Navy Mark 24 Mod 4 flares remained aboard the gunships.

Commanding personnel of the 17th SOS at the end of December were: Lieutenant Colonel Edward A. Elbert, Commander; Lt. Col. Alfred I. Flynn, Squadron Operations Officer; Lt. Col. John M. Fear, Squadron Navigator; Maj. Thomas V. Soltys, Squadron Executive Officer; Maj. Stanley M. Maillet, Squadron Administrative Officer; Capt. Thomas Hughes, Squadron Maintenance Officer; and MSgt James E. Manker, Squadron First Sergeant.

FOL B Flight commanding personnel at the time were: Lieutenant Colonel Bill R. Whitesell, who replaced Lt. Col. Flynn as Commander of "B" Flight while Flynn prepared to rotate back to the states; Flynn continued to serve as Flight and Squadron Operations Officer until his DEROS; and Maj. Stanley M. Maillet, Flight Administrative Officer.

FOL C Flight at Tan Son Nhut commanding personnel were: Lieutenant Colonel Tom A. Teal, Commander; Lt. Col. William B. Gregory, Operations Officer; and Maj. Earl J. Farney, Flight Administrative Officer.

From 1 October to 10 October, the seventeen (17) AC-119G aircraft of the 17th SOS were deployed as follows:

A Flight at Phu Cat – 5
B Flight at Phan Rang – 6 (plus one aircraft in phase)
C Flight at Tan Son Nhut – 5

From 10 October to 27 November, The seventeen AC-119G aircraft of the 17th SOS were deployed as follows:
A Flight at Phu Cat – 2
B Flight at Phan Rang – 3 (plus on aircraft in phase)
C Flight at Tan Son Nhut – 11

From 27 November until 29 December, the deployment of aircraft remained unchanged at Phu Cat and Phan Rang. Tan Son Nhut lost two aircraft when expanded phase inspection facilities were able to handle two aircraft at a time and the other aircraft was sent to Kadena AFB, Okinawa for Corrosion Control. During the remainder of the reporting period, aircraft were rotated to keep one in Corrosion Control at all times. Consequently, AC-119G aircraft deployment at the end of 1970 consisted of the following:
B Flight at Phan Rang – 5 (plus two aircraft in phase at Phan Rang)
C Flight at Tan Son Nhut – 9
Corrosion Control at Okinawa – 1

Training and upgrading aircrew and ground maintenance personnel within the squadron was enhanced with expanded missions out-country during the quarter. Adequate time was made available for beginning preparations for the VNAF training program in AC-119G gunships scheduled to begin on 1 February 1971. Maintenance of aircraft proved to be supreme as maintenance crew chiefs and their maintenance crews worked day and night to keep the gunships combat ready.

Lieutenant Colonel Tom Teal expressed his thoughts about the real everyday world of aircraft maintenance personnel in Fighting C Flight,

> The unsung and underappreciated men who kept us in the
> air and over Cambodia. It is hard to imagine how difficult it

is to prepare, get parts for and keep flying for months on end old propeller driven aircraft. To add to the luster of our C Flight maintenance were a lot of on-time takeoffs. Of course our backup system of standby or launch was a big help, but the maintenance task of readying six or eight combat ready sorties, fueled, armed, pre-flights, post-flights, and discrepancy free (gunships) per day was a gargantuan task that took steel nerves, an eye on the clock, and the dedication to work in rain, heat, night and tiring circumstances.[11]

During December 1970, the following 17th SOS flight crewmembers received the Distinguished Flying Cross:

1 December: Captain J.L. Hope and 1/Lt. P.C. Moran.

8 December: First Lieutenant R.C. Allen, 1/Lt. J.E. Gibson, 1/Lt. J.C. Williams, SSgt L.G. Kincaid, SSgt R.S. Friese, SSgt W.J. George, SSgt G.A. Renfroe, Jr., TSgt H.T. Coste, Jr., Maj. T.V. Soltys, 1/Lt. W.C. Lamont, 1/Lt. E.C. French, and Maj. W.W. Ware.

14 December: Sergeant L.A. Miner

27 December: First Lieutenant R.B. Sizemore, A1C W.M. Gelches, and Sgt R.K. Layton.

30 December: Sergeant R.J. Carlson, Jr., TSgt H.T. Coste, Jr., and 1/Lt. R.W. Mundle.

31 December: Staff Sergeant W.J. Drabek.[12]

FIFTEEN

New Year, New Mission

The 17th Special Operations Squadron started the new year of 1971 with high expectations and anticipation. Having completed one year and six months of successful combat operations in Southeast Asia since activation in June 1969, the Squadron faced the additional task of training the VNAF for eventual take-over of Shadow gunship operations.

During January, the 17th SOS at Phan Rang made final preparations for the February arrival of the first three VNAF aircrews to be trained in the AC-119 Shadow gunship as part of the VNAF I & M program (aka "Vietnamization" of the war). Squadron personnel were assigned for instructor duty and various other positions in the training school. Preparation for the VNAF I & M program involved major groundwork in the procurement of equipment and supplies, securing and preparing training facilities, and preparing instructional materials like lesson plans and training aids.

VNAF/USAF Joint Programmed Directive 71-106, 30 Nov 70, charged the 17th Squadron with VNAF combat crew training in the AC-119G. VNAF AC-119G aircrews started basic gunship schooling at Tan Son Nhut Air Base, Saigon. Fifty South Vietnamese pilots, half of them experienced in VNAF C-119G aircraft and the other half fresh from flight training in the United States joined recent graduates of navigator school in forming the nucleus of VNAF AC-119G gunship crews. AC-119 flight mechanics and illuminator (flare and searchlight) operators had also learned their specialties in the United States prior to teaming with pilots and navigators at Tan Son Nhut. Once brought together, each crew received additional training flying with American crews and final indoctrination before reporting to the 17th Special Operations Squadron, 14th Special Operations Wing at Phan Rang for the last phase of gunship training.[1]

When the 71st SOS AC-119 gunship force was forming and training in 1968, President Nixon had revealed plans for American troop withdrawals from Vietnam and for Vietnamization of the war. His plan for South Vietnam military forces called for the South Vietnamese to completely take over their fight against communist aggression, during and after complete withdrawal of American ground forces.

One of many I & M programs began in 1968 when handpicked VNAF C-47 crews were selected for transition to C-119G Flying Boxcars. VNAF air and ground crews received C-119 training in CONUS at Ellington AFB, Texas from USAF reservists from the 446th TCW and additional training by a detachment of USAF instructors stationed at Tan Son Nhut Air Base, RVN. By March 1968, sixteen C-119G aircraft were assigned to the VNAF 53rd Tactical Wing, 413th Transport Squadron (TS). Three more C-119Gs were transferred to the 413th in 1970. Top-quality VNAF pilots and aircrew members of the 413th TS would eventually enter 17th SOS gunship training at Phan Rang to become AC-119G gunship crews.[2] Some VNAF C-119G pilots were checked out in Phase I training at Clinton County AFB, Ohio, followed by Phase II aircrew training at Phan Rang.

A total of twenty-four VNAF gunship crews were scheduled for training in AC-119G Shadow gunships, initially to be ready for combat by 1 May 1972. But the ultimate plan and target date for the 17th SOS was to turn over all Shadow gunships and equipment with USAF-trained and qualified personnel to the VNAF by 1 September 1971. This was consistent with the Nixon administration's push for full-Vietnamization of the war that included bigger and better VNAF fixed-wing gunship capabilities. On that September date, the 17th Special Operations Squadron was scheduled to relinquish all AC-119G gunships plus specific maintenance and supply equipment to the VNAF who would then frag all AC-119G missions.

In addition to the VNAF training program for the 17th SOS at Phan Rang, 14th SOW still fragged 17th SOS "Bravo" Flight at Phan Rang for combat sorties in Vietnam and Laos that would expand further during the New Year. Fighting C Flight at Tan Son Nhut was still fragged to defend Cambodia. With deactivation of 17th SOS FOL Alpha Flight at Phu Cat Air Base at the end of December 1970, Bravo Flight at Phan Rang AB absorbed Alpha Flight assets of gunships and personnel.

The successful Cambodian Incursion in May and June 1970 had become advantageous for the I & M program for South Vietnamese armed forces. The diverted war from South Vietnam to Cambodia relieved the pressure of communist attacks in RVN. As a result, withdrawal of American forces and personnel from RVN could be accomplished without delay and the armed forces of South Vietnam could be sufficiently trained to assume major combat roles. Consequently under the consolidated I & M program, the VNAF had increased from twenty-two squadrons with 486 aircraft in mid-summer 1970 to 30 squadrons consisting of 706 aircraft by the end of 1970.

For 7th Air Force Commander General Lucius D. Clay, Jr., sharing facilities and services at air bases with VNAF personnel had become serious during the drawdown of American personnel during 1970 and would continue during 1971. Air bases in RVN deemed critical to USAF 7th AF operations while Vietnamization was taking hold included DaNang, Bien Hoa, and Tan Son Nhut.

In preparation for training VNAF crews in the AC-119 Shadow gunship, four 17th SOS Shadow gunship instructor crews were removed from combat operations and made instructor crews for the I&M Program at Phan Rang. An instructor crew consisted of one pilot (IP), one navigator (IN), one flight engineer (IFE), one gunner (IAG), and one illuminator operator (IIO). With the removal of twenty-one crewmen from combat operations, workloads on remaining combat crews in Bravo and Charlie Flights increased.

Lieutenant Colonel William E. Cosner was designated 14th SOW Chief of VNAF Training. 17th SOS personnel assigned to the original USAF cadre for the I & M Program were: Lieutenant Colonel J.M. Fear, I & M Project Officer; MSgt W.C. Rhoades, IFE; Maj. D. E. Fraker, Chief, VNAF Training & IP; MSgt L.D. Mott, IFE; Maj. W.E. Dickson, IP; TSgt J. Hallahan, IIO; Maj. W.A. Gericke, Jr., IN; SSgt J.J. Anderson, IFE; Maj. R.L. Lindley, IN; SSgt J.B. Osborne, I&M Clerk; Capt. B.S. Harmer, IP; SSgt J.R. Ramsey, Illustrator; Capt. W.H. King, IN; Sgt E.M. McCallion, IIO; and A1C C.S. Churchill, IIO.

The following 17th SOS Weapons Mechanics (Aerial Gunners) supported the I & M Program during the flying phases of training: Technical Sergeant. N.J. Evans, TSgt S.G. Jiminez, SSgt D.G. Fisher, SSgt W.J. George, SSgt G.R. Renfroe, Sgt R.M. Flak, Sgt M.G. Logan, Sgt W.J. Zito, and A1C J.R. Grieg.

I & M Program Phase I training at Phan Rang involved five days of ground school to introduce gunship tactics to each VNAF class. Phase II and III involved flight training, consisting of twenty-three missions per crew to develop gunship skills thru airborne demonstration and instruction by USAF instructor crews. Upon graduation from Phan Rang, VNAF crews would report to Tan Son Nhut for Phase IV training consisting of continued flight training to increase crew coordination until qualifying for combat ready status.

Between January and March, a total of seven AC-119G aircraft were released by USAF to become a part of the VNAF I & M Program. The gunships arrived from CONUS at Phan Rang without cockpit armor and none could be procured. The 17th petitioned 7th AF to allow these seven aircraft to be used for both training and combat missions provided that during daylight hours the gunship would fly no lower than "C" altitude (3500 feet). 7th AF approved the request with the stipulation that the aircraft be flown at "D" altitude (4500 feet) during daylight missions and at no lower than "B" altitude (2500 feet) at night. Cockpit armor was ordered for the seven gunships and was expected to arrive in a few months.

From 1 January to 24 February 71, AC-119G Shadow gunships of the 17th SOS were deployed as follows: "B" Flight, Phan Rang, 8 (plus two

gunships in phase); "C" Flight, Tan Son Nhut, 10; C & C, Kadena, Okinawa, 2; IRAN, Taipei, Taiwan, 1; and en route from CONUS.[3]

During this time, the 17th SOS possessed twenty-three G model AC-
119 Shadow gunships operated by fifteen American aircrews. With ten
gunships and twelve crews assigned to C Flight, 17th SOS and Bravo
Flight at Phan Rang possessed thirteen gunships for three USAF combat
aircrews, VNAF training, phase maintenance and corrosion control.

By 22 January 1971, all Fighting C Flight aircrews were faced with
increased workloads. The Flight had lost some of its most experienced
and valuable flight crew members from combat operations to form the
Shadow instructor crews for the VNAF I & M Program. With the loss of
key flight personnel to the VNAF training program plus the loss of aircraft commanders headed stateside, the Tactical Call Signs at 17th SOS
Fighting C Flight were updated in early February with the addition of
newly up-graded aircraft commanders and new instructor aircraft commanders in SECRET FLASH PT 00009 from 7th Air Force/DOPF to 14
SOW, 17 SOS and 18 SOS as follows:

Lt. Col. Teal, Shadow 05	Lt. Col. Gregory, Shadow 06
Lt. Col. James, Shadow 07	Capt. Cunningham, Shadow 11
Capt. Howze, Shadow 12	Capt. Heiner, Shadow 14
Capt. Smith, Shadow 15	Capt. Walker, Shadow 17
Capt. Gustin, Shadow 18	Capt. Weise, Shadow 19
Capt. Simmons, Shadow 21	Maj. Carter, R., Shadow 22
Capt. James, Shadow 24	Capt. Carter, Shadow 25
Capt. Van Over, Shadow 26	1/Lt. Fletcher, Shadow 27
Capt. Lefarth, Shadow 28	Capt. Batchelder, Shadow 29
Capt. McNamara, Shadow 30	Capt. Ruester, Shadow 31
1/Lt. Carlson, Shadow 32	1/Lt. Derr, Shadow 33
Capt. Walker, G., Shadow 35	1/Lt. Keller, Shadow 35.

Subsequently, Fighting C Flight was fragged for eight sorties per
twenty-four-hour day instead of seven; to pick up the slack. Now with
forty-eight flight officers to make up twelve complete combat crews to

man ten Shadow gunships was quite a change from the pre-Cambodia Campaign days back in June 1970 when C Flight was manned by six full combat crews with four extra pilots (two of which were flight commander White and incoming flight commander Teal and four extra navigators (two of which were flight administrative officers) to conduct combat operations with only five Shadow gunships. The closing of 17th SOS Alpha Flight at Phu Cat at the end of December 1970 and following reallocation of gunships and crews between Bravo and Charlie Flights had bolstered the number of Shadow gunships to ten and the number of aircrews to twelve at FOL Tan Son Nhut.

**

The dry season created by the northwestern monsoon was well entrenched in all of Southeast Asia military operating areas which produced favorable weather conditions conducive to enemy movement and combat operations. Commando Hunt V, the third large MACV air interdiction campaign against NVA dry season efforts to resupply their forces in South Vietnam, Cambodia, and Laos through southern Laos "Steel Tiger" region, had begun on 10 October 1970 and was still underway.

U.S. air support in Cambodia remained centered around Fighting C Flight AC-119G Shadow gunships based at Tan Son Nhut AB, RVN. Without interruption, Shadows of Saigon continued their twenty-four hours a day coverage over the country. Troops-in-contact still took first priority in missions of Shadow gunships, followed by convoy escort and armed reconnaissance in turn. On many occasions, the Shadow performed all three missions on one sortie.[4]

Armed reconnaissance and interdiction of enemy infiltration routes was performed during fragged sorties for Shadows in Cambodia when there was no requirement to support TICs or to provide armed escort for air, land, or riverine convoys. AC-119 Shadow gunships were required to stay within fifteen minutes flying time of the Phnom Penh/Kompong Cham region.

Seventh Air Force commanders employed the concept of immediate sorties to conserve resources in Cambodia. Using this concept, USAF A-37s, F-100s, and F-4s were able to strike the most lucrative targets while providing only critical air support without flying unnecessary sorties. In addition to tactical air strikes in Cambodia, USAF B-52s flew Arc Light strikes against known enemy locations.

***

As a first lieutenant Shadow gunship line pilot assigned to Fighting C Flight at TSN, I (yours truly) didn't always fully comprehend the "big picture" of the war in Southeast Asia, particularly Cambodia and the importance of 17th Special Operations Squadron operations. Consequently, I learned from reading *7th Air Force News* and *Stars & Stripes,* plus *Newsweek* and *Time* magazines purchased at the TSN air base newsstand. While pulling duty officer at Shadow Ops, I also learned from reading past and current action reports, some of which I typed. Classified reports ranged from secret to top secret.

While thinking that Shadow operations in Cambodia were still classified SECRET in late January 1971, I was shocked when I read a January news article in one of my favorite publications. I couldn't believe what was being divulged to the public about air operations in Cambodia. And the scary part was the reported source of information was the Pentagon. The Pentagon reported that U.S. air strikes in Cambodia had increased to their highest level since August 1970 when 1,770 sorties were flown by U.S. fighter-bombers, gunships and B-52 bombers. U.S. bombers and gunships flew close to 1,700 sorties during December 1970 and approximately 600 sorties were flown thus far in the first ten days of current month of January 1971.

Justification for the air campaign in Cambodia was stated using the Nixon administration's interpretation of congressional mandates prohibiting use of American ground troops in Cambodia, but allowance for use of American warplanes. The Vietnam War had certainly moved to Cambodia; a diversion from South Vietnam to protect U.S. ground troops and support personnel stationed in South Vietnam while withdrawal of U.S. ground troops from South Vietnam and Vietnamization of the war was taking place. So much for secrecy!

**

From January thru March 1971, the 17th SOS maintained a total of fifteen complete USAF combat crews; three at Phan Rang and twelve at Tan Son Nhut. The assigned personnel were qualified in their specialties and required only orientation and upgrading. No formal training was conducted within the squadron except for the VNAF I & M Program. In preparation for VNAF crews to fly with Fighting C Flight at Tan Son Nhut, starting 10 April, two additional instructor crews, consisting of pilots and navigators, were upgraded. These instructor crews would fly with the VNAF crews operating as a part of Fighting C Flight combat operations.

In-country training of USAF replacement personnel for the 17th SOS was headed by 17th Squadron Training Officer, Captain Arthur L. Law and C Flight Training Officer, Major Ralph Riojas. Extensive OJT training and testing programs proved satisfactory for replacement personnel trained in CONUS.[5]

Aircraft maintenance was superb with only minor problems. Many times aircraft replacement parts were not immediately available due to the age and special equipment of the gunship. Begging and borrowing spare parts from the VNAF C-119 unit stationed at Tan Son Nhut was not uncommon for Fighting C Flight gunship crew chiefs and mechanics. Fighting C Flight CO Lt. Col. Teal stated, "We were blessed to be co-located with a VNAF C-119 Wing on base [Tan Son Nhut] that was willing to share their aircraft parts with us. Propeller regulators were a big problem from time to time as well as spare engines. Our Air Force supply line would dry up at times on these as well as other parts due to excessive demand for them. The VNAF seldom turned us down. It was a sort of reverse Lend-Lease."[6] In the end, maintenance was able, through dedication and experience, to keep the fleet of gunships operational ready for combat missions.

Because of increased numbers of enlisted flight personnel assigned to Fighting C Flight at Tan Son Nhut after the beginning of the New Year, the shuttle bus schedule for enlisted flight crewmembers between off-base quarters at the Merlin Hotel and the TSN flight line was changed from running every hour to every half hour. Maintenance personnel continued living in non-air-conditioned Quonset huts on-base at TSN.

Bravo Flight continued support of its main civic action project of issuing scholarships under the Dollars for Scholars Program to students at Nguyen Tru High School in Phan Rang City. Charlie Flight continued its support of the Thong Thein Orphanages (Thong Thain Hoc Orphanage) in Saigon. The Flight provided medical assistance that included 50 pounds of medical supplies, over 100 articles of clothing, 100 pounds of cleaning materials, and 40 pounds of candy to the orphanage. During the TET celebration on 28 January, Fighting C Flight provided fresh fruit for the children.[7]

***

On the night of 23 January 1971, a Shadow gunship and a Rustic FAC working a TIC together about nine miles north of Phnom Penh witnessed the sky erupt with explosive lights to the south. Enemy rockets and mortars shot skyward from the vicinity of the airport as Shadow and Rustic concluded their TIC operations and flew toward Phnom Penh.

Cambodia's major airport was definitely under attack. Pochentong Airport at Phnom Penh was hit by NVA sappers under cover of a rocket attack, eliminating most aircraft of the Cambodian Air Force, which suffered the loss of sixty-one aircraft from an original inventory of eighty-seven. Destroyed in the satchel charge attack were the Russian MiGs, French Magisters, and most of the helicopters along with the Cambodian national airline Camboge that consisted of one twin engine jet transport French Caravelle. Of the remaining twenty-six aircraft, nineteen were operational (5 T-28, 4 C-47, 4 YAK-18, and 6 Horizon aircraft).[8]

Two more Shadow gunships from Tan Son Nhut were quickly dispatched to Phnom Penh by 7th Air Force to fire on enemy rocket sites and gun emplacements until the area around the airport was secure. Thereafter, Shadow gunships provided continual nighttime coverage to prevent a recurrence of the attack until Cambodian troops could adequately secure the area around Phnom Penh and Pochentong Airport.

The damage was done; the NVA had struck the Cambodians in the heart of Cambodian life. Their capital city of Phnom Penh was to become a city under siege just like their key province capital cities. NVA troops were effectively isolating Phnom Penh from its sources of food, fuel and supplies. The communist noose around Phnom Penh was tightening. Strangulation of the capital city was just a matter of time unless the tide of war could be altered in favor of the Khmer Republic.

Cambodia Route 4, the major highway between the nation's capital city and Kompong Som, the nation's major deep-water seaport along with its sole oil refineries and storage tanks located on the Gulf of Thailand, was highly vulnerable to NVA/Khmer Rouge attacks. Enemy ambushes and blockades of supply truck convoys destined for Phnom Penh along Route 4, particularly at the Pich Nil Pass, soon became common. Pich Nil Pass was located in the Elephant Chain of the Cardamom Mountains approximately sixty miles southwest of Phnom Penh.[9]

Fighting C Flight Shadow gunships were directed to provide air cover and direct fire support for Cambodian truck convoys on Route 4 (aka the "American Highway") that was constructed with U.S. financing during previous years of friendly relations with Prince Sihanouk. Shadows were also directed to provide direct fire support of ground operations conducted along Route 4 by units of the FANK and ARVN.

As early as September 1970, the FANK commander in charge of Route 4 security recommended closure of the highway at night because FANK troops were unable to insure its security. Enemy troops moved about with impunity from positions to the west on the Kiriron Plateau. By 24 November 1970, Route 4 was closed to friendly traffic because Pich Nil Pass was controlled by NVA forces. FANK counter-offenses to reopen the highway were immediately undertaken but after weeks of see-saw struggles with NVA forces, the offensive stalled short of the objective. Upon the arrival of ARVN units that reinforced the FANK, Pich Nil Pass was overtaken and returned to friendly control on 22 January.[10]

In a joint military campaign to eliminate communist attacks and blockades of truck convoys on the 115 miles of strategic Route 4 between Phnom Penh and Kompong Som, the republic's sole port facility, Cambodian and South Vietnamese forces launched operations on 2 January 1971. Two USN helicopter carrier warships, anchored off the Cambodian gulf coast provided support for the campaign. The campaign officially ended 23 days later on 25 January 1971.

During the Cambodian/South Vietnamese campaign to retake the Pich Nil Pass and open Route 4 from Phnom Penh to Kompong Som, Fighting C Flight Shadows from Tan Son Nhut operated day and night in support of the joint operation, especially when friendly troops made contact with enemy forces. Shadows were able to amass a substantial record of kills during aerial attacks.[11]

***

At Kompong Thom (KPT), approximately thirteen hundred soldiers filled the ranks of the FANK Tenth Brigade under command of Lt. Col. Oum. They defended the city against constant harassment and attacks from surrounding communist forces. The city remained a city under siege. Route 6 was still vulnerable to enemy attacks and unreliable as a supply route. The only reliable route for relief supplies was by waterways from the Tonle Sap during the wet season.

Decreased production in and transportation of agricultural products from the central region of Cambodia was impacting the stability of the nation. Communist troops concentrated on interrupting transportation routes and confiscating Cambodian goods by attacking Skoun at the junction of Routes 6 and 7 and Kompong Cham located on Route 7 at the Mekong River. Friendly commerce on the Mekong suffered from communist ambushes. The river was still a major infiltration and supply route for communist forces.

With shortages of food from the central region of the country and a shortage of fuel from its seaport at Kompong Som, Phnom Penh and its government strongholds at KPT, KPC, and Siem Reap were extremely pressed for food, fuel, and war supplies.

Safety of all relief convoys traveling by land or by water in Cambodia soon became a top priority. Convoys supplied the life blood for the new Republic and its Army, the FANK. Shadow escort missions for convoys became increasingly important as the Republic of Cambodia struggled to survive. Decisions were made to provide continuous aerial coverage of convoys with FACs and/or gunships with the capability to call-in other air support resources like fighter/bombers when needed.

Friendly convoys traversing the seventy miles of the Mekong River from the South Vietnam border to Phnom Penh were highly subject to enemy attacks by fire at practically any point on the waterway. Enemy

elements had relative freedom of movement throughout the area, especially in the dry season. For attacks on convoys, the enemy usually
chose narrow spots that provided protection from aerial observation and
at the same time, afforded adequate escape routes. All points on the
river were within recoilless rifle and mortar range. River width varied
from 400 meters to 2,000 meters during the dry season from November
to May. The terrain along the river was flat to gently rolling, with light
vegetation in most areas. Because of the poor drainage, there were many
swamps and extensive rice paddies in all areas along the Mekong.

To relieve Phnom Penh, riverine relief convoys of ocean-going
freighters and river barges plowed the brown waters of the Mekong
River from South Vietnam to the capital city of Cambodia to relieve
fuel, food, and munitions shortages. USAF C-130 and C-141 transport
planes flew some supplies into Pochentong Airport in spite of sporadic
NVA rocket and mortar attacks on the airport and city. The aerial supply
line was inadequate as were road convoys for the emergency relief effort
to sustain the threatened capital; plus exposure of U.S. transport planes
to enemy attack was deemed unwise. Therefore, the navigable Mekong
would become the major lifeline for the Khmer Republic.

In early January, the American Embassy in Phnom Penh reported critical shortages of petroleum, oil, and lubricants (POL) in the Khmer Republic (KR) that had resulted from successful enemy attacks on commercial
shipping vessels sailing the Mekong River inside Cambodia. The fact that
eight attacks between 26 November 1970 and 6 January 1971 on civilian
POL tankers transiting the Mekong between the KR-RVN border and Phnom Penh had effectively threatened to block vital POL and military
cargo into Cambodia. These attacks combined with the closure of Route 4
from the seaport city of Kompong Som prompted the United States, the
Khmer Republic, and the Republic of Vietnam to militarily protect
Mekong River convoys from Tan Chau, RVN to Phnom Penh. Thereafter,
the three nations agreed to a Combined Convoy Security Plan for the
Mekong River that was implemented on 12 January.

The Convoy Security Plan provided air and surface protection to military and commercial convoys on the Mekong River from Tan Chau,
RVN to Phnom Penh. Tran Hung Dao XVIII was the code name se-

lected by the South Vietnamese Navy (VNN) to represent the combined naval operations of both VNN and the KR. The operation entailed the assemblage of tankers, barges, and merchant ships at Tan Chau to form a convoy destined for Phnom Penh. The South Vietnamese Convoy Operations Commander was responsible for coordinating river, air, and riverbank defenses.[12]

Depending on convoy size, the number of VNN vessels covering the convoy varied in numbers but usually provided a group of advance, escort, and reaction vessels. For a convoy of ten commercial ships, the following was usually deployed: Advance vessels were comprised of four mechanized landing craft (LCM) which were modified for use as minesweepers and two river patrol boats (PBRs) followed by one Command and Control Boat (CCB) for the convoy commander, one monitor boat (LCM converted into a gunship) for heavy firepower, and three amphibious assault patrol boats (ASPB). These vessels cleared the river for mines and were a blocking force for shoreline attacks.

The escort group of VNN vessels included one large landing support ship (LSSL) used as the convoy flagship and four fast patrol craft (PCF) for speed and maneuverability. In addition, two PBRs were assigned to each commercial vessel in the convoy. It took twenty PBRs to provide escort protection for a convoy of ten ships.

The reaction group of VNN vessels was composed of one CCB for the Deputy COC, two ASPBs, and five armored troop carriers (ATC). The ATCs carried ARVN and FANK ground units which could be inserted on the riverbank if necessary. In addition to these units, ARVN units secured riverbanks from Tan Chau, RVN to Neak Luong, KR and FANK units insured security of riverbanks from Neak Luong to Phnom Penh.[13]

Air cover for the twenty-six-hour voyage of each convoy from the RVN/KR border to Phnom Penh was basically provided by U.S. Army and USAF assets. Seventh Air Force was tasked by the Commander, United States Military Assistance Command—Vietnam (COMUS-MACV) with providing continuous air support for all convoys. Under this task, 7th AF directed USAF FACs, flying O-2A and OV-10 aircraft and AC-119G Shadow gunships for continuous day and night coverage of convoys. The U.S. Army was tasked for continuous daytime coverage of convoys with Light Fire Teams (LFT) consisting of one UH-1H Command and Communications (C&C) helicopter, two OH-6A Light Observation helicopters (LOH-Scout), and two AH-1G Cobra gunships. Three LFTs were required to insure continuous daylight coverage of a convoy. The Army LFTs were stationed at Chi Lang and cycled between the convoy and Chi Lang for refueling.[14]

The first river convoy departed South Vietnam for Phnom Penh on 17 January. The convoy consisted of "ocean-going" cargo ships and river barges sailing under the yellow with three red horizontal stripes of the flag of the Republic of Vietnam. The convoy totaled forty-five vessels.[15]

Rules of Engagement for aircraft covering convoys during January permitted Shadow gunships, FACs or fighter aircraft controlled by FACs to return enemy fire for protection of the convoy when approved by the COC and the FANK liaison officer onboard the CCB. In situations where no radio communications existed between aircraft and the COC, gunships and FACs were permitted to expend ordnance to break enemy attacks only if the origin of enemy fire was unquestionably pinpointed.

The U.S. Navy provided advance notice to air support units one or two days prior to the launch of Mekong River convoys. Shadow gunships from Fighting C Flight were tasked with protecting river convoys with twenty-four hours a day high cover (3,500 feet AGL) combat air patrol (CAP). Shadows worked directly with various USAF FACs with radio call signs of Rustic, Tilly, Sundog, and later Black Pony orbiting at 2,500 feet AGL. During daylight, U.S. Army LFTs flew at and mostly below 1,500 feet AGL.

Shadow gunships had the assigned radio frequency to communicate directly with the convoy CCB, but without an interpreter onboard every Shadow, usually worked with the onsite FAC that carried an interpreter. The language of convoy commanders varied between Khmere, Vietnamese, and French. Mekong River convoy schedules were classified Top Secret, thus Shadows were again sworn to secrecy of missions.

Three days after the convoy security plan was approved and activated by COMUSMACV, the U.S. Navy requested an active roll in providing air coverage of convoys when USAF or VNAF assets were unavailable. Seventh Air Force claimed that sufficient USAF air assets were available, thus declining the assistance of the Navy. Navy air assets were thereby assigned standby alert status.

Approximately three weeks later in February, 7th AF air resources (FACs and Shadow gunships) in Cambodia were severely strained due to assigned tasks of providing air cover for TICs and road convoys. As a result on 28 February, COMUSMACV approved the employment of U.S. "Brown Water Navy" UH-1B "Sea Wolves" attack helicopters and heavily armed fixed-wing light attack OV-10 "Black Pony" FACs to cover and support Mekong River convoys.

At night, the U.S. Navy provided two Sea Wolves and two Black Ponies to accomplish low altitude coverage. The Navy aircraft cycled between the convoy and the Navy command and control vessel anchored on the RVN side of the Mekong at Tan Chau. The whole composite of aircraft from three U.S. services was designated an air cover package; controlled by 7th Air Force through TACCA.[16]

After weeks of convoy coverage, validation of targets for airstrikes was withdrawn from the COC and the FANK liaison officer and vested in the FANK liaison officer aboard an airborne tactical air control center and in the TACC at HQ 7th AF. Further control of air to ground attacks would eventually be established on 27 March because of increased friendly ground forces deployed along the banks of the Mekong from Tan Chau to Phnom Penh. The entire river route from Tan Chau to Phnom Penh would be declared a "no-fire" zone, requiring 7th AF TACC approval of any aircraft expending fire support for convoys.

The possible void of convoy air coverage in August was brought to forefront with forthcoming transfer of USAF AC-119G Shadow gunships to the VNAF scheduled for 10 September. Therefore on 28 August, COMUSMACV ordered U.S. Navy OV-10s fragged and placed on alert for immediate scramble while directing that an additional five USAF AC-119 Shadow aircrews be provided to ensure that five VNAF AC-119G sorties were flown daily (five in Cambodia of which three of the sorties would help cover Mekong convoys) until the VNAF was capable of assuming continuous night coverage of convoys.

By the end of September 1971, thirty-two convoys of approximately 640 commercial tankers, barges, and tugs would be exposed to enemy attack. Twenty-one ships sustained minor damage while four ships sustained heavy damage from a total of twenty-nine separate enemy attacks since January. During the nine plus months of air protection for Mekong River convoys, records show that U.S. Army Cobra helicopter gunships expended fourteen times on enemy troops, USAF Shadow gunships expended a minimum of seven times, and Navy Sea Wolves and/or Black Ponies expended two times.[17]

Considering the critical shortage of POL in Phnom Penh when air coverage of river convoys began in January and the fact that only one tug and one barge were destroyed out of approximately 640 commercial vessels attempting the round trip to and from Phnom Penh, there were no doubts that the mission was successfully accomplished. Over 2,240 aircraft sorties were flown in direct support of river convoys. Each Mekong River convoy consistently carried ten times as much POL as a regular thirty truck convoy from the nation's seaport Kompong Som.

Reduction in U.S. air assets, particularly with the scheduled transfer of AC-119G Shadow gunships to the VNAF on 10 September required a more active role by the VNAF and Khmer Air Force. The Khmer Air Force was incapable of providing additional support at the time; therefore, the most basic change in Mekong River convoy coverage was the transfer of night coverage to the VNAF AC-119G gunship squadron at Tan Son Nhut in September.

SIXTEEN

In–Country and Out–Country

During January and most of February, B Flight Shadows of the 17th SOS continued to support friendly Lima Sites on the Bolovens Plateau in Laos. Several major attacks against the sites were brought to a halt by the intervention of Phan Rang Shadows.

USAF FACs flying Cessna 0-2 Super Skymasters based at Pleiku owned the radio call sign of "Covey." Covey five-nine-one (591) droned through a January night sky in 1971 above the Ho Chi Minh Trail, looking for enemy movement but there was none. Thus, Covey 591 FAC, 1/Lt. Jim Roper, surmised, "They're hiding." Then Roper noticed multicolored flares popping-up ten miles ahead. His spotter onboard, named Reed, checked his map and concluded the flares were not from the Trail, but were from a Lima Site located on the Bolovens Plateau in southern Laos. With the radio frequency for the landing strip and the radio call sign "P.S. two-two (22)," Roper contacted the site to ask if they had a problem. Fear, approaching panic, came through the heavily accented reply. "Covey, this is site two-two. We have big problem. Big T-I-C."

Roper radioed airborne command center "Moonbeam" to report the situation. Moonbeam's reply was they would send some gunships to the site. Circling above two-two, Roper recognized from the firings of rifles, mortars, and recoilless weapons southwest of the air strip that the friendlies were vastly outnumbered and could be overrun at any time. Two-two confirmed Roper's assessment. "Affirmative. Big T-I-C. Maybe three battalions, NVA. Please make airstrike southwest."

Upon the arrival of an AC-119 Shadow, Roper detected a Texas accent from the Shadow over the radio. Appraising the situation, target area, and firing altitude, the Shadow was cleared by Covey 591 to fire upon confirmation of friendly troop's location. The Shadow confirmed, "Roguh, I have th' airstrip and th' friendlies around it. Lots o' muzzle flashes a couple hundred meters southwest in a large lahge semi-circle." Roper replied, "Affirmative, shoot southwest away from the friendlies." The Texan confirmed the radio call, "Roguh, We'll shoot 'em up for ya."

"Site two-two, Covey. Put your heads down. We shoot now."

"Okay, Covey. You shoot now," replied Site two-two.

Shadow fired its miniguns. Every fifth 7.62mm round was a red tracer. A red finger reached down and extinguished the NVA muzzle flashes like water on a fire. The deadly stream cut an arc across the southwest quadrant of the eerie scene.

"Covey, this is site two-two. Thank you very much."

Covey responded, "Mah sensors have movement within fifty meters of the fence."

"Negative. Outside fence all bad guy," responded two-two.

"Get down. We have to shoot close. Many enemy near the fence."

"Okay. Shoot close."

"Shadow, cleared hot."

"Roguh," confirmed the Texan as the lethal red finger reached down again and wiggled near the fence.

"STOP attack now! Covey, STOP now!" two-two frantically radioed.

"Is everybody okay?" Covey asked.

After a pause, two-two answered, "All okay. You shoot very close. Scare soldiers."

"Good work, Shadow. Friendlies thank you for saving their asses tonight."

"Roguh. Anything else we can do fer ya?"

An enemy mortar site southwest of two-two was identified and marked with a smoke by Covey. Covey warned two-two that Shadow would fire again. That was okay with two-two as long as it was 300 meters away from his position.

The Shadow radioed, "Let me turn on my flashlight." Like magic, a hundred-meter circle shone bright as daytime. "Yeah. We have movement. We'll shoot 'em up!" The red line smashed down and cut away swatches of jungle. Two silvery explosions flashed under the fiery finger.

"Shadow's winchestuh. R.T.B."

Covey 951 responded, "Thanks, Shadow. You saved some lives tonight.

A few days later, Roper read a *Stars and Stripes* article about the fierce fighting on the Bolovens Plateau at P.S. 22 in which 200 NVA were killed. Roper showed the article to Major Reed who stated, "Shadow should get the KBA credit for at least a hundred and ninety-nine of the enemy dead. We both know they were killed-by-air."

Close-air support (like Shadow gunships) brought a certain camaraderie to the war that was missing from the lonely interdiction mission.[1]

AC-119 Shadow and Stinger gunships successfully worked with Covey FACs. There existed a definite air of cooperation and mutual respect between AC-119 gunship crews and Covey FACs from many nights flying together on targets in Laos and Cambodia.

***

In Cambodia, a new ARVN campaign to eradicate remaining communist border sanctuaries was launched on 3 February. An ARVN force of 2,500 soldiers arrived in Kompong Cham Province to reinforce some 7,500 ARVN troops already deployed in the province. The operation was assisted by U.S. air support and 7,500 Cambodia FANK troops. ARVN units clashed with communist troops the next day, killing sixty-nine enemies while sustaining seven casualties. The objective of a 1,000-man FANK unit was the 9th NVA Division headquarters at Chup.

The FANK offensive stalled upon the death of Cambodian Brigadier General Neak Sam while fighting communists on 12 February. The ARVN campaign also stalled when the commander of South Vietnamese forces in Cambodia, Lieutenant General Do Cao Tri was killed in a helicopter crash on 23 February. As the offensive bogged-down for several weeks, Tri's replacement, General Nguyen Van Minh revised the strategy plans for the military operation.[2]

***

Shadows of Phan Rang were withdrawn on 23 February from supporting Lima Sites in southern Laos to give support to Operation Lam Son 719. Most probable due to the absence of gunship support, the Bolovens Plateau and its Lima Sites would fall to enemy attacks on 9 March 1971 and remain in enemy hands thereafter.

On 25 February, two Shadow gunships and three crews from Phan Rang were assigned TDY to DaNang Air Base to relieve Stinger gunships of ground alert status for South Vietnam Military Region I (aka I Corps). 18th SOS Stinger gunships at DaNang were fragged to fly night air cover for ARVN troops invading Laos on Route 9 in Operation Lam Son 719, to cut through the Ho Chi Minh Trail. From 25 February to the end of March, TDY Shadows from 17th SOS B Flight from Phan Rang AB while stationed at DaNang flew thirty-six sorties, including three medical evacuation sorties. Bravo Flight Shadows were credited with killing 118 enemy troops within I Corps.[3]

18th SOS AC-119K Stinger gunships had been flying their primary mission of truck hunting in the Steel Tiger and Barrel Roll areas of Laos during January and first half of February. Because of Operation Lam Son 719, the FOL at DaNang was fragged to support the ARVN operation and the FOL based at Nakhon Phanom Royal Thai AFB, Thailand was diverted from truck hunting to supporting friendly ground forces operating in the Plain de Jarres of northern Laos. Increased truck kills by AC-119K gunships during the first two months of 1971 was attributed to the new 20mm mix of API and HEI ammunition carried onboard all Stingers.

On 28 February while flying nighttime CAP over and ahead of an ARVN armored column and infantry advancing westward on Route 9 during Lam Son 719, Stinger 04 was credited with destroying eight

NVA PT-76 tanks with the 20mm mix of API and HEI ammunition near Hill 31 in Laos. The eight tank kills were confirmed at daylight by the ARVN ground commander.[4]

***

Flying CAP missions around Phnom Penh and over Cambodia Route 4 on the Kiriron Plateau became routine for Shadows from Tan Son Nhut by the latter half of February. The capital city had been on high alert since the attack on Pochenong in late January. Sporadic communist rocket and mortar attacks terrorized the city. FANK troops had clashed with enemy forces in several battles near Phnom Penh.

The South Vietnamese had reinforced the FANK effort to open and secure Route 4 from Phnom Penh to the Cambodian seaport of Kompong Som located on the Gulf of Thailand (Siam). For the first time in nearly two months, a truck convoy hauling gasoline from Kompong Som to Phnom Penh had safely arrived intact during the first week in February.

Shadows worked with USAF OV-10 Rustic FACs covering Phnom Penh and Route 4 truck convoys both day and night from the beginning of February. Shadows occasionally worked with U.S. Navy OV-10 Black Pony FACs during night missions in southwestern Cambodia.

Sometimes, Shadows had an interpreter onboard who could speak French to communicate with Cambodian commanders who spoke French, but could not speak English. When there was no interpreter onboard, the Shadow relied on FACs with an interpreter onboard for situation reports and target identification from ground commanders who could not speak English.

Radio communication with Cambodian ground commanders and even convoy commanders was much more productive than with South Vietnamese ground troops operating in Cambodia. Shadows usually had radio frequencies for communicating with the Cambodians, whereas, ARVN radio communication for ground operations and VNAF air operations were conducted on frequencies undisclosed to Shadow gunships. In spite of dealing with the four languages of English, Khmere, French, and Vietnamese, Shadows accomplished quite a bit in protecting the truck convoys and helping friendly ground troops with opening Route 4.

The enemy still concentrated on stopping Cambodian POL truck convoys headed for Phnom Penh. During a day mission to cover a truck convoy that was approaching the infamous ambush area of Pich Nil Pass on Route 4, my Shadow 27 was surprised to meet head-on the O-2 FAC covering the convoy. The near-miss was over before we knew it. After the convoy had safely passed through the ambush sites, we were to remain in the vicinity in case the convoy was attacked later. Following Route 4 through the Elephant Chain of the Cardamom Mountains to the southwest, we decided to recon Kompong Som. Many photographs were taken as we flew above and around the tranquil seaport. The city was beautiful with beach resorts and blue gulf waters. The place had thus far escaped the ravages of war.

When an oil storage tank burns, pitch black smoke mushrooms skyward like a volcanic eruption. The plume of smoke can be seen for miles and miles, especially when airborne at 3,500 feet above the ground.

On a bright moonlit night on 1 March, my Shadow 27 was conducting armed recon around Phnom Penh and Pochenong Airport when we received a radio call from the ABCCC "Ramrod," directing us to divert our mission to Kompong Som. A U.S. Navy FAC radio, call sign Black Pony, had requested fire support for Cambodian troops engaged in a TIC, defending the tank farm and refinery against enemy attacks at Kompong Som. My copilot, Lieutenant Marty Noonan, and I could see dark black columns of smoke on the horizon as we raced full speed above Route 4 toward the seaport city.

There was no interpreter onboard our gunship so we had to rely on the FAC's communication with friendly ground forces. Upon Noonan contacting Black Pony on the radio, the FAC gave us a quick sit-rep on our way in, so we completed our strike checklist and were prepared to fire once over the TIC. Upon arriving over the target area, we could clearly see heavy ground fighting with streams of red tracers from friendly troops and streams of green tracers from enemy troops shooting back and forth. Explosions from RPGs and enemy mortars were impacting within the oil storage tank farm. We could also vividly see the burning storage tanks and smell the toxic smoke fumes bellowing up to our firing altitude of 3,500 feet. Our firing circle to attack enemy locations involved flying through the smoke on part of our orbit. Around and around we flew firing on enemy troops and mortar positions while breathing and tasting oil smoke. Enemy positions were easily identifiable from the air with the glow of burning oil tanks. Telltale green tracers and mortar flashes marked enemy locations. The Shadow 27 crew attacked the enemy until the assault was broken-off. No enemy anti-aircraft fire was encountered. Another target was identified by Black Pony and with the little amount of ammo remaining; we fired on the SEL until Winchester. A secondary explosion erupted from the target. There was no Shadow gunship to replace us, so we thanked the Navy pilot and high-tailed it straight back to Tan Son Nhut below Bingo fuel and were lucky to safely land amidst severe thunderstorms surrounding the airport.

Heavy shelling the next night on 2 March by NVA and Viet Cong forces on the oil refinery at Kompong Som destroyed 80% of the Khmer Republic's main fuel storage facility.[5] From that time forward, Mekong River relief convoys hauling POL to Phnom Penh from South Vietnam became extremely critical for the Republic's survival.

* * *

Classified SECRET FLASH PT 05065 from 7th Air Force/DOPF to 14 SOW, 17 SOS, and 18 SOS stated in SPIN 5 that effective 1 March, fixed-wing gunships operating in RVN and Cambodia...AC-119G sorties can be planned for four hours and AC-119K sorties for four hours. Actual sortie duration may be dependent upon tactical, weather, fuel consumption, and crew duty time limitations. DOCT Senior Duty Officer may authorize scrambles if crew duty is extended. Airborne crews in combat duty that may exceed crew duty time will notify DASC one hour prior to the expiration of crew duty. DASC will relieve crew or request crew duty time extensions from DOCT as may be appropriate.

Missions diverted to convoy escort by Airborne TACC call sign RAMROD, or specifically fragged as convoy missions will contact

RAMROD prior to TOT, requesting latest convoy position and any additional instructions including convoy commander FM radio frequencies if changed. Convoy escorts on Mekong will contact convoy commander when overhead convoy.

At 17SOS C Flt, Tactical Call Signs are assigned to Aircraft Commander with Shadow Prefixes:

Lt. Col. Teal: Shadow 05	Lt. Col. Gregory: Shadow 06
Capt. Blanton: Shadow 10	Capt. Cunningham: Shadow 11
Capt. Howze: Shadow 12	Capt. Heiner: Shadow 14
Capt. Smith: Shadow 15	Capt. Rapuzzi: Shadow 16
Capt. Walker: Shadow 17	Capt. Gustin: Shadow 18
Capt. Wiese: Shadow 19	Capt. Simmons: Shadow 21
Maj. Carter, R.: Shadow 22	Maj. Marples: Shadow 23
Capt. James: Shadow 24	Capt. Carter: Shadow 25

***

In addition to combat missions flown by 17th SOS B Flight aircrews out of Phan Rang and DaNang, the 17th SOS at Phan Rang started the Improvement and Modernization Program of VNAF AC-119G Crew Training on 1 February with the first three VNAF aircrews. After completion of ground school on 5 February, the first training sortie was launched at 0900 hours on 6 February. Each crew flew a total of twenty-three missions during the initial flying training phase, usually four hours per sortie. Most of the training missions were flown in designated training areas that were also known enemy locations (KEL). During the last portion of flying training, fragged combat missions were flown with targets provided by II DASC.

VNAF training at Phan Rang was a three phase program. First, a week of ground school was conducted; then basic flying training with emphasis on instrument and emergency procedures. The third phase concentrated on combat tactics during actual combat missions. Phase IV of training was conducted with Fighting C Flight at TSN AB.

According to 17th SOS Instructor Navigator Major William Gericke, training of the VNAF crewmembers was quite an experience. It brought out the best in everyone. Major Gericke wrote the following:

The first hurdle was to convince the GI types that their lives were not in jeopardy by flying on integrated crews. You might have a Vietnamese pilot and an American pilot, for instance. Nearly all the VNAF pilots had excellent command of the aircraft and their flying skills were superb. They had flown the cargo version (C-119G) for years. And their safety record was tops. After a VNAF pilot, Captain Bich demonstrated his expertise bringing in a crew with an engine out, we heard no more about safety. Actually, in comparison to the U.S. pilots, the VNAF were substantially more seasoned. It showed in their well-coordinated pylon turns in firing orbits.

But from there, the situation deteriorated. All checklists had to be run in English. And some of the VNAF spoke little, let alone read English. Neither the instructors nor the ground commanders could easily understand.

Navigators were held in low esteem (i.e., trash). It was bad enough to be a pilot in a non-fighter aircraft, but a navigator, unheard of. In fact, they didn't have them at all until 7th Air Force insisted that they man the gunship with a standard crew. The VNAF navigators went into combat with roughly twenty hours of experience. The pilots preferred to disregard the navigator and do their own pilotage (navigating). If one of them got tired, they'd turn the controls over to the other pilot and go to sleep. According to one instructor, "The pilot is a character. When he gets tired, he just quits! Tonight he ran the VNAF flight engineer out of his seat and just crumped out in it for the last forty-five minutes of the mission."

We (USAF) just were not used to running a railroad like this. Not on combat sorties anyway. But then, we had a one-

year tour with the end in sight. The VNAF were faced with
an entire career of fighting.

One of our instructors once asked a VNAF gunner to
wake up an officer. They were in the firing circle. The gunner indicated he was prohibited from touching an officer. If
they had to abort a takeoff, many of them felt it was unlucky
to try again on the same day. I'm not saying they were
derelict in duty; their ways were simply different.

They (VNAF) didn't like night sorties and were very family oriented. Our military ways of putting job first and family
second just didn't sell.

Overall however, progress was satisfactory. The VNAF
crews could do the job, alone. We could see some further
problems downstream, though. The Cambodians didn't want
Vietnamese of any kind firing guns over their territory. Not
on a routine basis. They would frequently query us about this
in flight. It was a trifle embarrassing to say the least because
most of the crews were now integrated.

Communication between USAF instructors and VNAF
students was the major problem, especially with enlisted
VNAF crewmen. VNAF officers were generally fluent in the
English language while some were excellent. Even so, during
tactical flight conditions, the American instructors usually
handled radio communications. Flying experience varied
among the VNAF students. VNAF pilots were highly qualified, having logged thousands of hours flying the C-119G
while becoming instructor pilots for the Flying Boxcar.
Overall, VNAF crewmembers possessed a positive attitude
with a will to learn through hard work.[6]

Interestingly, a VNAF AC-119 gunship student crew, only half-way
through their training schedule, were airborne within forty minutes of being scrambled on 5 March with USAF instructors from Phan Rang aboard.
A beleaguered ARVN unit located fifteen miles southwest of Dak To in II

Corps Kontum Province lost their English-speaking interpreter during
heavy fighting. Without their interpreter, they were unable to communicate
with the USAF Shadow gunship flying overhead. The ARVN unit was in
a critical combat situation and needed immediate gunship help.

VNAF Major Dang Van Duc was the AC-119G gunship aircraft commander on the scrambled mission #4220. USAF Major Donald D.
Fraker (Shadow 63) of Grover, Colorado was the 17th SOS instructor
pilot onboard the gunship. Major Fraker stated, "Even though the VNAF
crew was still on training status, they did a 'Number One' job. Major
Duc acted as interpreter and the rest of the crew worked rather
smoothly. Seeing what goes on during an actual combat mission was a
valuable experience and will help them greatly during the rest of their
training. I think the student crew could have handled the whole mission
if necessary. They have applied themselves very well in the whole training program and were eager to fly this one. This was the first VNAF
crew to fly combat in the Shadow gunship. We are all very impressed by
their performance." Time on target was from 2340 to 0115 hours. The
ground commander radio call sign was Process Romeo.

Major Duc, the VNAF flight training officer for the 17th SOS, remarked, "The mission went very well, the coordination was all very
good and we worked effectively. The ARVN ground troops were surrounded by the enemy who were about 800 meters out from their camp.
The whole area was very mountainous and there were many fires from
earlier artillery and air strikes in the area. I contacted the ground unit
and they marked their position. We got into position and the first shots
were right on target. Even though the enemy troops were in such close
proximity to the ARVNs, we didn't have any trouble keeping the guns
on the enemy. Our hits were accurate and we put 7,000 rounds in on enemy positions before coming home. This kept the enemy off guard long
enough for the ARVN to regroup and plan their next move. The crew
did a very good job; they found out about all the coordination needed to
work together effectively."[7]

Major Duc was designate commander for the 819th Combat
Squadron, the first VNAF AC-119G gunship squadron which was

scheduled to start forming at Tan Son Nhut Air Base, Saigon upon completion of training at Phan Rang. Having served 16 years in the VNAF, Major Duc was a seasoned pilot with over 11,000 total flying hours in the C-47 Skytrain, C-119G Flying Boxcar, and the C-123 Provider before starting the AC-119 Shadow gunship program.

On 22 February, additional AC-119G aircraft for the I & M Program began to arrive at Phan Rang AB from CONUS. By the end of March, the 17th SOS would gain five additional AC-119G aircraft for the VNAF aircrew training program.

The first three VNAF crews graduated from Phase III training at Phan Rang on 24 March. RVN Vice President Nguyen Cao Ky attended the graduation ceremony. Upon completion of training at Phan Rang, the three VNAF crews moved to Tan Son Nhut where they began Phase IV training, flying fragged combat missions for Fighting C Flight at Tan Son Nhut with American instructors onboard.[8]

***

On 14 March, Major General Earnest C. Hardin Jr., Vice Commander, Seventh Air Force, presented the 14th Special Operations Wing and subordinate units (including 71st SOS) with the Presidential Unit Citation covering the period 21 June 1968 to 30 June 1969. On that date (14 March), Colonel Mark W. Magnan assumed command of the 14th SOW, replacing Colonel Alfred F. Eaton.[9]

By the end of March 1971, the 17th SOS reported 22 AC-119G gunships with two back-up gunships in Phase (maintenance). Squadron personnel totaled 108 officers and 176 airmen. Lieutenant Colonel Ed Elbert remained at the helm of the 17th. Lieutenant Colonel Joseph R. Dixey had replaced Lt. Col. Alfred I. Flynn as 17th Squadron and B Flight Ops Officer. Lieutenant Colonel Carl W. Brage had assumed the duties of Squadron Chief Navigator on 27 February, replacing Lt. Col. N. Fear, and Maj. Philip E. J. Lee assumed duties of Squadron Executive Officer, replacing Maj. Thomas V. Soltys.

B Flight Commander at Phan Rang was Lt. Col. Bill R. Whitesell. 17th Squadron key personnel performed B Flight duties that corresponded to their Squadron duties (e.g., Ops Officer, XO, MO, etc.).

Lieutenant Colonel Tom Teal commanded C Flight with Ops Officer Lt. Col. Bill Gregory; Adm. Officers, Majors Earl Farney and James A. Rash; Flight First Sergeant, TSgt James F. Culbertson; and Flight Adm. Specialist, Sgt Robert P. Allen.

Squadron manning stabilized at or near the 289 personnel authorized. The number of Illuminator Operators reached the minimum necessary to provide one IO for each combat crew. A shortage of IOs would continue without adequate numbers of replacements.

Awards and Decorations for 17th SOS personnel in the month of January included the following crewmen receiving the DFC: 12 January: Captain B.S. Harmer, Capt. G.A. Totten, 1/Lt. R.J. Mills, 1/Lt. S.R. Podelski, Maj. F.D. Richards, TSgt E. Williamson, SSgt W.L. Patterson, A1C R.S. Lyall, SSgt R.M. Pommerelle, TSgt C. Ellis, Maj. D.L. Fraker, 1/Lt. E.B. Menarchik, Maj. B.M. Bell, Maj. J.B. Nicol, TSgt G.F. Gourley, SSgt M.D. Henness, A1C R.G. Lyall, A1C W.M. Gelches, A1C P.K. Brown, A1C D.C. Roach, SSgt R. Mikolowski, SSgt W.J. Drabek, 1/Lt. B.B. Napier, Maj. J.H. Oswald, and 1/Lt. R.E. Coe.

On 12 January, Capt. John L. Hope received the Silver Star. On 19 January, Maj. R. Ribinski was awarded the DFC. On 30 January, Sgt J.A. Clark, SSgt D.L. Emmons, TSgt M.B. Mullen, and Lt. Col. L.H. Christopherson were awarded DFCs. Also on 30 January, A1C J.O. Hughes and A1C J.W. McAdams, Jr. were awarded Air Force Commendation Medals (AFCM) and on 30 January, Capt. J.R. Mely, Jr. was awarded the BSM.

During the month of February, DFC medals were awarded to the following: Staff Sergeant O. Townsend, Jr. and Sgt J.R. Weaver on 10 February. On 19 February, A1C F.J. Sledzinski, Capt. P.L. Conklin, TSgt. W. Besaw, and Capt. W. Forbis.

17th SOS personnel receiving awards during March were as follows: 16 March, Distinguished Flying Crosses were awarded to A1C R.E. Grimsley, Sgt J.R. Weaver, SSgt O. Townsend, Jr., 1/Lt. D.B. Menarchik, Capt. D.A. Rapuzzi, 1/Lt. W.L. Sasz, Capt. J.M. Cachuela, 1/Lt. R.E. Poe, Capt. J.S. Sawtelle, and Capt. B.H. Blanton. On the 16th, the Air Force Commendation Medal was awarded to Capt. W.H. Bottoms, Jr.

On 17 March, DFCs were awarded to the following: Master Sergeant D.S. Feasel, 1/Lt. R.J. Mills, Jr., SSgt S.B. Walley, Maj. J.F. Stewart,

Jr., 1/Lt. S.R. Podielski, SSgt R. Coaturier, SSgt M.D. Henness, TSgt
A.T. Brown, and SSgt R. Mikolowski. On the 18th of March, 1/Lt. R.I.
Choate and Maj. R.S. Carter received DFCs. Captain D.A. Rapuzzi,
Maj. D.D. Frazier, Capt. G.A. Totten, Capt. W.S. Cunningham, Capt.
B.H. Blanton, and Lt. Col. W.B. Gregory were awarded DFCs on 21
March. On 28 March, 1/Lt. B.B. Napier, Sgt K.B. Henning, and Sgt R.S.
Friese received DFCs. Also on the 28th, Sgt B.L. Lucky received the
Air Force Commendation Medal.[10]

Fighting C Flight BDA Report for January thru March 1971 from
14th SOW History included:

SORTIES:	JAN*	FEB	MAR	TOTALS
Scheduled	255	224	248	727
Flown	247	220	242	709
Total Hours	1,116.2	967.3	869.4	2,952.9
Time on Target	749.6	588.9	674.4	2,012.9
Firing Sorties	166	174	178	518
7.62mm Expended	1,802,763	2,388,940	2,111,530	6,303,233
20mm Expended	57,892	-------	------	57,892
Flares Launched	1,063	1,024	989	3,076
Markers Dropped	48	78	91	217
Trucks Damaged 2-Wheel Vehicles	12	12	20	44
Destroyed/Damaged "Other Vehicles"	20	2	22	44
Destroyed/Damaged	22	2	6	30
Sampans Destroyed	4	40	3	47
Sampans Damaged	23	11	18	52
KBA	227	158	56	441
WBA	0	17	87	104
AAA REACTIONS				
Aircraft Fired At	15	11	11	37
Daytime	6	6	7	19
Nighttime	9	5	4	18
Hits	1	0	3	4

*January figures include AC-119 Stinger gunships flying two sorties per day from TSN.[11]

***

During the first three months of 1971, Cambodia was still the exclusive operating area for Fighting C Flight with eight fragged missions per day providing continuous coverage. Shadows from Saigon played major roles in many operations in Cambodia. Capping truck convoys on Route 4 from Kompong Som to Phnom Penh as well as Mekong River convoys from South Vietnam to Phnom Penh received major emphasis. Supplies of food, ammunition, and petroleum hauled by road and river convoys were absolutely essential for continued existence of Phnom Penh and the Khmer Republic.

Fighting C Flight had unquestionably accomplished its mission in Cambodia during the months of January, February, and March 1971. Flying 709 combat missions during the three month period, C Flight BDA included 44 trucks damaged, 44 two-wheel vehicles and 30 other vehicles destroyed or damaged, 47 sampans destroyed, 52 sampans damaged, 12 secondaries, 441 enemy troops killed by air and 104 enemy wounded by air.[12]

Combined BDA reports for Shadow gunships supporting Cambodian and South Vietnamese forces in Cambodia between July 1970 and March 1971 show that Shadow gunships were credited with destroying or damaging 609 enemy vehicles, destroying 237 sampans while damaging another 494, and killing 3,151 enemy troops.[13]

To summarize, enemy attacks throughout Cambodia had significantly increased during the first three months of the New Year. Shadows were constantly on the run, chasing and attacking Charlie. Seventh Air Force intelligence briefings for Shadow pilots and navigators now encompassed the latest war news from Cambodia which had been reported in the *Stars and Stripes* and in the *7th Air Force News*.

A fifty-truck convoy traveling on Route 4 from Kompong Som had made it safely to Phnom Penh, but two other convoys were ambushed, both sustaining losses before breaking through. A road convoy ambush on Route 6 north of Skoun had developed into a full scale battle in which the mass of enemy troops were finally driven away with U. S. fighter strikes and Shadow gunships. Fighting C Flight's Operations Officer, Shadow 06 aircraft commander Lt. Col. Bill Gregory, and his crew proved to be highly effective during the TIC at Skoun. NVA and Viet Cong forces had again attacked Kompong Som, shelling and destroying a major portion of the oil refinery and fuel depot while inflicting heavy casualties on the Cambodian defenders.

Communist forces continued harassing Cambodian government-controlled province capitals with rocket and mortar attacks during darkness while conducting hit and run sapper attacks on smaller government garrisons and outposts. Laos Lima Sites and government outposts on the Bolovens Plateau had fallen after near nightly attacks by communist forces. Phan Rang Shadows had been withdrawn from night duty on the Bolovens to cover for AC-119K Stinger operations in I Corps during Lam Son 719.

In support of South Vietnamese ground forces invading Laos to attack the Ho Chi Minh Trail, 7th Air Force Headquarters ordered stepped-up armed recon under ROE Freedom Deal for Shadow missions on Cambodia's eastern province roads and trails. The NVA had firm control over the northeastern provinces of Tattana Kiri, Mondul Kiri, and Stoeng Treng while still maintaining dominion over the 600 mile border area with South Vietnam. Communist troops, whether NVA, VC, or Khmer Rouge ruled the countryside from Siem Reap and the Angkor Wat ruins in northwestern Cambodia to Svay Rieng located in the Parrot's Beak, strategically astride the Saigon-Phnom Penh Highway 1. The large French-owned Chup rubber plantations north of the highway were under communist control. Kratie was now firmly established as Headquarters for the South Vietnamese National Liberation Front (aka Viet Cong).

The ARVN assault on the Ho Chi Minh Trail that began on 8 February had slowed considerably after initial successes because of fierce resistance from the NVA resulting in bloody battles and heavy losses for both sides. Operation Lam Son 719 would end on 24 March as the last ARVN units pulled out of Laos under heavy communist assaults. Officially, the operation ended on 6 April 1971.

Khmer Republic Premier Lon Nol had suffered a major stroke on 8 February. Lon Nol delegated his leadership duties as Premier to his Deputy Premier Sisowath Sirik Matak in order to fly to Hawaii for treatment and recovery from his misfortune. In addition to losing the leadership of Lon Nol, Cambodia also lost the leadership of a top FANK general on 12 February. Brigadier General Neak Sam was killed while fighting communist troops in Kompong Cham Province. The future of the new republic was shaky to say the least.

There had been no progress toward a settlement in the war at the deadlocked Paris Peace Talks. That didn't matter for the Khmer Republic. The Talks between negotiators from the United States, South Vietnam, North Vietnam, and the Liberation Front Viet Cong did not address the war in Cambodia. President Nixon had stated that U. S. troops would remain in South Vietnam until North Vietnam released all American POWs. Except for support from the United States and the Republic of Vietnam, the Khmer Republic stood alone in its quest for freedom.

Shadowmen marveled at the vulnerability of Cambodia. Without the help of the United States and South Vietnam, there seemed to be no way the Khmer Republic and the Lon Nol government would survive the relentless communist onslaught. Even though the majority of seven million Cambodians were under government control, Lon Nol's government had absolutely no control over eastern provinces and for the most part, the nation's countryside.

Communist forces were using superior tactics of guerrilla warfare; attacking government garrisons, ambushing water and land transportation routes while effectively laying siege to strangle major population centers. Cambodia was definitely the underdog, but maybe, just maybe with continued support of the U. S. and the South Vietnamese, the Cambodians could weather the storm to eventually win their war against the communists.

Shadow "Charlie Chasers" parked in revetment ready to launch. Armor plating in two lower windows were installed to protect the pilot and cockpit crew from enemy ground fire. There was absolutely no protection from enemy ground fire in the open doorway for the NOS operator. All nose art on AC-119 gunships was eventually removed after claims that the painted white images of "Shadow" and "Charlie Chasers" could be seen by enemy anti-aircraft gunners even in the darkest of nights.

SEVENTEEN

Shadow Treadmill and Vietnamization

O n 29-30 March, NVA and VC troops again seized control of a ten-mile stretch of Route 4 near Phnom Penh when a Cambodian convoy of several battalions was blocked and pushed back toward the capital city. The fight for control of strategic Route 4 would be ongoing through April.[1]

On 3 April 1971, Cambodia Route 4 was again closed by the destruction of a bridge west of Pich Nil Pass, and by 10 April, Route 3, the alternate route for the pass, was closed by numerous road cuts and downed bridges. Thus the LOC was again denied friendly use. FANK operations to reopen either or both routes before the wet season were still underway at the end of April.[2]

The Shadows of Fighting C Flight at Tan Son Nhut continued the grueling treadmill to provide twenty-four-hour-a-day CAS for troops-in-contact, road and riverine convoys, cities and towns in Cambodia. Armed reconnaissance was part of most every mission.

The first three I & M Program graduating VNAF classes from Phan Rang arrived at Tan Son Nhut on 10 April to begin Phase IV training with Fighting C Flight which involved more flight training to increase VNAF crew coordination until qualified for combat ready status. VNAF crewmembers were scheduled to fly with American AC-119 Shadow combat crew instructors.

During the first three weeks of April, the two Shadow gunships and three crews from Phan Rang 17th SOS B Flight were still providing TIC alert for Corps I and II out of DaNang AB, RVN. These crews and aircraft had been dispatched to DaNang during Operation Lam Son 719 in February to relieve Stinger gunships at DaNang of TIC alert, so the Stingers could support the ARVN offensive thrust into Laos. Extensive coverage was provided by Shadow gunships operating out of DaNang for Fire Bases 5, 6, and Mary Ann. On 23 April, the Shadows returned to Phan Rang AB as Operation Lam Son 719 terminated.

At Phan Rang, the 17th SOS was primarily tasked and involved with training VNAF aircrews and support personnel in accordance with the I & M Program. Frag orders from Seventh AF included an alert frag for Phan Rang Shadows to provide continuous night TIC support for MR II. The alert frag ordered that an aircraft and crew would assume ground alert status from 1130-2200Z or by airborne training aircraft flying throughout this time period or a combination of both. Training aircraft were required to have onboard USAF Instructor Crews, who would assume active control of the aircraft in the event the gunship was diverted to an actual TIC situation and the TIC was closer than 1,000 meters to friendly forces.

VNAF student crews #4 through #10 arrived at Phan Rang AB on 2 April and completed their training on 8 June. USAF 17th SOS instructor crews at Phan Rang numbered #4 through #7 responsible for training VNAF crews #4 thru #10 were as follows:

Crew #4: IP Maj. Donald D. Fraker, IN Maj. John D. Berrier, IFE SSgt James J. Anderson, IIO TSgt James Hallahan, IAG SSgt Ralph M. Flak.

Crew #5: IP Maj. William E. Dickson, IN Maj. Lawrence W. Barber, IFE MSgt Leon D. Mott, IAG Sgt Robert G. Lyall.

Crew #6: IP Cpt. Barry S. Harmer, IN Maj. Richard D. Bode, IFE MSgt William C. Rhoades, IIO Sgt Calvin S. Churchill, IAG SSgt Doughlas G. Fisher.

Crew #7: (IP) Maj. Jerry W. Marples, (IN) Maj. Daniel W. Pruitt, IFE TSgt Donald A. McMullen, IIO SSgt Richard W. Hall, IAG Sgt Ronald W. Schultz.

VNAF crews #11 thru #17 arrived at Phan Rang on 18 May and assumed the responsibility of II Military Region (II Corps) combat frags when VNAF crews #4 thru #10 completed Phase III training on 8 June. USAF 17th SOS instructor crews at Phan Rang numbered #8 thru #11 for VNAF crews numbered #11 thru #17 were as follows:

Crew #8: IP Cpt. Richard S. Howze, IN Maj. James A. Rash, IFE TSgt. Franklin D. Gentry, IIO SSgt Bryan P. McAnulty, IAG Sgt Michael J. Drzyzga, Jr.

Crew #9: IP Cpt. Victor H. Heiner, IN Maj. George E. Bethke, IFE TSgt Douglas E. Gorsuch, IIO Sgt Lonnie L. Harper, IAG SSgt George R. Renfroe, Jr.

Crew #10: IP Cpt. William S. Cunningham, IN Cpt. Joseph L. Hill, IFE MSgt Lawrence W. Crawford, IIO Sgt Kenneth P. Stearn, IAG SSgt Douglas G. Fisher.

Crew #11: IP Cpt. Gary A. Totten, IN Cpt. Gary L. Willman, IFE MSgt Thomas E. Collum, IIO SSgt Steven C. Jarnagin, IAG Sgt James R. Greig.

VNAF crews #18 thru #24 commenced training at Phan Rang on 25 June with a completion date for Phase II & Phase III training on 27 August 1971. USAF 17th SOS instructor crews at Phan Rang numbered 12 thru 15 for VNAF crews numbered 18 thru 24 were as follows:

Crew #12: IP Maj. Jerry Marples, IN Maj. Dan Pruitt, IFE TSgt Garrettson F. Gourley, IIO SSgt Richard Hall, IAF Sgt Ron Schultz.

Crew #13: IP Maj. Gene M. Donahue, IN Maj. Lawrence Barber, IFE TSgt Elliott Williamson, Jr., IIO SSgt Donald R. Somerville, IAG Sgt Robert G. Lyall.

Crew #14: IP Cpt. Herbert K. Wiese, Jr., IN Maj. John D. Berrier, IFE TSgt Albert F. Leach, IIO SSgt Francisco Rodriguez-Rivera, IAG SSgt Ralph Flak.

Crew #15: IP Cpt. Douglas L. Batchelder, IN Maj. Richard Bode, IFE SSgt Kelly McNeil, IIO Sgt Edward McCallion, IAG TSgt Joseph C. Wells.[3]

***

On 1 May, the AC-119G gunship I & M Program for the VNAF took over all combat frags for the 17th SOS at Phan Rang. VNAF crews and their USAF instructors were fragged for three night sorties, providing airborne alert throughout the hours of darkness. If there were no requirements for TICs or TACEs (Tactical Emergencies), the Shadows fired on known or suspected enemy locations after receiving proper clearances from local Province Chiefs in Corps II and III.

On some occasions more than three sorties were flown due to critical ground action. In these instances, the Shadow would stay on target longer than normal, recover and re-arm at a nearby base and then re-launch for continued support of allied troops. In addition to providing fire support for allied ground troops, the Shadow provided perimeter illumination, on request, for Phan Rang AB and nearby army camps. All of these missions were invaluable ingredients in the VNAF training program.

A VNAF student crew was involved in a short round incident in which two Republic of Korea Army (ROKA) personnel were wounded on 27 April. Investigation findings conclusively proved that the incident was not due to aircrew error.[4]

***

During April and most of May, Fighting C Flight flew eight combat frags per day. One sortie per day was manned by VNAF crews with USAF instructors onboard. On 26 May, one frag was dropped and the flight time per sortie was fragged for 4.5 hours in order to continue the twenty-four-hour coverage desired. It became necessary to reduce the number of fragged missions to seven frags per day because of the manning situation in the 17th SOS. Several more crew members were moved to Phan Rang from Tan Son Nhut to become VNAF training instructors. With impending deactivation of the squadron, there was no 17th SOS replacements inbound.

Additional VNAF crews reported to Tan Son Nhut following their graduation from Phan Rang and subsequently the VNAF flew three of the seven combat frags assigned to C Flight. Again, USAF instructors accompanied VNAF crews on these missions. Night sorties were exclusively manned by USAF crews.

***

In April 1971, Fighting C Flight held another Dining-In Awards Banquet at the TSN Officers Club. Flight Commander Lt. Col. Teal stated, "I inquired at 7th AF if General Clay, the Commander, would like to attend, pin on medals, etc. He sent word that he would like to attend and would accept a Shadow One award, pin on medals, etc. Of course, the 14th SOW Commander, DCO, and DCM also would attend and participate. We invited the TSN Base Commander, in appreciation for the Shadow Party Hootch, so he could be thanked publicly by our unit. I was not prepared for his reply when I introduced him at the head table, thanked him for the Party Hootch, when he said in front of God and everyone that he would have liked to have fired me, long pause, but only to hire me to work for him."[5]

In addition to 7th AF Commander General Lucius D. Clay, Jr., 14th SOW Commander Col. Mark W. Magnan and Cambodian FANK Commander at KPT (Hotel 303) Lt. Col. Lieou Phin Oum were distinguished guests at the Dining-In.

Upon completion of his twelve-month tour of duty in April 1971, Lt. Col. Tom A. Teal departed Vietnam for another assignment in CONUS,

(*Left to right*): Shadow Pilot Lt. James Keller, Lt. Col. Lieou Phin Oum (Hotel 303), and 7th AF Commander General Lucius Clay at the spring 1971 Shadow Dining-In/Awards Banquet held at the Tan Son Nhut Officers Club.

only to return to Vietnam seven months later as the 56th SOW Stinger Gunship Detachment 1 Commander at DaNang. Promoted to full colonel, Teal was the last USAF commander at DaNang and turned the base over to the VNAF commander in March 1973.

***

Lon Nol recovered from his 8 February stroke and returned to Cambodia in mid-April 1971. Planning started thereafter for another major offensive named Chenla II in which the objectives resembled the same objectives of Chenla I. Operation Chenla I that ended in mid- December 1970 had been declared successful by the leader. Again, opening the highways leading to Kompong Thom from Skoun and Kompong Cham, stopping the flow of enemy supplies from the Kompong Chhnang region, and regaining control of the agriculture rich central region were the major objectives. The operation officially began on 20 August 1971.[6]

In May, another significant operation supported by Fighting C Flight Shadows was the joint Cambodian-South Vietnamese operation launched on 20 May by Cambodian troops to clear Route 3 as an alternate supply route between Phnom Penh and Kompong Som. Route 3 to Kompong Som would avoid enemy ambushes experienced on Route 4 through the Elephant Chain of the Cardamon Mountains. Just west of Phnom Penh, convoys turned southward off Route 4 to pass Strang, then drive through Chhuk, Kampot, Bokor, Veal Renh, Prey Nop, and Ream to reach Kompong Som for supplies. Shadow gunships provided air coverage of the operation, especially during hours of darkness, to avert any enemy counter-attacks on the advancing government forces.

Also during May, a Mekong River convoy barge packed full of munitions took a direct hit from enemy fire and exploded into a dangerous fireworks display. Fortunately, the remainder of the convoy made it safely to Phnom Penh.

On 19 May, Fighting C Flight AC-119G aircraft #53-1115 Shadow 21 was hit by one round of a suspected .51 caliber machine gun during a return flight from Cambodia to Tan Son Nhut. The round went through the nose of the aircraft, causing minor damage. No crew injuries resulted.

Between 26 and 31 May, an estimated force of 1,000 NVA troops captured the strategic rubber plantation town of Snoul, defeating and driving away some 2,000 ARVN troops in spite of U.S. air strikes supporting the ARVN. The capture of Snoul gave the communists control of parts of Routes 7 and 13, leading into South Vietnam in addition to large amounts of military equipment and supplies abandoned by ARVN troops.

On 31 May, Lon Nol and the Khmer Republic called for peace talks between warring factions in Cambodia if all NVA and VC forces withdrew from the country. The communists rejected the offer.[7]

***

NVA and Viet Cong units tried to consolidate strategic positions in

Cambodia before the southwest monsoon "wet" season took full effect
in June. As a consequence, Shadows close-air support on numerous battles between enemy forces and allied troops resulted near Phnom Penh.
Possibly the most important battle was for control of the strategic Vihear
Suor Marshland, located east of and well within rocket range of the capital city. The battle began on 1 June and eventually involved approximately 2,000 NVA troops opposed by the Cambodian artillery fire bases.
The heaviest fighting occurred about thirteen miles east of Phnom Penh
near the village of Vihear Suor. Hotel 26 was the radio call sign of the
Cambodian FANK commander. FANK forces were in continuous radio
contact with Shadow gunships on station resulting in a rapid response by
Shadows whenever contact was made with the enemy. FANK losses were
held to a minimum and all fire support bases remained under control of
friendly forces. FANK commanders in the area attributed this success to
effective air support which was immediately available when requested.

On 7 June, AC-119G Shadow aircraft #52-9942 was hit in the right
boom by one round from a .30 caliber machine gun. The battle damage
was found during post flight inspection.

Aircraft Commanders in Fighting C Flight assigned tactical radio call
sign numbers with Shadow prefixes in June 1971 were as follows:

Lt. Col. J. James: Shadow 05	Lt. Col. Bill Gregory: Shadow 06
Capt. Cunningham: Shadow 11	Capt. Heiner: Shadow 14
Capt. Smith: Shadow 15	Capt. Walker: Shadow 17
Capt. Simmons: Shadow 21	Capt. James: Shadow 24
Capt. Carter: Shadow 25	Capt. Van Over: Shadow 26
Capt. Lefarth: Shadow 28	Capt. McNamara:Shadow 30
Capt. Ruester: Shadow 31	Lt. Carlson: Shadow 32
Maj. Donahue: Shadow 33	Capt. Walker: Shadow 35
Lt. Keller: Shadow 36	Lt. Letterman: Shadow 38
Capt. Garcia: Shadow 39	Capt. Beatty: Shadow 40
Lt. French: Shadow 41	Lt. Marr: Shadow 42
Capt. Stahl: Shadow 44	Lt. Noonan: Shadow 45 [8]

***

On 30 June 1971, a fifty-one-truck convoy departed Phnom Penh on Route 4 for Cambodia's major seaport, Kompong Som. Enemy forces were spotted at a point on Route 4 by an USAF FAC covering the convoy. The FAC suspected the enemy were preparing to ambush the convoy and requested strike aircraft to the site. An AC-119 gunship from Fighting C Flight was diverted from a target northeast of Phnom Penh to the ambush area. The convoy had not reached the suspected ambush site and the FAC decided to investigate further before clearing the Shadow to fire. The FAC's suspicions were confirmed and he cleared the Shadow to attack the enemy forces. The AC-119G attacked the enemy troop concentrations and saturated the area with 7.62mm bullets while receiving heavy ground fire, including 12.7mm automatic weapons (AW) fire in return. The Shadow continued to engage the enemy until the last truck in the convoy had safely passed the ambush zone.

When the AC-119G Shadow gunship returned to Tan Son Nhut Air Base, it had flown for 5.3 hours and expended 31,500 rounds of 7.62mm ammunition. The extended loiter capability and devastating firepower of the Shadow had again proven the effectiveness of fixed-wing gunships.[9]

The 17th SOS quarterly report for April, May, and June 1971 included a total of 918 combat sorties flown, 9,493,500 7.62mm rounds expended, 5,719 flares launched, and 391 TICs in which Shadows were engaged. Total BDA included 18 trucks, 12 carts, 19 other vehicles, 131 sampans, 103 boats, and 723 KBA. Fighting C Flight BDA report for April through June 1971 reflected essentially the same as the 17th SOS report: 18 trucks, 12 carts, 10 other vehicles, 131 sampans, 103 boats, and 723 KBA. No distinction was made on the report as to destroyed or damaged targets. Phan Rang BDA information was not available in the report most likely due to the VNAF I & M Training Program at Phan Rang taking over all combat frags on the first of May.

Major problem areas continued to be aircraft engines and propeller systems. The R3350-93 and the R3350-95W engines proved to be more reliable than their predecessor R3350-89B engines. Aircraft 52-5925 was modified by removal of the four-blade Aero-Products propeller and its regulator and the installation of the three-blade Hamilton Standard propeller system. The modified aircraft was quieter while having a slightly increased payload and a reduced fuel consumption rate.

A new flare, the LUU-2, was introduced for test purposes on 18th SOS Stinger gunships based at NKP. Test results proved outstanding. The LUU-2 flare burned longer and brighter than the MK-24 flare with a decreased dud rate. Consequently, the LUU-2 eventually replaced the MK-24s as the old flares were expended.[10]

With the influx of VNAF flight crews at Tan Son Nhut, USAF flight crew personnel assigned to Fighting C Flight on 20 May totaled 14 pilots, 12 copilots, 24 navigators, 11 flight engineers, 31 gunners, and 10 illuminator operators. By 30 June, aircrew personnel had dropped to 11 pilots, 10 copilots, 17 navigators, 6 flight engineers, 23 gunners, and 7 illuminator operators.

The programmed phase-out of the 17th SOS resulted in negative replacement personnel for those returning to CONUS at the end of tour completion. This plus the I & M Program requirements resulted in heavy demands on USAF aircrew members to utilize their limited free time in learning and accomplishing additional and administrative duties.[11]

By the summer of 1971, the top secrecy of Mekong River convoys had faded away as reports of convoys even graced the headlines of the *Stars and Stripes*. In spite of dangerous working conditions, news reporters were becoming more prevalent in Cambodia. Some reporters had already paid the ultimate price or would eventually pay the ultimate price for their daring quests of news information about the war in Cambodia.

The drawdown of American airmen crewing and maintaining AC-119G Shadow gunships obviously affected 17th SOS combat operations. Vietnamization of the war was paramount! Even so, the achievements of the squadron were directly attributed to the dedication to duty and unselfish professionalism exhibited by remaining USAF Shadow aircrews and support personnel.

VNAF crews assumed the responsibility of more combat frags at Tan Son Nhut from USAF crews in June. At this time, four of the seven combat frags were being flown by VNAF crews with a USAF instructor pilot and instructor navigator onboard.

As of 30 June, the I & M Program at Phan Rang had progressed as scheduled with combat missions providing VNAF student crews with valuable training. On 2 July, Shadow 71 was diverted by II DASC to Firebase Fuller in MR I. When the crew arrived over the firebase, they found the friendly troops being overrun by a large enemy force. The VNAF copilot and navigator contacted the Vietnamese ground commander and quickly determined the situation. Clearance to fire under the direction of the ground commander was obtained and Shadow 71 began placing a stream of bullets into the enemy force, disrupting their advance and preventing them from mounting a sustained attack. The attack was repelled and in a sweep of the area the following morning, the friendly forces credited Shadow 71 with thirty enemy bodies and numerous blood trails.[12]

EIGHTEEN

Shadows Become Black Dragons

During the last three months of operations for the 17th Special Operations Squadron in Southeast Asia, changes in personnel created by individuals with a DEROS from the Squadron resulted in the following list of key squadron personnel at Phan Rang Air Base (as recorded in the final quarterly report for July, August, and September 1971): 17th SOS Commander Lt. Col. Edward A. Elbert Jr. (DEROS 8 July) and 17th SOS Commander Lt. Col. Glenn R. Loveall (9 July–31 Aug). Other key personnel serving the squadron until deactivation were: Lieutenant Colonel Carl W. Brage, Sq. Nav., SEFE Nav., Adm. and Exec. Officer; Capt. Gary A. Totten, Operations Officer; MSgt George C. Stout Jr., First Sergeant; Capt. Thomas R. Hughes, Maintenance Officer; and CMSgt Oliver C. Bell, Maintenance Superintendent

Lieutenant Colonel James W. "Bill" James continued as flight commander of FOL Fighting C Flight at Tan Son Nhut. Major Gene Donahue replaced Lt. Col. William Gregory as C Flight operations officer on 10 August. Other positions in the Flight included: Technical Sergeant James Culbertson, Flight First Sergeant; Maj. Howard Nolan, Administrative Officer; and Sgt Haskett and Sgt Cotton, Administrative Specialists.[1]

The mission of the 17th SOS operations at Tan Son Nhut remained unchanged during July, August, and September 1971 as outlined in 7th

AF Operation Order 538-69, "Gunship III (AC-119G/K)" on a priority
basis: 1) Close fire support of friendly troops in contact, 2) Close fire
support of U.S. and friendly military installations including forts and
outposts., 3) Close fire support of strategic hamlets, villages and district
towns, 4) Pre-planned armed recce and interdiction of hostile areas and
infiltration routes, 5) Search and Rescue support, 6) Night armed escort
for road and close off-short convoys, 7) Illumination for night fighter
strikes, and 8) Harassment and interdiction.[2]

The inactivation of the 17th SOS as directed in 7th AF Programmed
Action Directive (PAD) #71-7-17 demanded constant coordination to
keep abreast of the multiple changes and to seek guidance on problems
created by and unsolved by the PAD. The phase-down decreased personnel placing heavy workloads on remaining members of the organiza-
tion. The initial plan called for a complete stand-down for combat missions at the Tan Son Nhut FOL. This changed however, and the combat
missions continued, necessitating the return of four instructor crews to
the MOL (military operating location). This further increased the work-
load of the I & M Program instructors remaining at Phan Rang in the
form of many more additional duties to effect the phase-down. Maintenance excelled as evidenced by their outstanding operational ready rates
of 76.7% and 79.1% for July and August. During this period, three-
blade Hamilton Standard propellers with two modifications on four aircraft were accomplished during twenty-eight phases. Simultaneously,
maintenance prepared all twenty-four aircraft for transfer to the VNAF
819th Combat Squadron.[3]

Fighting C Flight flew seven missions per day averaging 4.5 hours per
mission while providing twenty-four-hour coverage over Cambodia.
Three of the missions were flown by USAF crews and four missions
were flown by VNAF crews with a USAF instructor pilot and instructor
navigator onboard. On 25 July 71, VNAF crews began flying six of the
seven sorties with a USAF instructor pilot and instructor navigator onboard and one sortie per day was flown by a USAF crew.

Shadow gunships from Tan Son Nhut supported a major FANK operation conducted in the vicinity of Kampong Chhnang on 25 July. Ten

FANK battalions, covered by FAC Rustic 16 and Shadow gunships, started a military offensive thrust from three locations; Tang Kouk on Highway 6, Ekon, and Kampong Chhang. The objective of this operation was to secure and establish a friendly fire base at the city of Prey Kri, located to the southeast of Kampong Chhang in the center of a major enemy infiltration route. Once established, using the radio call sign of Hotel Kang Rey, the fire base would disrupt and attempt to block the flow of enemy supplies through the area that had long been an enemy strong hold. This operation was a complete success. Shadow gunships provided direct fire support for the base during all enemy attacks and were credited with deterring any further attacks that were expected from enemy troops.

During this time, Kompong Thom (KPT) remained under siege but not without territorial gains around the city by KPT garrison troops. Colonel Oum was still the brigade commander for troops defending the province capital. The KPT garrison had extended its control to five miles around the city, but was still devoid of resupply by land routes.

High altitude supply airdrops delivered by Cambodian C-47s and USAF C-130s helped in spite of losing half of the airdrops to enemy troops because of inaccuracy. Low altitude drops from USAF C-130s proved highly successful as all supplies landed within KPT city limits. Riverine operations also supplied KPT with necessary supplies by running convoys of small boats from Kompong Chhnang up the Tonle Sap and then eastward on the Stung Sen River to KPT.

To create an aircraft landing strip just north of KPT, Colonel Oum used a portion of Highway 6 for construction of a runway plus taxiways. Bricks from destroyed houses in KPT were used for the runway surface and leveled with a GMC truck loaded with forty people for extra weight. Cambodian Air Force C-47s used the runway to fly in supplies for KPT.[4]

Colonel Oum made several trips during the summer to Bien Hoa and Tan Son Nhut for briefings and to escort Cambodians to be trained on Rustic FACs and Shadow gunships for more effective air support/ground communication coordination. Normally, Oum incorporated in his trips the personal acquisition of firearms to take with him on the flight back to Cambodia. Shadow 28 pilot, Captain Ralph Lefarth wrote about one of Oum's visits to Tan Son Nhut: "One day on the crew bus, on our way to Base Ops., we saw Colonel Oum (Kampong Thom garrison commander—Hotel 303) carrying an arm load of odds and ends of contraband arms he had collected in Saigon. This included sawed-off shotguns, AK47s, etc. Upon seeing Oum and his weapons, one of the Nav's on the bus said, 'Boy, it looks like he's going to fight a war.' The whole bus broke into laughter, knowing that was exactly what he was doing with the stuff. Needless to say, we liked Colonel Oum and Colonel Oum liked us Shadows. If we had an empty room in our barracks, he stayed with us when he was in Saigon."[5]

August 15th was the date set for standing down and the beginning of a transition period lasting until 10 September at which time the VNAF, operating as the 819th Attack Squadron, would take control of Fighting C Flight operations with selected instructors from the 17th SOS remaining as advisors.

Nonetheless, on 15 August 1971, in order to provide continuing gunship air cover in Cambodia, a directive was received by the 17th SOS from 7th AF to continue flying fragged missions past 15 August. But due to the reduction in USAF manning and VNAF preparation for a transition period, Fighting C Flight's fragged sorties per day was reduced from seven sorties to five sorties per day starting on 15 August. Of the five sorties, two missions were flown by USAF crews and three missions were flown by VNAF crews with USAF instructors. This schedule continued until Fighting C Flight operations were turned over to the VNAF in September.

The first I & M Program AC-119G gunship was ferried from Phan Rang to Tan Son Nhut on 15 August and was accepted by the VNAF on 17 August. The day was the beginning for the VNAF 819th Hac Long "Black Dragons" Squadron of AC-119G gunships. Commander of the new squadron was Major Dang Van Duc. Captains Pham Bich and Nguyen Van Hong were assistant squadron CO and squadron operations officer, respectively.

USAF personnel assigned to 17th SOS FOL C Flight at Tan Son Nhut had dwindled to nineteen pilots and fourteen navigators which included the flight commander Lt. Col. James, an operations officer, an administrative officer, and a duty officer. There were six flight engineers, six illuminator operators, and nineteen airborne weapons mechanics (aka aerial gunners), two of which were permanently grounded and two of which were assigned to munitions loading on a rotating basis. Three personnel were assigned to the flight as operations and administrative specialists and two life support specialists were assigned to take care of flight crew personal equipment. There were also four interpreters assigned to the flight. Alert status for flight crews at Tan Son Nhut was discontinued on 15 August 71.[6]

Cambodia still remained the exclusive operating area for the 17th SOS FOL at Tan Son Nhut. Supporting fire bases and towns with military significance as well as ground operations initiated by the Cambodian government were of primary importance. The southwestern monsoon season (wet season) brought-on strong winds, heavy rain, and storms which hampered flying conditions. Weather dominated Shadow operations during the months of July and August.

Due to the flying conditions encountered during the monsoon season, effective air support was many times limited and at times impossible. The weather was also a factor in the reduced AAA reactions, KBA, WBA, and enemy traffic damaged or destroyed on the lines of communications. During July and August, twenty-six gunships reported enemy anti-aircraft (AA) fire with two of the gunships taking hits without any crew injuries/loss or significant damage to the aircraft.

Major Alfred "Al" Breaud and Capt. James Garcia were in charge of extensive OJT training and testing of VNAF students at Fighting C Flight during Phase IV of I & M training. Aircraft maintenance officer, Capt. Eugene Corbett ensured continuous gunship coverage in the AO by having OR aircraft parked in the revetments. Corbett's responsibilities also included the training of VNAF maintenance personnel to take over the aircraft after the transition.

With an adjusted transition completion target date of 10 September, the transition of AC-119G Shadow gunship operation and maintenance control from USAF personnel to VNAF personnel had begun on 15 August. Transition included preparation of gunships for transfer to the

VNAF inventory such as removing USAF markings from aircraft and painting on VNAF markings and changing some equipment like secure voice capability.

***

During August in Cambodia, the FANK undertook a major military offensive labeled Operation Chenla II. Instigated by Khmer Republic Prime Minister Lon Nol upon his return in April to Phnom Penh after successful stroke rehabilitation in Hawaii, the plan encompassed opening supply routes to besieged government troops and to regain control of the country's heartland.

Operation Chenla II was initiated with basically the same objectives as those of Operation Chenla I in 1970. Chenla II had three major objectives: 1) Clear approximately seventy miles of Highway 6 from Skoun to Kompong Thom and clear Highways 7 and 21 from Kompong Cham to Kompong Thom, 2) stop movement of enemy supplies from the northeast to the Kompong Chhnang region at the southern tip of the Tonle Sap, and 3) regain control of the central agricultural region of Cambodia. Chenla II was very ambitious considering the reality of Cambodian military strength. Actual troop strength was consistently over-reported by many Cambodian field commanders.

Operation Chenla II officially started on 20 August 1971 with the Force Armee Nationale Khmere (FANK) (aka Cambodian Army) fighting northward on route 6 from Tan Kouk located north of Skoun on Route 6 to Kompong Thma where they arrived on the first of September. In the meantime, a brigade task force from Kompong Thom under the direction of Colonel Oum (Hotel 303) drove fifteen miles south on Route 6 to meet up with the main FANK column at Kompong Thma on 5 October.[7]

Meanwhile, another FANK unit advanced northward on Route 21 from Kompong Cham to join up with FANK forces from Kompong Thma who were moving southward on Route 21 from Kompong Thma. Strong NVA resistance along Route 21 stymied FANK advances from both directions, thus keeping control of the road between Kompong Thma and Traeung in enemy hands. During the FANK advance up Route 21 in September from

Traeung, Rustic 07 was shot down. The pilot and translator bailed-out over Kompong Cham and were safely rescued uninjured by the townspeople before USAF "Jolly Green" rescue helicopters arrived to fly the two back to their home base at Bien Hoa AB, RVN.[8]

On the afternoon of 23 August 1971, Fighting C Flight instructor pilot Captain Ralph Lefarth (Shadow 28) flew with a VNAF crew aboard an AC-119G gunship with Vietnamese markings. Following is Capt. Lefarth's account of the mission over Cambodia in support of Operation Chenla II:

> I was monitoring the Vietnamese crew from the jump seat. Things were quiet for over two hours; then a FAC radioed us asking, "Shadow 28, do you normally trail smoke off your left engine?" The Vietnamese copilot answered, "Roger that" before going back to sleep. Engine instruments showed no signs of a problem. I raced down the ladder to the gun compartment and saw a ribbon of blue-black smoke trailing us as far as I could see. I ran back to the cockpit and started trying to identify a cause of the problem. The (Shadow) instructor navigator confirmed the nearest emergency airport was Phnom Penh.[9]

Upon safely landing at Phnom Penh's Pochenong Airport, Shadow 28's left engine oil quantity gauge read zero. After hours of waiting for evacuation, Lefarth and the crew were transported back to Tan Son Nhut via a USAF C-130. The crippled AC-119 gunship parked at Pochenong was recovered three weeks later.

By October, all USAF Shadow gunships were officially VNAF Black Dragon gunships, but American Shadow instructor/advisor pilots and navigators were still flying with some Black Dragon crews with Shadow radio call signs of the onboard USAF instructor/advisor pilot. Shadow gunships of Fighting C Flight continued flying in support of the FANK and Operation Chenla II under aircraft markings of the Republic of Vietnam. As an example, Capt. Lefarth would finally fly his last combat mission as an in-

structor/advisor pilot for VNAF Black Dragon crews on 9 October 1971.
On that night, Lefarth flew with VNAF crew #18 on a very quiet CAP mission over Saigon. Shortly thereafter, after having flown 204 AC-119G gunship combat missions in SEA during his tour of duty in Vietnam, the Captain boarded his Freedom Flight for the long trip home to Missouri.

AC-119 Shadow gunships supported Operation Chenla II often under extremely adverse flying conditions and heavy enemy ground fire. Within the Andong Plantation, a long held enemy headquarters area, immediately to the east of Highway 6, FANK forces were met with stiff resistance, but with Shadow coverage and TAC air support directed by Rustic FACs, FANK casualties were relatively light.[10]

***

I & M Program Phase II and III training of the 24 VNAF AC-119G aircrews was completed at Phan Rang on 27 August 1971. By 31 August, five of the seventeen VNAF crews at Tan Son Nhut were completely qualified to conduct missions on their own. During the entire VNAF I & M training program, the 17th SOS Shadows at Phan Rang continued to provide illuminator and fire support for allied forces in Military Region II and on few occasions outside the MR.[11]

With the imminent inactivation of the 14th Special Operations Wing at the end of September 1971, 7th Air Force on 25 August 1971 transferred the 18th Special Operations Squadron of AC-119K Stinger gunships to the 56th Special Operations Wing at Nakhon Phanom (NKP) Royal Thai Air Force Base (RTAFB), Thailand. A detachment (Det.1) of 18th SOS Stingers remained stationed at DaNang (30 Sep '71 – 31 Dec '72) and a FOL was established at Bien Hoa AB, NVN.

***

On 9 September 1971, the last gunship of 24 AC-119G Shadows was transferred to and accepted by the Republic of Vietnam Air Force (VNAF) at Tan Son Nhut Air Base, RVN. Fighting C Flight's six Shadow gunships plus eighteen Shadow gunships of the 17th SOS and Bravo Flight at Phan Rang were formally turned over to the VNAF 5th

Event at the Tan Son Nhut Air Base Officer's Club commemorating the USAF turn-over of 17th SOS Shadows to the VNAF. (*Left to right*): 17th SOS C Flight Commander Lt. Col. James "Bill" James, VNAF General Nguyen Cao Ky, 7th AF Commander General Lucius Clay, VNAF 819th "Black Dragon" Combat Squadron Commander Maj. Dan Vang Duc, and Vice-Commander Capt. Phan Bich.

Air Division, 53rd Tactical Wing, 819th Hac Long (Black Dragons) Attack Squadron at Tan Son Nhut Air Base, Saigon. The AC-119G Shadow gunships were summarily renamed Black Dragon gunships. A total of twenty-four AC-119G gunships now displayed the insignia of the VNAF.

On 10 September 1971, deactivation ceremonies for the 14th SOW were held at Phan Rang Air Base. General John D. Levelle, 7th AF Commander, and Lieutenant General Tran Van Minh, VNAF Commander, addressed the Wing expressing thanks for a job well done. 14th SOW aircraft conducted a fly-over for the event. Upon the official deactivation of the 14th Special Operations Wing, the 14th Field Maintenance Squadron (FMS), the 17th Special Operations Squadron, and Headquarters 14th Special Operations Wing were officially deactivated. 14th SOW Commander Colonel Mark W. Magnan received the Legion of Merit during the ceremony.

Also on 10 September 1971 at Tan Son Nhut, the last USAF AC-119G Shadow gunship combat mission was flown by Fighting C Flight Commander Lt. Col. James William "Bill" James as aircraft commander of Shadow 05 with an All-American crew. Crew members included: Capt. Gary Walker, copilot; Capt. Warner Giles, navigator; 1/Lt. Pete Clark, night observation scope operator; SSgt Kenneth Vanderhoff, flight engineer; SSgt Earl Murray, illuminator operator; TSgt Charles White and SSgt Eugene Lee, gunners. The mission was launched at 0400 hours for armed recon over Cambodia, but when diverted to a TIC in support of Hotel 40, James and his crew did what all Shadow crews were expected to accomplish; they silenced enemy guns and mortars and drove away the attacking enemy forces with withering firepower. Thus, with this final USAF AC-119 Shadow gunship mission, the saga of the USAF 71st and 17th Special Operations Squadrons and the Shadow "Charlie Chasers" came to a successful end.

The 17th Special Operations Squadron's final BDA report that only included the months of July and August was:

	July	August	Total
Sorties Scheduled	217	185	402
Sorties Flown	214	182	396
Firing Sorties	166	149	315
Time on Target	643.9	546.0	1,189.9 (hours)
Total Rounds	2,214,974	1,783,467	3,998,441 (7.62mm)
Flares Launched	880	792	1,672

Dud Flares	71	72	143
Troops-In-Contact	96	73	169
Trucks Damaged	1	0	1
Carts Damaged	3	3	6
Other Vehicles	2	3	5
Sampans	42	38	80
Boats	10	10	20
KBA*	78	70	148
WBA	9	150	159

Confirmed by Ground Commanders

AAA Reactions

Daytime	7	15	22
Nighttime	4	11	15
Gunships Fired At	11	26	37
Gunships Hit**	1	1	2

** Both gunships hit during nighttime missions.[12]

***

With deactivation of the 14th SOW and the 17th SOS, Shadow gunship personnel still in-country were orphans without an "official" USAF designated unit. Most Shadows did not know that they had become part of operations and support personnel for the 377th Combat Support Group (CSG) based at Tan Son Nhut Air Base after the deactivation of the 17th. The 377th CSG was assigned to 7th Air Force, the air arm of Military Assistant Command—Vietnam (MAC-V) at TSN responsible for operations and maintenance of the USAF portion of TSN. Responsibilities included housing, maintenance, base defense, and liaison with VNAF, and support of numerous organizations including 7th AF. In 1971, the 377th was responsible for supporting flight operations of T-39, C-54, C-118, and C-130 aircraft of the 834th Air Division.

17th SOS instructor/advisor personnel listed as operations and support personnel for the 377th CSG in the *History of the 17th SOS* for 1 July—10 September 1971 were:

Pilots: Captain Douglas L. Batchelder, *Capt. James W. Carter, *Capt. James G. Garcia, Jr., *Capt. Victor H. Heiner, Capt. Richard S. Howze, *Capt. James E. Keller, *Capt. Ralph R. Lefarth, *Capt. Jay R. Simmons, *Capt. Gary J. Walker, and Capt. Herbert K Wiese, Jr.

Navigators included: Major Lawrence W. Barber, *Maj. George E. Bethke, Maj. Richard D. Bode, *1/Lt. David A. Harley, Capt. Joseph L. Hill, *1/Lt. Walter T. Howland, *Maj. Howard R. Nolan, Maj. Daniel W. Pruitt, *Maj. James A. Rash, *Maj. Ralph O. Riojas.

Flight Engineers included: Master Sergeant Laurence W. Crawford, *TSgt Franklin D. Gentry, TSgt Albert F. Leach, SSgt Kelly McNeil (NMI), and SSgt Kenneth G. Vanderhoff.

Illuminator Operators included: Staff Sergeant Richard A. Hall, SSgt Steven G. Jarmagin, Sgt Edward McGallion (NMI), *SSgt Ray B. Mandeville, *SSgt Grover J. Poe.

Aerial Gunners included: *Airman First Class David W. Dieher, *SSgt Jeffrey A. Anderson, *TSgt Samuel G. Jimenez, *SSgt Eugene A. Lee, *A1C Larry W. Payne, *SSgt Vernal D. Tuttle, TSgt Joseph C. Wells, *TSgt Charles A. White, *TSgt Jerry D. Williams, *SSgt David H. Zimmer.

Administrative Personnel included: Staff Sergeant Norman M. Wills, Jr., *Sgt Norris J. Cotton, Jr., *Sgt John L. Haskett.

Operations Clerks: *Sergeant Manuel J. Ramendez (Sp?) and SSgt Clement E. Hill.

Life Support: *Staff Sergeant William J. Timpkins, *Sgt. John A. Barfield, *Sgt. Michael C. Martin.

Maintenance Personnel at Phan Rang for the 377th CSG were TSgt Quenton H. Baccus, TSgt Wesley H Stinson, and SSgt Richard H. Boston. [*Denotes personnel assigned to Tan Son Nhut FOL.] [13]

Fighting C Flight Commander Lt. Col. James William "Bill" James remained in Vietnam as a Senior Advisor to the 819th Attack Squadron, VNAF (Black Dragons) until February 1972.

The last and final quarterly historical report of the 17th SOS for the 14th SOW History was compiled by Maj. Lawrence W. Barber, 17th SOS historical officer; Capt. Jay R. Simmons, TSN FOL historical officer; and Sgt Roberto Rodriguez.

Epilogue

B y October 1971, KPT was being resupplied via Route 6 from Skoun in spite of NVA troops controlling the surrounding territory. Eventually, NVA forces destroyed a bridge on Route 6 south of Skoun to deny use of the route by FANK relief columns. Rustic FACs had moved from Bien Hoa Air Base, RVN to Ubon Royal Thai Air Force Base, Thailand and USAF Shadow gunships no longer existed, having been replaced by VNAF AC-119 Black Dragons.

Other NVA attacks on Route 6 resulted in the Cambodian garrison at Rumlong located between Skoun and Kompong Thma to become completely isolated. Battles raged on for control of routes leading to Kompong Thom and the agriculture region of central Cambodia. In spite of gallant efforts by Rustic FACs and USAF A-37 Hawk fighter/bombers from Bien Hoa, the end was nearing. First, after two weeks of attacks, Rumlong fell to NVA forces in mid-November, followed in the first week of December of the capture of Baray and Kompong Thma.

Lon Nol's Operation Chenla II had failed when military operations ceased on 3 December 1971. Control of Route 6 and the rice crop in central Cambodia still belonged to the NVA. Supply routes into Laos were now open for the dry season resupply of NVA troops.

Fighting in Cambodia raged on into January 1972. Ubon-based Rustic FACs continued providing aerial reconnaissance and support for the FANK. USAF AC-119K Stinger gunships based at NKP, Thailand and AC-130 gunships at Ubon were on-call to defend Cambodian cities and FANK garrisons.

The 18th SOS AC-119K Stinger gunships stationed at NKP and air bases at DaNang and Bien Hoa in RVN were also playing key roles in the Commando Hunt VII Campaign, the Spring Offensive launched by enemy troops on 30 March 1972, and the Linebacker Campaign between May and October 1972.

Early in 1972, concentrations of NVA troops in South Vietnam were primed for an Eastertide Offensive to claim as much territory as possible in the Republic of Vietnam for peace negotiation purposes. On 1 May 1972, Quang Tri fell to the NVA but was retaken by ARVN troops in a counterattack with the support of offshore U.S. Naval bombardment and USAF B-52 strikes. NVA attacks on Kontum were finally repelled.

NVA forces were fully employed in South Vietnam, using conventional warfare weapons such as tanks and artillery pieces. Anti-aircraft guns and SA-7 Strella heat seeking missiles protected ground operations against air attacks. At An Loc, NVA troops attacked with all available weapons. While flying a daylight mission near An Loc on 2 May 1972, an AC-119K gunship, Stinger 41 was shot down by NVA .37mm anti-aircraft guns. Seven Stinger crewmen bailed-out and were rescued. The Stinger's pilot, copilot, and flight engineer went down with the gunship. The loss marked the last daylight mission fragged for Stinger gunships.

In December 1972, talks at the Paris peace negotiations stopped. President Nixon consequently ordered the bombing of Hanoi and Haiphong in Operation Linebacker II. Thanks to brave B-52 crewmen, like former AC-119 Shadow gunship combat crewmembers Maj. Earl Farney, Capt. Don Craig, and Capt. Don Carlson, the eleven-night "Christmas" Bombing Campaign by B-52s conducted in late December 1972 forced North Vietnam back to the peace conference table in Paris on 8 January 1973 that resulted in the signing of the Paris Peace Accords on 27 January 1973 by the United States, South Vietnam, Viet Cong (NLF), and North Vietnam. The peace agreement called for an in place cease-fire in Vietnam on 27 January with a cease-fire date of 23 February in Laos. No cease-fire in Cambodia was declared because Cambodia was not represented at the Paris Peace Conference. Thus, Cambodia was still at war with no cease-fire in sight as Nixon announced the cease-fire agreement for Vietnam to the world via television on 24 January 1971.

Consequently, Cambodia became the major battleground between communist and free world forces in Southeast Asia. AC-119K Stinger gunships stationed at Nakhon Phanom RTAFB, Thailand and AC-130 Spectre gunships roamed the skies over Cambodia for enemy targets identified by Rustic and Nail FACs. The NVA and Khmer Rouge noose around Phnom Penh grew tighter and tighter as time marched forward. The Khmer Republic had shrunk down to control of Phnom Penh, Kompong Thom, and Siem Reap. In early July 1973, President Nixon announced the date of 15 August 1973 for cessation of U.S. air activities in support of Cambodia (i.e., The Khmer Republic).

With the signing of the Paris Peace Accords, all military action in Vietnam was suspended effective on the signing date of 27 January 1973. On that day, the last combat mission by a Stinger gunship crew exclusively manned by Americans was flown by the 18th SOS FOL Detachment at Bien Hoa, landing just forty-five seconds before the required grounding time of 0600 hours for all armed aircraft in Vietnam.[1]

On 29 March 1973, the last U.S. military personnel departed South Vietnam. United States strike aircraft including 18th SOS AC-119K Stinger gunships of the 56th Special Operations Wing headquartered at NKP, Thailand continued support for the Cambodian Army until 15 August 1973 when the U.S. Congress, in violation of its treaty obligations, cut off all military support and aid to the Republic of Vietnam and to the Khmer Republic.

Under "Project Enhance," dated 1 October 1972, the twenty-two remaining AC-119K Stinger gunships in the USAF inventory were transferred to the VNAF 821st Tinh Long Attack Squadron of the 53rd Tactical Wing, 5th Air Division. Stinger instructor crews were charged with training VNAF aircrews in the AC-119K gunship. The last VNAF combat training mission for Detachment 1 at Da Nang was flown on 1 March 1973.

Four of the twenty-six C-119G "Flying Boxcars" converted into AC-119K Stinger gunships were lost during the three years, three and one-half months of combat duty in Southeast Asia. The 18th Special Operations Squadron was deactivated on 31 December 1972.

Ignoring the Paris Peace Accords signed in January 1973, the North Vietnam Army and the Viet Cong eventually resumed full-scale war on

South Vietnam. The Khmer Rouge continued to wage bloody war on Cambodia and its courageous people who dreamed of living in peace and freedom from communism. Both nations finally collapsed under the onslaught of communist troops.

On 17 April 1975, Phnom Penh surrendered to the Khmer Rouge and its leader Pol Pot. Phnom Penh became a ghost city as Pol Pot and the Khmer Rouge led Cambodians into "The Killing Fields."

Surrounded by 13 NVA Divisions, Saigon surrendered to North Vietnam on 30 April 1975 and was renamed Ho Chi Minh City by the North Vietnamese in honor of their revolutionary leader. The Republic of Vietnam (South Vietnam) no longer existed.

USAF Brigadier General Harry C. "Heinie" Aderholt could not have said it better: "The U.S. had let down its allies." The general was a dynamic leader and driving force in USAF Air Commando/Special Operations warfare during the Vietnam War that earned him the title of "Air Commando One."

Afterword

For combat action in Southeast Asia from 1 Jun 69 thru 30 Sep 71, the 17th Special Operations Squadron was issued the Presidential Unit Citation and the Air Force Outstanding Unit Award with Combat "V" Device for action between 1 July 1970 and 30 June 1971. The 17th SOS was also awarded the Republic of Vietnam Gallantry Cross with Palm for action between 1 June 1969 and 30 September 1971.

Campaign Streamers awarded to the 17th Special Operations Squadron were: Vietnam: TET 69/Counteroffensive, Vietnam Summer/Fall 1969, Vietnam Winter/Spring 1970, Sanctuary Counteroffensive, Southwest Monsoon, Commando Hunt V, and Commando Hunt VI.

The 14th Special Operations Wing was awarded the Presidential Outstanding Unit Citation on January 1, 1971 for highly successful and noteworthy accomplishments in the war effort.

Fifty-two USAF C-119G "Flying Boxcars" were converted to twenty-six AC-119G Shadow gunships and 26 AC-119K Stinger gunships. Twenty-four of the twenty-six 71st SOS/17th SOS AC-119G Shadow gunships and twenty-two of the twenty-six 18th SOS AC-119K Stinger gunships survived combat operations in Southeast Asia from 1969 to 1972.

The 71st Special Operations Squadron was re-activated at Kirtland Air Force Base, New Mexico on 20 May 2005. Assigned to the 58th Special Operations Wing, the 71st was the first USAF unit to receive Bell/Boeing CV-22 Osprey aircraft. The 71st accompanies the 550th SOS and its H/MC-130P Combat Shadow and MC-130 Combat Talon II aircraft at Kirtland. The 58th SOW is a Flying/Aircrew Training Unit of the Air Education and Training Command (AETC).

The 17th Special Operations Squadron was re-activated at Kadena Air Base, Okinawa on 1 August 1989. As a squadron of the 353rd Special Operations Group, the 17th SOS fly MC-130P aircraft called "Combat Shadows." The mission of the squadron is multi-tasked from infiltration to exfiltration of special ground units, aerial refueling of helicopters, and humanitarian assistance all over the Pacific region. During Japan's earthquake/tsunami in 2011, the 17th SOS was instrumental in opening the airport at Sendai for emergency operations within hours of the catastrophe. During the past twenty-two years, the 17th has trained and advised dozens of foreign militaries through Joint Combined Exchange Training (JCET).

The future and importance of USAF Special Operations continues to grow with time. Long will be the need for freedom loving people to have a diversified military force that includes manned and unmanned aircraft to support and conduct military operations.

***

John Paul Vann was one of the most knowledgeable and respected American advisors in Vietnam until his death in 1972. He remarked in the early years of U.S. involvement in Southeast Asia that the Vietnam War was a political war that called for discrimination in killing. The best weapon for killing would have been a knife, but beyond the knife, the side-firing USAF gunship and the USA helicopter gunship were probably the closest that air power could come to Vann's knife.

Chapter Notes

Prologue
1. Smith, Jerry. "Adieu at Dien Bien Phu," VIETNAM, pp. 48-53.
2. Grant, Rebecca. "Dien Bien Phu," Air Force Magazine, pp. 78-84.

Chapter I: Emergence of USAF Fixed-Wing Gunships
1. Ballard, Jack S., *Development and Employment of Fixed-Wing Gunships 1962-1973*, pp. 34-35.
2. Ibid., pp. 51-52.
3. Ibid., p. 57.

Chapter II: Gunship III
1. Pyle, James, 71st SOS Activation. *www.71stsos.com/biography.html*

Chapter III: Call to War
1. Hamilton, William, AC-119 Memoir. www.ac-119gunships.com
2. *Ibid.*
3. *Ibid.*
4. *Ibid.*

Chapter IV: 71st SOS Combat Operations
1. Emma, Frank, Memoir. *AC-119 Gunship History Book 1968-1973*, pp. 78-79.
2. Hamilton, William, Memoir. *www.ac-119gunships.com*
3. Gabor, Louis. Interview.
4. *Happy Valley Weekly*, Phan Rang AB, RVN, 1969.
5. *Ibid.*, 5 June 1969.
6. *Ibid.*
7. 71st SOS Mission Review. *www.71stsos.com*

Chapter V: 17th SOS Activation and Take-Over
1. Hamilton, William, Memoir. *www.ac-119gunships.com*
2. Farney, Collection, unpaginated.

3. *Ibid.*

4. Hamilton, William, Memoir. *www.ac-119gunships.com*

Chapter VI: Good Morning Vietnam, 1970

1. Alau, Hank, Memoir. A*C-119 Gunships History Book 1968-1973*, p. 24.

2. Chandler, Allen, Memoir. *AC-119 Gunships History Book 1968-1973*, pp. 48-51.

3. Bokern, Robert, Memoir. *AC-119 Gunships History Book 1968-1973*, p. 44.

4. Nolan, Keith, *Into Cambodia*, pp. 46-48.

5. *Ibid.*, p. 55

6. Farney, Collection, unpaginated.

7. Phu Cat AB Newspaper, "Cobra Courier," 18 May 1970.

8. Lavell, Kit, *Flying Black Ponies*, pp. 64-65.

9. Lloyd, Alwyn, *Fairchild C-82 Packet & C-119 Flying Boxcars*, pp. 122-123

10. Farney, Collection, unpaginated.

11. Bokern Memoir.

12. Chandler Memoir.

Chapter VIII: The Cambodia Incursion

1. *History of 17th SOS*, 1 April to 30 June 1970, unpaginated.

2. Shaw, *The Cambodian Campaign*, p. 73.

3. Nolan, *Into Cambodia*, p. 348.

4. Nalte, *Air War over South Vietnam*, p. 199.

5. Alau, Memoir. *AC-119 Gunships History Book 1968-1973*, pp. 24-25.

6. Davis, Interview.

7. CHECO Report #52, pp. 34-71.

8. Shaw, *op. cit.*, p. 145.

9. Nalte, *op. cit.*, p. 202.

Chapter IX: Secret Shadows Cover Cambodia

1. *History of 17th SOS*, 1 July to 30 September 1970, unpaginated.

2. Wood, *Call Sign Rustic*, p. 1.

3. Teal, Memoir, unpaginated.

4. *Ibid.*

5. Shaw, *The Cambodian Campaign*, pp. 140-145.

6. Lloyd, *Fairchild C-82 Packet & C-119 Flying Boxcar,* p. 123.

7. Nolan, *Into Cambodia*, p. 439.

8. Wood, *op. cit.* pp. 78-79.

9. Farney, Collection, unpaginated.

10. Lloyd, *op. cit.*, p. 122.

11. CHECO Report, Cambodian Campaign, p. 34.

12. Nalte, *Air War over South Vietnam*, pp. 203-204.

13. *Ibid.* p. 205.

14. *History of 17th SOS*, op. cit.

15. Nalte, *op. cit.*, p. 207.

Chapter X: Fighting C Flight

1. *History of 17th SOS*, 1 October to 31 December 1970, unpaginated.

2. Farney Collection, unpaginated.

3. Nalte, *Air War over South Vietnam*, p. 208.

4. Farney, *op. cit.* unpaginated.

5. Teal, Memoir, unpaginated.

6. Wood, *Call Sign Rustic*, p. 79.

7. *History of 17th SOS, op. cit.*

8. Teal, *op. cit.*

Chapter XI: Guardian Strikers

1. Nalte, *The War against Trucks*, p.144.

2. Nalte, *Air War over South Vietnam*, p. 204.

3. *History of 17th SOS*, 1 July to 30 September 1970, unpaginated.

4. Farney, Collection, unpaginated.

5. Gericke, Memoir.

6. Farney, Collection, unpaginated.

7. Teal, Memoir. unpaginated.

8. *Nalte, op. cit.*, pp. 209-210.

9. *History of 17th SOS*, op. cit.

Chapter XII: Fearless Fliers

1. *History of 17th SOS*, 1 October to 31 December 1970, unpaginated.

2. Wood, *Call Sign Rustic*, p. 87.

3. Lefarth, Memoir.

4. *Ibid.*

5. *History of 17th SOS, op. cit.*

6. *Ibid.*

7. *Ibid.*

8. *7th AF Commando Hunt V Report*, May 1971, p. 111.

9. *History of 17th SOS, op. cit.*

10. *7th AF Commando Hunt V Report, op. cit.*, p. 113.

11. Wood, *op. cit.*, pp. 90-93.

12. *History of 17th SOS, op. ci*t.

13. *Ibid.*

14. Nalte, *Air War over South Vietnam*, p. 208.

Chapter XIII: Shadows over Laos

1. *History of 17th SOS*, 1 October to 31 December 1970, unpaginated.

2. *Ibid.*

3. Safreno Memoir

4. Wood, *Call Sign Rustic*, p. 98.

5. *History of 17th SOS*, op. cit.

Chapter XIV: Recognition and Reports

1. Nalte, *Air War over South Vietnam*, p.237.

2. Teal, Memoir. unpaginated.

3. Farney, *Shadows of Southeast Asia*, unpaginated.

4. Teal, *op. cit.*

5. Farney, *op. cit.*

6. *Ibid.*

7. *7th AF Commando Hunt V Report*, May 1971, p. 113.

8. *History of 17th SOS*, 1 October to 31 December 1970, unpaginated.

9. *7th AF Commando Hunt V Report*, op. cit.

10. *History of 17th SOS, op. cit.*

11. *Teal, op. cit.*

12. *History of 17th SOS, op. cit.*

Chapter XV: New Year, New Mission

1. Nalte, *Air War over South Vietnam*, p. 218.

2. Lloyd, *Fairchild C-82 Packet & C-119 Flying Boxcar*, p. 142.

3. *History of 17th SOS,* 1 January to 31 March 1971, unpaginated.

4. *7th AF Commando Hunt V Report*, May 1971, p. 113.

5. *History of 17th SOS, op. cit.*

6. Teal, Memoir. unpaginated.

7. *History of 17th SOS, op. cit.*

8. *7th AF Commando Hunt V Report, op. cit.*, p. 114.

9. Wood, *Call Sign Rustic*, p. 103.

10. *7th AF Commando Hunt V Report, op. cit.*, pp. 111-112.

11. *History of 17th SOS, op. cit.*
12. CHECO Report, "Aerial Support for River Convoys," pp. 1-2.
13. *Ibid.*, pp. 2-3.
14. *Ibid.*, p. 4.
15. *Wood, op. cit.*, p. 105.
16. CHECO Report, *op. cit.*, p. 7.
17. *Ibid.*, pp. 13-14.

Chapter XVI: In-Country and Out-Country

1. Roper, *Quoth the Raven*, pp. 115-117.
2. *Interactive Wartime Chronology Vietnam 1971*, p. 276.
3. *History of 17th SOS*, 1 January to 31 March 1971, unpaginated.
4. Fletcher, "Tank Busters," *VIETNAM*, pp. 26-33.
5. *Interactive Wartime Chronology Vietnam 1971, op. cit.*, p. 277.
6. Gericke, Memoir.
7. *History of 17th SOS, op. cit.*
8. *Ibid.*
9. *Ibid.*
10. *Ibid.*
11. *Ibid.*
12. *Ibid.*
13. Lloyd, *Fairchild C-82 Packet & C-119 Flying Boxcar*, p. 123.

Chapter XVII: Shadow Treadmill and Vietnamization

1. *Interactive War Chronology Vietnam* 1971, p. 279.
2. *7th AF Commando Hunt V Report*, May 1971, p. 112.
3. *History of 17th SOS*, 1 April to 30 June 1971, unpaginated.
4. *Ibid.*
5. Teal, Memoir, unpaginated.
6. Wood, *Call Sign Rustic*, p. 112.
7. *Interactive Wartime Chronology Vietnam 1971, op. ci*t., p. 283.
8. *History of 17th SOS, op.cit.*
9. CHECO Report "fixed-wing Gunships in SEA," p. 22.
10. *History of 17th SOS, op. cit.*
11. *Ibid.*
12. *Ibid.*

Chapter XVIII: Shadows Become Black Dragons
1. *History of 17th SOS*, 1 Jul - 10 Sep 1971, unpaginated.
2. *Ibid*.
3. *Ibid*.
4. Wood, *Call Sign Rustic*, p. 109.
5. Lefarth, Memoir.
6. *History of 17th SOS*, op. cit.
7. Wood, *op. cit.*, p. 112.
8. Wood, *op. cit.*, p. 114.
9. Lefarth, *op. cit.*
10. *History of 17th SOS, op. cit.*
11. *History of 17th SOS, Ibid.*
12. *History of 17th SOS, op. cit.*
13. History of 17th SOS, op. cit. pp. 29-32

Epilogue:
1. *AC-119 Gunship History Book 1968-73*, p. 13.

Bibliography

Primary Sources

Alau, Henry "Hank" D. Kailianu. Memoir, "Shadow (We Own The Night)." Oct 1969 – Sep 1970.

Bokern, Robert. Memoir

Chandler, Allen. Memoir.

Davis, Dennis L. Interview.

Emma, Frank. Memoir.

Farney, Earl J. Unpublished Manuscript "Shadows of Southeast Asia," Personal Collection of Documents, Records, Letters, and Transcriptions from Tape Recordings of Interviews and Events.

Fraker, Donald. Memoir.

Gericke, William. Memoir

Gabor, Louis. Interview.

Hamilton, William. Memoir, "Shadow AC-119: A History." Dec 1968 - Dec 1969.

Lefarth, Ralph. Shadow Memoir.

Safreno, Robert. Memoir.

Teal, Tom A. *Memoir, Shadow Gunships at Saigon and Distant Places Apr 1970– Apr 1971.*

Government Publications, Documents, and Reports

CHECO Report, USAF Support of Special Forces in SEA, 10 Mar 1969.

CHECO Report, Fixed-wing Gunships in SEA (Jul 69–Jul 71), 30 Nov 1971.

CHECO Report, Cambodian Campaign, 28 Apr–30 Jun 1970, The Vietnam Center and Archive, Texas Tech University.

CHECO PACAF S.E.A. Report, Aerial Protection of Mekong River Convoys in Cambodia, 1 Oct 1971, The Vietnam Center and Archive, Texas Tech University.

CHECO Report, USAF Tactical Reconnaissance in Southeast Asia, July 1969–June 1971, 23 Nov 1971, The Vietnam Center and Archive, Texas Tech University.

Commando Hunt III Report, Headquarters Seventh Air Force, May 1970, The Vietnam Center and Archive, Texas Tech University.

Commando Hunt V Report, Headquarters Seventh Air Force, May 1971, The Vietnam Center and Archive, Texas Tech University.

Corona Harvest Project, Pacific Air Forces (PACAF), *United States of America Operations in Laos: 1 Jan 70–30 Jun 71*. Maxwell AFB, AL, 1971.

History of the 17th Special Operations Squadron, 14th Special Operations Wing, 7th Air Force, 1 January to 31 March 1970. Maxwell AFB, AL. **

History of the 17th Special Operations Squadron, 14th Special Operations Wing, 7th Air Force, 1 April to 30 June 1970. Maxwell AFB, AL. **

History of the 17th Special Operations Squadron, 14th Special Operations Wing, 7th Air Force, 1 July to 30 September 1970. Maxwell AFB, AL. **

History of the 17th Special Operations Squadron, 14th Special Operations Wing, 7th Air Force, 1 October to 31 December 1970. Maxwell AFB, AL. **

History of the 17th Special Operations Squadron, 14th Special Operations Wing, 7th Air Force, 1 January to 31 March 1971. Maxwell AFB, AL. **

History of the 17th Special Operations Squadron, 14th Special Operations Wing, 7th Air Force, 1 April to 30 June 1971. Maxwell AFB, AL. **

History of the 17th Special Operations Squadron, 14th Special Operations Wing, 7th Air Force, 1 July to 10 September 1971. Maxwell AFB, AL. **

National Archives, Nixon Presidential Materials, NSC Files, NSC Institutional Files (H-Files), Box H-219: DOD Foreign Relations Department, 1969-1976, Vol. VII, Vietnam July 1970 – January 1972, p. 60-61.

* *Project CHECO: Contemporary Historical Examination of Current Operations. Project conducted and reported by HQ PACAF Directorate of Operations Analysis, CHECO/Corona Harvest Division.*

***Project Corona Harvest Reports: USAF and Air University system to evaluate the effectiveness of air power in Southeast Asia.*

Secondary Sources

Websites and E-Mails
AC-119 Gunships Homepage: *www.ac-119gunships.com*

Air Force Historical Research Agency, Factsheet: 17 Special Operations Squadron: *www.afhra.af.mil/factsheets/factsheet.asp?id=9847*

Interactive Wartime Chronology Vietnam 1971: *http://members.aol.com/warlib/v1971.htm*

71st Special Operations Squadron Homepage: *www.71stsos.com*

353rd Special Operations Group, 17th Special Operations Squadron, Fact Sheet: *www.353sog.af.mil/library/index.asp.*

Magazines, Presentations, and Journals
Berube, Claude G. "Ho Chi Minh and the OSS." *Vietnam Magazine* Vol. 22, No. 4 (December 2009) 52-56.

Berube, Claude G. "Ho, Giap and Me." *Vietnam Magazine* Vol. 24, No. 2 (August 2011) 38-41.

Fletcher, Larry Elton. "Tank Busters Over Laos." *Vietnam Magazine* Vol. 18, No. 6 (April 2006) 26-33.

Grant, Rebecca. "Dien Bien Phu." *Air Force Magazine* Vol. 87, No. 8 (August 2004) 78-84.

Hemingway, Al. "Answer to a Soldier's Prayer: Sacking NVA Sanctuaries in Cambodia, 1970." *VFW Magazine* (May 2010) 16-22.

Kolb, Richard K. and Von Lunen, Kelly. "America's Advisory War in Vietnam, 1962-64: A GI's Combat Chronology." *VFW Magazine* Vol. 98, No. 10 (August 2011) 30-34.

Smith, Jerry V. "Adieu At Dien Bien Phu." *Vietnam Magazine* Vol. 21, No 3 (October 2008) 48-53.

Newspapers, Media Reports, and Press Releases

7th Air Force Times/Southeast Asia

Stars & Stripes Vietnam Bureau

Happy Valley Weekly, Phan Rang AB, RVN

Cobra Courier, Phu Cat AB, RVN. Vol. 2, No. 2, May 18, 1970

Books

AC-119 Gunship Association, *AC-119 Gunships History Book 1968-1973*. Jefferson City, Missouri: Brown Printing Company, 2009.

Ballard, Jack S. *The United States Air Force in Southeast Asia: Development of Fixed-Wing Gunships*, 1962-1972. Washington, D. C.: Office of Air Force History, 1982.

Churchill, Jan. *Hit My Smoke*. Manhattan, Kansas: Sunflower University Press, 1997.

Conboy, Kenneth and Bowra, Kenneth. *The War in Cambodia 1970-75*. London: Osprey Publishing Ltd, 1989.

Davis, Larry. *Gunships: A Pictorial History*. Carrollton, Texas: Squadron/Signal Publications, Inc., 1982.

Deac, Wilfred P. *Road to the Killing Fields*. College Station: Texas A&M University Press, 1997.

Fall, Bernard B. *Street Without Joy*. Harrisburg, PA: Stackpole Co.,1961

Fletcher, Larry Elton. *Shadows of Saigon: Air Commandos in Southeast Asia*. Philadelphia, Pennsylvania: Xlibris Corporation, 2001.

Fletcher, Larry Elton. *The Shadow Spirit: Flying Stingers & BUFFs in S.E.A.* Philadelphia, Pennsylvania: Xlibris Corporation, 2004.

Gurney, Gene. *VIETNAM: The War in the Air*. New York, New York: Crown Publishing Inc., 1985.

Halberstam, David. *The Best and The Brightest*. New York: Ballantine Books, 1993.

Hass, Michael E. *Apollo's Warriors: United States Air Force Special Operations during the Cold War*. Maxwell Air Force Base, Alabama: Air University Press, 1997.

Head, William P. *Shadow & Stinger: Developing the AC-119G/K Gunships in the Vietnam War*. College Station, Texas: Texas A&M University Press, 2007.

Kamm, Henry. *Cambodia*. New York: Arcade Publishing Inc., 1998.

Kelley, Michael P. *Where We Were in Vietnam*. Ashland, Oregon: Hellgate Press, 2002.

Lavell, Kit. *Flying Black Ponies*. Annapolis: Naval Institute Press, 2000.

Lloyd, Alwyn T. *Fairchild C-82 Packet and C-119 Flying Boxcar*. Hinckley, England: Midland Publishing and Aerofax, 2005.

Mutza, Wayne. *GUNSHIPS: The Story of Spooky, Shadow, Stinger and Spectre*. North Branch, Minnesota: Specialty Press, 2009.

Nalty, Bernard C. *Interdiction in Southern Laos*. Washington, D.C.: Air Force History Office, 1988.

Nalty, Bernard C. *Air War over South Vietnam 1968-1975*. Washington D. C.: Office of Air Force History, 2000.

Nalty, Bernard C. *The War against Trucks—Aerial Interdiction in Southern Laos 1968-1992*. Washington D.C.: Office of Air Force History, 2005.

Nolan, Keith William. *Into Cambodia*. Novato, CA: Presidio Press, 1990.

Roper, Jim. *Quoth the Raven*. Baltimore: America House Book Publishers, 2001.

Rustic Forward Air Controller Association, Inc. *The Rustics*. www.lulu.com, 2011.

Shaw, John M. *The Cambodian Campaign*. Lawrence: University Press of Kansas, 2005.

Tran, Hoi B. *A Vietnamese Fighter Pilot in an American War*. Xlibris Corporation, 2011.

Trest, Warren A. *Air Commando One: Heine Aderholt and America's Secret Air Wars*. Washington and London: Smithsonian Institution Press, 2000.

Wood, Richard. *Call Sign Rustic: The Secret Air War over Cambodia, 1970-1973*. Washington and London: Smithsonian Institution Press, 2002.

Glossary of Terms and Acronyms

A & I	Armed Recce & Interdiction
AA	Anti-Aircraft (Enemy Guns)
AAA	Anti-Aircraft Artillery
ABORT	To Terminate Aircraft Mission or Takeoff
AB	Air Base
ABCCC	Airborne Communications Command Center
AC	Aircraft Commander Pilot or Attack Cargo Aircraft
ADVON	Advanced (Elements of Military Unit)
AF	Air Force
AFB	Air Force Base
AFLC	Air Force Logistics Command
AFVN	Armed Forces Vietnam Radio/TV Network
AG	Aerial Gunner/Airborne Weapons Mechanic
AGATE	TACC Radio Call Sign at Tan Son Nhut
AGE	Aerospace Ground Equipment
AGL	Above Ground Level
AIR COMMANDO	Special Operations Personnel
ALERT	Aircrew Personnel Status for Instant Response
ALLEY CAT	Radio Call Sign for 7th ABCCC EC-130 at Udorn, Night Barrel Roll/Northern Steel Tiger, 237.0 UHF
ALPHA PAPA	Ambush Patrol
ALPHA SIERRA	Air Strike
ANGELS	Radio Slang for Aircraft Flight Altitude
AO	Area of Operation
APC	Armored Personnel Carrier
API	Armor Piercing Incendiary Ammunition
APO	American Military Postal System
ARC LIGHT	B-52 Bombing Strike

ARTY	Artillery
ARVN	Army of Republic of (South) Vietnam
AVNK	Cambodia Air Force
BANDIT	Enemy Aircraft
BASKETBALL	Radio Call Sign for C-130 Flare Ship
BATTALION	Army Unit 300 to 1,000 Soldiers
BDA	Bomb (Battle) Damage Assessment
BIG BLUE	Large River
BINGO FUEL	Fuel Remaining Onboard Aircraft is Just Enough to Return and Land at Home Air Base with a Set Minimum of Fuel Reserve Remaining for Unforeseen Circumstances Requiring Landing at Alternate Air Field. (For AC-119G, Reserve Minimum 1,000 gallons of avgas).
BLACK PONY	Radio Call Sign for US Navy OV-10 Strike Aircraft Stationed at Vung Tau, Can Tho, and Binh Thuy, RVN. Primary Air Support for Riverine Operations
BLIND BAT	Radio Call Sign for C-130 Flare/FAC Ship
BOONIES	Jungle
BRIGADE	Army Unit 3,000 to 5,000 Soldiers. Composed of Battalions and Support Elements
BUSH	Jungle
CA	Combat Assault
CANDLESTICK	Radio Call Sign for UC-123K Flare Ships of the 606 SOS Based at NKP
CAP	Airborne Alert, Flying Predetermined Track or Position, Combat Air Patrol
CAS	Close-air Support
CASI	Continental Airlines Service International
C & C	CorrosionControl of Aircraft Fuselage/Systems Performed at Kadena AB at Okinawa for AC-119s
CEL	Confirmed Enemy Location
CHARLIE	Nickname for Viet Cong, North Vietnam, Khmer Rouge Troops
CHECO	Contemporary Historical Examination of Current Events
CHECK FIRE	Cease Fire

CIA	Central Intelligence Agency
C.I.D.G.	Civilian Irregular Defense Group
CIDER	Radio Call Sign for 02 FAC In-Country
CO	Commanding Officer
CLICK	One Kilometer (1.6093 km = 1 mile)
COMBAT EYE SPOT	Radar Directed Bombing Techniques Encountered During Gunship Operations
COMMANDO HUNT	Air Interdiction Campaign
CONUS	Continental United States
CORPS	Military Regions I, II, III, IV of South Vietnam
COVEY	Radio Call Sign for O-2 & OV-10 FACs of the 20th TASS Stationed at DaNang
CR	Combat Ready
CROWN	Radio Call Sign for Search & Rescue HC-130
DASC	Direct Air Support Center
DELTA OSCAR	Duty Officer
DEROS	Date of Estimated Return from Overseas
DFC	Distinguished Flying Cross
DMZ	Demilitarized Zone
DUST OFF	Army Medical Evacuation Helicopter or Mission
ETA	Estimated Time of Arrival
ETD	Estimated Time of Departure
FAC	Forward Air Controller
FANK	Force Armee Nationale Khmere (Cambodian Army)
FAST MOVER	Jet Fighter-Bomber Aircraft
FE	Flight Engineer
FEET DRY	Flying Over Land
FEET WET	Flying Over Water Just Off the Coast of Vietnam
FIGMO	Forget It, I've Got My Orders
FINI-FLIGHT	Last Flight of Duty Tour Before DEROS
FLIR	Forward Looking Infrared Radar
FMS	Field Maintenance Squadron
FNG	Friggin' New Guy
FOL	Forward Operating Location
FOX-MIKE	FM (Frequency Modulated) Radio

FRAG	Fragmentary Portion of Air Operations Order (i.e., a Tactical Air Mission (Sortie) Pre-Assigned by TACC).
FRAGGED AF	Missions (Sorties) Scheduled by 14th SOS; 7th
FREE FIRE ZONE	Enemy Areas Not Requiring Clearance to Fire
FREEDOM DEAL	Code Name for US Air Interdiction Operation in Cambodia
FREQ	Radio Frequency
FSB	Fire Support Base
FUNNY PAPER	Map (1*50,000)
GCA	Ground Controlled (Radar) Approach for Landing
GCI	Ground Controlled Intercept (e.g., CORPS radar sites such as Panama and Portcall)
GI	Government Issue (Issued by Uncle Sam)
GLO	Army Ground Liaison Officer
GOOK	Derogatory Slang for Communist Troops
GROUND POUNDER	Slang for Non-Flying Military Personnel
GRUNT	A Term of Endearment for the American G.I. on the Ground, Living In and Slogging Through the Rain and Mud. He was the Man that Airmen always Worked for First.
GUARD CHANNEL	Universal Radio Frequency for Emergencies.
HAMMER	Radio Call Sign for FACs of the 23rd TASS Stationed at Quang Tri, RVN
HEAVY ARTY	B-52 or Fighter/Bomber Strikes
HEI	High Explosive Incendiary Ammunition
HF	High Frequency Radio
HIGHERS	Higher Ranking Personnel in Chain of Command
HILLSBORO	Radio Call Sign for 7th ABCCC EC-130 based at Udorn, Southern Steel Tiger, 125.0 Victor (VHF), 266.9 Uniform (UHF)
HOLD	Maintain Orbit over Fixed Point (Awaiting Arty Clearance) or Set up a Racetrack Holding Pattern (For CAP)
HOME PLATE	Landing Air Base or Home Air Field
HOOCH	Booze or Alcoholic Drink

HOOTCH	Hut or Building
HOTEL	Radio Call Sign Prefix for Cambodian Commanders
I.F.F.	Identification, Friend or Foe for Aircraft
IFFV	1st Field Force, Vietnam (US Army Command for II Corps. DASC Alpha Supports IFFV
IFR	Instrument Flight Rules
IG	Inspector General
I & M	Improvement and Modernization Program
IN-COUNTRY	Within South Vietnam Borders
INDIAN COUNTRY	Enemy Territory
INN KEEPER	CH-47 Chinook Helicopter
INTEL	Intelligence
IO	Illuminator Operator
IRAN	Inspect and Repair As Necessary
JOLLY GREEN	Radio Call Sign for SAR HH3 or HH-53E Helicopters (40th ARRS, NKP)
KBA	Killed By Air
KEL	Known Enemy Location
KR	Khmer Republic
KHMER ROUGE	Cambodian Communist
KHMER SEREI	Free Cambodians
KIA	Killed In Action
KILOMETER	1000 Meters (.6 mile)
KING	Radio Call Sign for SAR HC-130P (Former Call Sign "Crown")
KLICK	Term Used by GIs for one Kilometer (km)
KNOTS	Nautical Miles per Hour
KPC	Kompong Cham (Cambodia)
KPT	Kompong Thom (Cambodia)
LIMA SITE	Laos—Short Landing Strip, Usually Dirt, Used as a Resupply Point for Royal Laotian Forces
LIMDIS	Limited Distribution
LITTLE BLUE	Stream
LOACH (L.O.H.)	Nickname for OH6 Light Observation Helicopter

L.O.C.	Line of Communication (road, trail, river)
LRP	Long Range Patrol Team (Army)
LZ	Landing Zone
MACV	Military Assistance Command Vietnam
MARK-6 (MK-6)	Ground Marker (Smoke Flare, 30 to 45mm)
MARK-24 (MK-24)	Illumination Flare (2 to 3 mm)
MAY DAY	International Distress Call on Radio
MEDEVAC	Medical Evacuation
METER	1.09 yards or 3.28 feet
MIA	Missing In Action
MIKE-MIKE	Slang for Millimeter
MISSION	Flight Objective, Used Interchangeably With Sortie
MISTY	F-100 FAC
MM	Millimeter
MOL	Main (Military) Operating Location
MOONBEAM	Radio Call Sign for 7th ABCCC EC-130 based at Udorn, Night Southern Steel Tiger, 266.9
MOONSHINE	C-47 Flareship
MOS	Military Occupation Specialty
MOU	Memorandum Of Understanding
MOVER	Ground Vehicle
MR	Military Region aka Corps
NAIL	Radio Call Sign for 0-1/0-2/OV-10 FACs 23rd TASS, NKP—Operating in Laos/Steel Tiger
NAV	Navigator
NCO	Non-Commissioned Officer
NKP	Nakhon Phanom Royal Thai Air Force Base
NORS	Not Operational Ready - Supply
NOS	Night Observation Scope or Night Observation Scope Operator
NVA	North Vietnam Army
O CLUB	Officers Club
OJT	On-Job Training
ON STATION	At Assigned Position or Location in AO

OPS	Operations
OPORD	Operational Order
OR	Operational Ready
ORI	Operational Readiness Inspection
OUT-COUNTRY	Outside South Vietnam Borders
PACAF	Pacific Air Forces
PAD	Programmed Action Directive
PADDY CONTROL	Radio Call Sign for Bien Thuy Radar Ground Control, 619th TCS, Det. 3, Binh Thuy/Can To, 242.4
PAMPER CONT'L	Radio Call Sign for 621st TCS, Quang Tri
PANAMA CONT'L	Radio Call Sign for Radar Ground Control 621st TCS, DaNang, TACAN Ch. 77, 367.8, 376.9
PANEL	Highly Reflective Beads on Cloth Backing to Mark Ground Position of Friendly Troops
PAPA PAPA	Slang for Phnom Penh
PARROT	Slang for I.F.F./S.I.F.
PARIS CONTROL	Radio Call Sign for Saigon Radar Control Center, 619th TCS – TSN, TACAN Ch. 102/ 268.1- 347.9— 235.9
PAWNEE TARGET	Radio Call Sign for 19th TASS Ground Control at Tay Ninh City, TOC
PCS	Permanent Change of Station
PEACOCK	Radio Call Sign for Radar Ground Control, 619th TCS, Det. 10, Pleiku, TACAN Ch. 107, 248.8, 318.9
PEDRO	Radio Call Sign for USAF Base Emergency and Rescue Helicopter HH-43
PHASE	Periodic Required Aircraft Maintenance
PIDGEONS	Radio Slang for Headings and Distance to a Point
PIPPER	The Center Dot in a Gunsight Crosshairs
PJSS	PACAF Jungle Survival School
POPEYE	Flying Instrument Flight Rules
POW	Prisoner of War
PSYOPS	Psychological Operations
PUSH	Radio Frequency (usually FM)
RANCH HAND	C-123 Spray Birds (Agent Orange)
RECCE	Short for Reconnaissance
RECON	Short for Reconnaissance

RED LEG	Artillery
REGENERATE	Land, Refuel, Rearm, and Takeoff Again
REGIMENT	Army Unit of Approximately 1,660 Soldiers
RLAF	Royal Laotian Air Force
ROE	Rules of Engagement
ROGER	Slang for Understand
RPG	Rocket Propelled Grenade
RPM	Revolutions Per Minute
R & R	Rest and Recuperation
RTB	Return To Base
RUSTIC	Radio Call Sign for 0-2 & OV-10 FACs 19th TASS at Bien Hoa, RVN. Relocated Oct.1971 to Ubon, Thailand, Freq. 359.9/272.8
RUSTIC ALPHA	Radio Call Sign for 19th TASS Rustic Relay Radio Station Located atop Nui Ba Den Mountain
RVN	Republic of Vietnam (South Vietnam)
SAC	Strategic Air Command
SAM	Surface to Air Missile
SAR	Search And Rescue
SCRAMBLE	To Respond to Action ASAP
SEA	Southeast Asia
SECONDARY	After-Explosion from Hit on Initial Target
SEL	Suspected Enemy Location
SHADOW	AC-119G Gunship
SHADOW BOX	Armed Recce Areas for Shadow Gunships in South Vietnam
SHORT	Slang for Being Close to DEROS
SHORT ROUND	A Round Fired by Friendly Forces That Causes Casualties among Friendly Forces
SIT-REP	Situation Report
SLR	Side Looking Radar
SOG	Studies and Observations Group
SOP	Standard Operating Procedures
SORTIE	One Scheduled Mission for One Aircraft
SOS	Special Operations Squadron
SOW	Special Operations Wing
SPAD	A-1E Attack Aircraft Used for Rescue Cover

SPEAK	U-10 Psyop Aircraft
SPECTRE	AC-130 Gunship
SPOOKY	AC-47 Gunship aka Puff or Puff the Magic Dragon
STAN/EVAL	Standardization/Evaluation
STINGER	AC-119K Gunship
STOL	Short Takeoff and Landing Aircraft
SUNDOG	Radio Call Sign for 0-2A FACs of 19th TASS
SWIFT	Harbor Patrol Boats
TAC	Tactical Air Command
TAC-AIR	Tactical Air Support
TACAN	Tactical Air Navigation System
TACC	Tactical Air Control Center
TACE	Tactical Emergency
TASS	Tactical Air Support Squadron
TCS	Tactical Control Squadron
TCTO	Time Compliance Technical Order
TDY	Temporary Duty
TIC	Troops-In-Contact (with enemy troops)
TILLY	Radio Call Sign for O-2A FACs, 19th TASS Thuy, River Convoy Escort Support
TOC	Tactical Operations Center
TOT	Time On Target
TRIPLE A	Anti-Aircraft Artillery
TSN	Tan Son Nhut Air Base
TUOC	Tactical Unit Operations Center
TURN-AROUND	To Fly Another Mission Immediately After Competing First Mission
UDL	Unit Detail Listing
UHF	Ultra High Frequency Radio
UNIFORM	UHF Radio
USAF	United States Air Force
U.S.	United States of America
USO	United Service Organization
VC	Viet Cong or Vietcong/Vietnamese Communist

VICTOR	VHF Radio
VICTOR SITE	Vietnam – Short Landing Strip, Usually Dirt
VFR	Visual Flight Rules
VHF	Very High Frequency Radio
VNAF	South Vietnam (RVN) Air Force
VNN	South Vietnam (RVN) Navy
WBA	Wounded By Air
WILLY PETE	White Phosphorous Ground Marker
WINCHESTER	Term Used for "Out of Ammunition"
WRAMA	
XO	Executive Officer

About the Author

Former United States Air Force Captain Dr. Larry Elton Fletcher flew 177 combat missions as a pilot in AC-119 Shadow gunships during his tour of duty in Vietnam with the 17th Special Operations Squadron Forward Operating Location "Fighting C Flight" at Tan Son Nhut Air Base, Saigon, Republic of Vietnam, from May 1970 to May 1971. He was awarded the Distinguished Flying Cross with Oak Leaf Cluster and the Air Medal with eight clusters for missions flown in Southeast Asia. Fletcher was nominated for Pacific Air Forces Outstanding Junior Officer of the Year.

After five years of active military service from 1968 to 1973, Fletcher returned to the teaching profession and public school administration, and earned a Doctor of Education degree from the University of Missouri, Columbia. He retired from public education in 1997 to pursue a writing career. His first novel, *Shadows of Saigon: Air Commandos in Southeast Asia,* was published in 2001 and its sequel, *The Shadow Spirit: Flying Stingers & BUFFs in SEA,* was published in 2004. As history book project coordinator, Larry spearheaded the *AC-119 Gunships History Book 1968-1973* for the AC-119 Gunship Association, which was published by the Association in 2009. Larry and his wife Sue reside at Lake of the Ozarks, Missouri.

CPSIA information can be obtained at www.ICGtesting.com
Printed in the USA
LVOW05s0329180214

374138LV00001B/2/P